Aut

Jan Hann (JanHann), is known for her Memoirs and Artwork; but with her Poetry and Research, her pseudonym is generally written as BODINE HÖFT.

KNOCK THE DOOR

MEMOIR OF THE 60s

JanHann

NUSEARCH BOOKS

KNOCK THE DOOR

A NUSEARCH BOOK

This is a true story. With the exception of the author,
all names are fictitious. All photographs are authentic,
however, apart from the author, all faces have been masked
for protection of identity.

First paperback edition 2022

Book design by Publishing Push
ILLUSTRATIONS BY JanHann
unless otherwise stated.

ISBNs:
Paperback: 978-1-80227-253-6
eBook: 978-1-80227-294-9

AUTHOR'S FACEBOOK: Jan Hann/menu/pages/bookshop

A True Story – Memoir.
This historical novel is set in 1960s England.
It tells of a roller-coaster love affair
of an entrepreneur in London
making a successful career
when everything takes an unexpected turn.

Dedication

Dear Rebekah,
When I first began writing this memoir, you were still in my womb.
Many years have now passed and the possibility is that,
you may no longer want to know about these things.
But one day, somehow, somewhere, sometime, we may meet.
And then, I can tell you all about my memoir.
And you can ask me what you want.

What I need to say to you Rebekah is that:
I have always thought of you and loved you.
And I will always think of you and love you.
From your birth mother
Janet.

Contents

Acknowledgements

MANY THANKS TO THE FOLLOWING: to my daughters Michéle and Monique. They have always been by my side during the many years that it has taken to fulfil this dream. Without their loyalty and patience, this work would never have become complete.

I am very grateful to all the people who have kindly shared their work for the public's interest; and especially to those persons whose research and pictures I have referred to as guidance throughout my work.

Lastly, but certainly not least, I am indebted to the Publishers, for without them, this work would have taken much longer – if at all! Their skills, their temperament, stimulation and encouragement, all of which kept me motivated, regardless of good days and bad days throughout my goal. I highly recommend *Publishing Push* and its Team to anyone that feels they have a story to share.

CHAPTER ONE

College Life

May: 1964

Clothes were rapidly stripped off whilst other articles of clothing were carefully being slipped on. The small, crowded room was very hot and stuffy due to lack of ventilation, but no-one cared on this particular day because everyone was on a 'high.' All around the outer edge of this dressing room were mobile rails packed full of clothes and close by each one would be a tall, delicate female model along with her dresser. Models were swaying, twisting, pouting or grooming themselves, and all the while, they would watch themselves in their long, slim, full-length mirrors. Each dresser hurriedly bustled around, making a show of frantic activity with coat-hangers and clothes, hair-adornments, shoes and all the other exciting paraphernalia that would help make it a perfectly beautiful groovy day.

The day had come at last for the student's fashion show!

One or two students checked lists for co-ordination to fix timing against the correct order of garments, whilst models were promptly called in to keep the sequence of instructions running smoothly. From one side of this backstage space, they would leave with the use of the so-called *catwalk*.[1] At the other end of this catwalk, the mannequins would return to the dressing room via a back location, looking very quiet and serious in most cases, yet proud of themselves, whilst getting increasingly excited as the evening ticked on. The Head of the Fashion Department of Southampton College of Art had chosen wisely, for this special 'Saturday Clothes Show' was being held in a castle. Only fragments of the medieval castle remain visible in Southampton today, but it was enough to make it a truly historical day![2&3]

It had been an extremely warm May day which must have been one of the reasons why there was such a wide audience within the castle grounds, and in the cool of the evening, the crowd appeared very relaxed. Nevertheless, if you listened intently, you might vaguely hear the words:

"Please don't fall over, please don't fall over, please don't fall over!"

There were jaunty clothes, sportswear, nightwear, cotton dresses, fun gear and suits. They continued to gush out of the dressing area in a colourful billowy mosaic - complete with the additional colour hues of spotlighting and the appropriate sounds of pop, jazz, classical, orchestral and even solo songs.

Suddenly, the music changed dramatically, with which a tall, slim model ventured out onto the gangway. She was displaying a kind of soft black two-piece evening wear, and as she sauntered casually along this narrow platform in a manner of no particular purpose, the audience were distracted towards revealing glimpses of this tubular outfit. Running down the entire length were white satin stripes that seemed to come from a white silky rosette, which sat proudly on the right shoulder. The skirt revealed a long left-side

Figure 1 'Shapes of Things to Come'

split, while the model wore black fingerless satin gloves and rod-like high-heeled shoes. But it was the style - the asymmetrical design of the garment - that had stirred the crowd's curiosity, and even more so - the hat!

As the outfit's designer, I had worked really hard to create this moulded cocktail cap. If I had been a professional milliner or hatter as they were called, I would have been expected to design, make, trim, and sell hats. They would have been made for all kinds of people: women, men and children alike - although some definitions tend to restrict the term to a female clientele. These types of hats were often decorated with ornaments, jewels or even feathers, as well as a veil. They were closely related to fascinators, which were extravagant hairpieces worn on the side of the wearer's head and attached to a band or a clip. In the case of the model's cocktail cap, it was characteristic of a cloche hat - more simply known as 'cloche,' which is a fitted, bell-shaped hat for women. They first became popular around the 1920s to early 1930s and were typically worn low on the forehead, with the wearer's eyes only slightly below the brim. The cloche had its second appearance in the 1960s as with this fashion show in Southampton. It reappeared again in the late 1980s and was also featured in the autumn 2007 collections of many designers.

Figure 2 Hats

The audience were greatly pleased with the outfit. They were murmuring, fidgeting and turning from left to right. Some of them were clapping and stomping their feet on the ground, whilst others were standing and whistling and waving their arms in the air. Reporter's cameras had been clicking and flashing in every direction, and all in all, the show seemed to have been a very prosperous one.

Back in the college a few days later, all appeared normal until Amanda, the head of department, walked into the tailoring room. She was carrying a newspaper known as the *Evening News* under her arm. She strode over to the front of the room and spoke to the teacher. He was a timid man, a dedicated tailor, plus determined not to lose his job. Their conversation lasted for a few minutes, and then Amanda turned around and faced the group. Mr Hollywell looked up and, taking control of the class, told everyone to stop work. Amanda proceeded to talk about the fashion show. Everyone listened intently with which she held up the newspaper and pointed to an article bearing the following title:

College Fashion Show – A Success!

As a group, we became excited; we were very proud of ourselves and our publicity. As each of us students put our pressing and sewing to one side, we made our way out to the front. We huddled close together to read the article, and there, in the midst of the write-up, was a photograph of my black and white evening two-piece.

Figure 3 Black & White outfit

There were murmurs and giggles and chatter as everyone passed comments, and then it was time for a break. The twelve of us – eleven females and one male – all proceeded to leave the room. We made a lot of noise as we walked along the corridor; after all, we had a lot to talk about. Our excitement was going to be the peak of our conversation with the other students in the Art section – once we got down into the college canteen. Amanda stood in her office doorway as we wandered by; and as I was passing, she called softly to me and beckoned me into her office:

"Come," she said, "sit down."

This was not the first time that I had entered this office. I flashed back to the previous time…

I had applied to the college for a studentship via my school headmistress… but let me explain how that happened.

At the age of eleven, I had found it very difficult to settle down at my new secondary school, and so I kept running away. After a while, the headmistress found a way to curb my problem - she became my *other* mother. Wherever I sat to eat my school dinner, the headmistress would turf out the child beside me and sit *herself* down in that place - and this became the mode for the first twelve months of my secondary school life. During this period, Miss Sears, the headmistress, got to learn quite a bit about me as a young pupil and one of the things that she noticed was that I seemed to overcome my anxieties in my Art Lessons. At around the age of fourteen years, I was told that I had achieved an award along with approximately five other students. The school was going to fund all six of us to attend Saturday Morning Classes at the reputable Winchester College of Art.[4] The purpose being was to improve our artistic skills. These sessions were to continue until I almost left school, and I must admit that I have *always* felt so lucky to have been able to be trained there!

Besides these Saturday morning classes at Winchester College of Art, it was also Miss Sears that arranged an application for me to attend an interview at the College of Art in Southampton. This time, it was for a potential course for a future career. At the age of sixteen, and because of my uneasiness, I had arrived together with my mother for the college interview, plus my *Simplicity Sewing Book* - to show how eager I was to join the Dress Design Course!

It was James J. Shapiro (1909–1995) who founded the Simplicity Pattern Company in 1927. Like most home sewing patterns, they are made of tissue paper, which is a thin paper or light-weight crêpe paper, or sometimes made from recycled paper pulp. The first thing that has to be done when using these patterns is to place one onto a piece of fabric and pin it down securely. The sewer then cuts along the printed lines adhering to the instructions and stitches the shaped cloth pieces together to create the finished clothing. Each Simplicity pattern comes with its own step-by-step guide for cutting, stitching and assembling the garment, which makes everything seem much simpler.[5]

My college interview was held in the *Dress & Design* office. The head of the department had accepted both mine and my mother's information, and together with the appropriate qualifications, I was entered to start college life, full-time, in the September of that year – 1963. Oh, and I was told:

"You won't need to bring your Simplicity Sewing Book with you next time you come because you are going to be taught how to create your own designs and how to make your own patterns for them!"

How wonderful is that?

Figure 4 A Simplicity Sewing Book

Shortly afterwards, I became a commuter at seventeen years of age.

So, here I was again being invited to walk through this same office door, some eight months after my acceptance to the Dress Design Course.

I sat down gingerly.

"We had a visitor to the college yesterday," Amanda said. "It was an enquiry on your black and white evening wear." She continued. "The lady wants to buy it; is that alright with you, Jan?"

I looked up at her excitedly, "Well, yes, of course," I said, "that will be fine by me!"

We discussed a price together by working out the cost of materials and the time taken to produce the garment, plus accessories, plus profit, with which Amanda told me that she would get back to me a little later.

A few days later, and all had gone well - the business transaction was complete, and the result was a success.

October 1964

The weeks and summer holiday came and went, and it was around the first few weeks back at college in October 1964. Amanda walked into our classroom with three business-looking men. They had loud voices and appeared extremely confident - excited too, it seemed, to be in our college - especially in a room full of young women. Amanda spoke to our teacher, and we were told to stop work and listen.

I was still very reserved in those days, definitely not worldly, more of a book worm, in fact, *Readers Digest* - that was me. I was wearing a dark brown skinny-ribbed jumper and a mustard corduroy skirt with brown suede shoes. I felt very smart. I had got the hang of not having to wear a school uniform anymore, plus the freedom and flexibility of college life - especially as a commuter - and I liked it very much. In those days, I had very long, sleek, straight black hair, which I would divide into two halves along the centre of the top of my head and have like a curtain arrangement across my forehead. All of which was held into place using a dark brown velvet headband.

"These men are from *Southern Television*," Amanda said. "They want to do a programme on the life of a fashion design student here at the college! One student is going to show the producers what type of work they do in a week of their college life!"

"I've already chosen a student," Amanda continued. "The student is going to be Marina!"

She was her favourite, you see.

However, these men were not going to let Amanda choose. There seemed to be some kind of controversy, a dispute or disagreement, between the three of them.

Then, much to my amazement, these males came over to me quite positively and said, "Would you like to show us your student work?"

I was dumbfounded. I was also in a difficult situation - I didn't want to upset the head of department; we needed to abide by her rules.

The man who had spoken to me went back to Amanda to have a discussion, and with that, she told the whole class to take a break. As they all went out of the room, Amanda closed the door - but not before providing me with a few cautious glances.

This man sat on the edge of my desk, and I felt extremely nervous - he was too close!

He had a bag with him, and he proceeded to open it whilst his colleague watched from a distance.

He delved into his briefcase, pulling out a microphone, which he put in front of me on my desk. He continued to put his hand back into his bag, and this time, he pulled out a kind of woolly mitten, which he put onto the end of this piece of equipment.

He looked at me and said, "Do you know who has spoken to me through this microphone?"

I shook a 'No' with my head.

"One of the Beatles - Paul McCartney!" he said. "When I film you, I will be using this same mouthpiece that I used for Paul!"

I looked down, away from him, and reflected on Paul McCartney: he was a singer and multi-instrumentalist in the group known as the Beatles, which had become a worldwide phenomenon. Alongside John Lennon, he was half of one of the world's most successful songwriting teams in history.

I kept my head down and replied very meekly, "I don't think that the head of department wants you to use me for your documentary."

He gulped, "Yes, she does," he replied. "I've had words with her, and she is happy about it now!"

He proceeded to tell me of lots of other well-known people that had spoken to him using the same mouthpiece until he eventually ended with, "Just think how proud your mum and dad will be when they see you on the television."

He stood up and put his hand out for me to shake. "That's a deal then, Jan!"

I stood up as well, shaking a lot, and put out my hand. "Well, yes, of course," I replied. "Oh! Um! Thank you!"

And so, I ended up on a programme called *Here and Now* for approximately fifteen minutes. I took the viewers through making my own tie-and-dye materials. I also showed them how to use a spinning wheel - an implement for spinning yarn - using selected sheep's wool from the fences of fields in my own hometown. I produced two garments for the viewers from these particular fabrics, and by the end of the week, they were ready for wearing - with the help, of course, from the ones that I had made earlier! This is because, in reality, it had actually taken me nearly a month!

It's surprising how things work in TV Productions, isn't it?

Nevertheless, my family and I eagerly sat around our nine-inch Bush Television Box to watch the finished production.

There was no such thing in those days as video recorders, so it was a one-off!

Figure 5 Television set

One of the things that I didn't realise at the time was that Southern Television was comparatively new in those days. The three-man team were Bob Walker (senior cameraman), Ben Brightwell (sound recordist), and Barry Allsopp (assistant cameraman). Initially, they were involved with news assignments for locally made programmes, but their workload increased with the launch in 1961 of the *Day by Day* local news feature. They were a familiar sight in the area, travelling in a blue Morris Oxford with the Southern TV logo on it. I personally remember some of the programmes on Southern Television, such as *Emergency-Ward 10, Huckleberry Hound, The Flintstones, The Beverly Hillbillies* and *Rawhide*. Of course, I am not going to forget Wednesday's viewing, which included: 4.45 pm *Small Time;* 5.00 pm *Zoo Time.* At 5.55 pm was the ITN *News* followed by 6.05 pm *Day by Day.* And, of course, at 6.45 pm: ***Here and Now*** with Terence Carroll and Uffa Fox.[6]

Needless to say, this particular television programme was to cause friction between Amanda and me, for some reason. Life at the college became not so happy for me after this, yet, from it, my confidence was growing.

February 1965

It was now February 1965, and in the midst of the winter term, the class had been busy designing various clothes - sheets and sheets, in fact. Together, with the skills of the teacher, the designs had been whittled down to a workable and viable few, with which the instructor would then leave the choice to the student. I knew which one I wanted to make, especially as I would be the wearer and owner of the garment. This is because our clothes, this time, were being prepared for the City & Guilds of London Institute.

The name of our examination was called 'Dress.' Mine was to be made using thin, smooth, soft bone-coloured flannel material, with a minute brown fleck woven into the fabric. The slim-fitting shirt-dress would have straight sleeves that ended in a long, pleated, frilled cuff, which, as the hand was held up, the frill would drop outwards, like an upside-down umbrella, exposing a chocolate brown inner lining. I was really excited and set to create the pattern. Soon, it was time to cut it out, then tack it all together, ready for its first fitting.

Our fitting room was really just a corner of the classroom. A tall, square rail stood there with a curtain hanging from it, which could be pulled all around the rail to turn the corner into an enclosed dressing cubicle.

It was my turn for a fitting. I got inside this space and started to undress. I suppose I must have been taking a long time - as always - because I liked to fold up my clothes and put them on a chair so that they didn't get dusty. All of a sudden, the curtain is being pulled open wide, and my teacher is standing there.

She appeared with an O-shaped mouth as she said, "Janet! Why are you wearing a corset?"

I just stared at her trying to cover myself up.

"Why are you wearing a corset?" She asked again in a demanding voice with her hands on her hips.

I didn't know what to say. After all, I had always worn such things, and even at school, I would wear a liberty bodice with draw-strings to lace it shut.

I slumped onto the chair to conceal myself better, but this teacher was not going to let go until she received an answer.

"Tell me, *why* are you wearing a corset, Janet?"

"My mother says so," I replied.

"But why?" she said in horror.

"Well, because my mother wears a corset too."

"Yes, well, perhaps your mother needs one, but not you, at *your* age. Besides, you have a slim figure; it doesn't make sense! Take it off!" she said. "I refuse to fit your dress with it on!" And with this, she closed the curtain.

I sat there, not knowing what to do for the best.

Eventually, I knew that I had to make a move; otherwise, my tutor would get cross, and I might not even be permitted to continue with my dress.

I stood up, and with both hands, I gripped the lower edge of the corset and tugged downwards from both sides. It was always a struggle. Gradually, it chugged its way down my body in starts and stops until it reached my feet, where I was able to step out of it.

I felt quite bare when the tutor came in.

"What is that neck scarf doing tied around your undergarment - your brassière?" she asked.

I looked down at what she was pointing to.

"It helps to flatten my bust," I said.

"Well, I need that off as well!" she replied.

I felt awkward; I stood there red with shame as she moved in closer to fit my dress. This woman, a mere stranger at that, was touching my flesh!

Nevertheless, the garment fitted well, but it was my rump that I worried about and, well, my boobs which were both now able to bounce. After all, things like these were always held in tight enclosures and never allowed to move - well, wobble.

As I started to slip out of my dress, the teacher looked back at me in the cubicle, saying, "And don't wear all that paraphernalia again - just panties and brassière next time when we do the final fitting."

I sat down on the chair. 'What should I do?' I thought to myself. 'Put it all back on for now? That would be best and think about it for later.'

I strapped my breasts in under tight control, and I gripped, pulled and jostled with my boned corset until it eventually reached right up to the top, alongside the lower-level edge of my bra. I tugged downwards at the legs - it was most important that my hips were encased.

Straight down, a tubular body, that's what I was aiming for - and always had!

I told my mother when I got home, and of course, she was very angry. You see, she saw these things as 'Vulgar' and 'Too Sexy.'

The next day, my mother seemed to have calmed down quite a bit. I think she must have had words with my father, and he wanted me to make something of my life. So, nothing more was mentioned, and I nervously left those hand-trappers off.

At first, I was severely affected by the experience - I was embarrassed - and then it was amazing. It was as if I'd been released into freedom, a sense of exposure and interaction with the natural elements.

I felt like a bird: a fledgling that had just discovered the power of its wings.

Very sensual, really!

The Corset Controversy

Corsets in those days had been variously called by such names as *a pair of bodies* or *stays* (although I have found out recently that some people would call them "hand-trappers" – and very appropriately so too). They were worn by European women from the late 16th century onward, changing their form as fashions changed. In spite of radical changes to fashion geographically and temporally, the corset assumed its dominant role for the rest of the 19th century. Designed to emphasise the waist by minimising it, corsets would constrict the waistline in order to achieve a slender silhouette. Doctors and much of the press deplored the garment in spite of its continued use.

The Corset Controversy was concerned with supporters' and detractors' arguments for and against wearing a corset. Otherwise known as the "corset question," the controversy spilt over multiple publications, countries and decades. Of particular concern was the issue of tight lacing.

Figure 6 "A cutting wind, or the fatal effects of tight-lacing,"
a satirical cartoon from around 1820 (adapted)

There were countless denunciations. One such appeared in the *Chicago Tribune*:

'*THE SLAVES OF FASHION*: through Long Centuries Women Have Obeyed Her Whims'

Yet, some women professed to enjoy the practice. A letter to the *Boston Globe* read:

'I myself have never felt any ill effects from nearly 30 years of the most severe tight lacing...'

One reader wrote to *The Toronto Daily Mail* insisting that only those who have been systematically laced up in proper stays from their childhood are capable of forming a rightful judgment on this subject. She hoped they would allow tight lacers the opportunity of defending themselves against the enemies of trim little waists.

Figure 7 A rendering of an Edwardian Corset

It was expected that women would wear corsets, and it was part of a mother's duty to her female offspring to have them wear the garment. Just how and when might depend on the mother, the daughter, the place and the time. However, some things were much the same everywhere. For example:

Laura Ingalls Wilder was an American author who wrote a series of children's books based on her childhood in a pioneer family. *Little Town on the Prairie* is set in 1880 in South Dakota in an area recently settled. The family had four daughters, Mary, Laura, Carrie, and Grace, the youngest. Mary, the eldest, tries on a dress that is found not to fit until her corset is laced more tightly, leading to the following conversation:

"I'm glad I don't have to wear corsets yet," said Carrie.

"Be glad while you can be," said Laura. "You'll have to wear them pretty soon."

"You should wear them at night," Ma said.

Mary did, but Laura could not bear them on at night. It was the torment of the steels that would not let her draw a deep breath. And so, *always* before she could get to sleep, she had to take off her corsets.

"What your figure will be, goodness knows," Ma warned her. "When I was married, your Pa could span my waist with his two hands!"

In some cases, mothers started their daughters wearing corsets in early childhood. *The New York Times* described the practice in its Fashion section:

'From the time an infant wears dresses, a kind of broad belt is used, with shoulder pieces. To this, the child's undergarments are buttoned. Little girls wear these until they are about 7 years of age. From this time, the belt has rather more shape, and the back part is supported on both sides by whalebone or a very soft steel spring. From the age of 10 to 12 years, another bone is added in the back. Corsets for young ladies have busks, narrow whalebones, and very soft steel springs. Ladies' corsets of satin or other material have jointed busks and are drawn in over the hips, making the front of the corsets very long.'

Another account from a young lady reads:

'A friend of mine has a wonderfully slender figure, which she says is the result of her mother putting a flannel band around her when she was only a year old to mould her soft bones. At six, she wore a corded corset with whalebones, and at thirteen, her mother had her daughter tightly laced, making her waist only fifteen inches.'

Mothers typically put their daughters into serious corsets in their teens or sometimes in their pre-teens. They sought advice in their local newspapers, giving rise to heated discussions.

In fashionable London, tight lacing of teen-aged daughters was considered an important matter. One of the most exclusive corsetieres in Oxford Street, who is the authority for the statement, said:

"Today, I provided three pairs of corsets of graduated sizes, and the young miss wore sixteen-inch corsets laced close to, the week before last at the Buckingham Palace Garden Party. She and her mother were so delighted with the effect that the girl came to me a day or two later to be measured for a pair of fifteens for dress occasions."[7]

Figure 8 "Small waist sizes 15 to 23 inches"

October 1965:
A Hint at my Future Career

One day, a professional fashion artist came to the college and gave us a talk about her career as a fashion illustrator for a local newspaper. I found her very interesting and was immediately taken aback by her drawings. I wanted to learn more about her work as a career, and I told her so. She said that if enough of us were interested, the college would employ her to give us training on an evening class basis. Straightaway, I was eager, and the next thing to do was to ask my grandmother, who lived in Eastleigh, if I could stay with her one evening each week to reduce my travelling time, plus of course, it would give my grandmother some company during this period as well. It seemed that there were a few other students just as enthusiastic as me to do some evening classes, and so twilight sessions were set up.

In those days, my grandmother would take a kitchen chair and put it in her walk-in pantry, where her provisions of bread, butter, cakes, meat, cheese, eggs, crockery, cutlery, etc. were kept, and there she would sit and knit. At the end of the pantry, a window led onto the front garden and gate and the pavement and road. People would walk past going about their daily business. They never knew that my grandmother was watching from behind the pantry's net curtain. She told me it was her form of company and entertainment because she never had many visitors, apart from the milkman, baker, rent-man, postman and coalman. Pantry watching is a bit like watching television today, isn't it? Only for real!

Ernie: The Fastest Milkman in the West

"Ernie" is an innuendo-laden comedy or novelty song, written and performed by the English comedian Benny Hill. The song was first performed on television in 1970, and released as a successful recording, topping the UK Singles Chart in 1971.

Story line
The lyric's story line is inspired by Benny Hill's early experience as a milkman for Hann's Dairies in Eastleigh, Hampshire. The Market Street that is mentioned in the lyrics is a real-life street in Eastleigh. The song tells the fictional exploits of Ernie Price, a 52-year-old (68, in the original television version) milkman who drives a horse-drawn milk cart. It relates his feud with the bread delivery man ("Two-Ton Ted" from Teddington) and their efforts to win the heart of Sue, a widow who lives alone at No. 22, Linley Lane.
When Ted sees Ernie's cart outside Sue's house all afternoon, he becomes enraged and violently kicks Price's horse, Trigger. The two men resort to a duel, using the wares they carry on their respective carts for weapons, and Ernie is killed by a rock cake underneath his heart, followed by a stale pork pie in his eye - although in the original television version it was a fresh meat pie. Sue and Ted then marry, but Ernie's ghost returns to haunt them on their wedding night.[7]

Figure 9 Ernie: The Fastest Milkman in the West[8]

Prior to this, my Nan had things such as seaweed hanging up on a nail outside the back door. The purpose of this was to tell us what sort of a day it was going to be, weather-wise, and if we heard thunder and rumbling in the sky, that was God moving His furniture about! There would be the washtub and the mangle on a Monday. Those were the times when you needn't lock your door. Those were the days when it was smoked haddock for tea on a Saturday and where we checked the football results from the wireless; when we would play cards altogether and draughts in the evening whilst we sucked liquorice imps and then had Horlicks at bedtime. In those days, it was more to do with interaction and communication: a sense of belonging and joining in with each other as a family when doing these things, rather than the activities themselves. Once upstairs, there was the geyser (apparatus for heating water) located over the family bath.[9] It would have a long, stretched stocking over its tap so that the running hot water wouldn't splash us as children.

Figure 10 A Geyser

In the children's front bedroom, there was an enamel potty placed underneath the bed. The bed itself had a feathered mattress, and sometimes we would use a warming pan to make it extra warm before we clambered in.

Figure 11 Bed, potty & rag doll

Cosy Days!

However, now, everyone had gone, and my grandmother lived all alone in Eastleigh.[10]

Pantry Watching

amazon.co.uk/VintageKnitting Needles

My Nan's pantry has cutlery, crockery and food in there,
and besides this, she has a kitchen chair.
There she would sit for an hour and knit,
and do, write and say, what're she thought fit.

At the end of the pantry was a net curtain,
so, to see my Nan was impossible – that's for certain!
My Nan would knit to the sounds of click-click!
If it weren't click-click, it would be "Tut! I've dropped it!"

"Oh! That's the eleven o'clock bus and again Sam's missed it!"
"If he'd come three minutes sooner he'd have caught it!"
" Good Lord, Margaret's late and sheesh, she's put on weight!"
Clickety-click, clickety-clack.
"Ah! Here comes Kate!" "How about that!"

Poem by JanHann

Figure 12 Pantry Watching

I really enjoyed the evening classes. I adored making drawings and bringing the garments to life. It wasn't just a case of designing and sketching sheets of outfits on paper anymore; these same clothes were now taking shape being worn by models as well. This fashion illustrator was very passionate about her work too. I liked the way she told us to bring in some action.

"Don't do static poses," she had said. "Make them come alive! Puff up the hairstyles! Show that there is a wind that blows their hair about! Provide different expressions on the models' faces!"

Figure 13 Two girls on a motor-bike

I was fascinated with the way I was now turning my unique designs into life drawings and for advertising or publicity purposes - to make the viewers want to purchase these clothes for themselves. My drawings were now being shaped in such a way that it was for making money - a business! However, it wasn't to be for long because the student numbers soon dwindled to just three of us, and sadly, these evening classes soon came to an end. Nevertheless, I had been given a chance to whet my appetite for creating a skill of this kind, and I really loved making the mannequins come alive on paper in my own unique way!

Figure 14 The Latin Look

Gibson Girl

The Gibson Girl was the personification of the feminine ideal of physical attractiveness as portrayed by the pen-and-ink illustrations of artist Charles Dana Gibson during a period that spanned the late 19th and early 20th century in the United States and Canada. The artist saw his creation as representing the composite of "thousands of American girls."

Figure 15 An adaptation of an iconic Gibson Girl

The image that appeared in the 1890s combined elements of earlier images of contemporary female beauty, including the "fragile lady," who took the basic slender lines, and a sense of respectability and the "voluptuous woman," who took on a large bust and hips but was not vulgar or lewd. From this combination emerged the Gibson Girl - a tall, slender girl, yet with ample bosom, hips and buttocks.

She was a member of the upper-middle-class society, always perfectly dressed in the latest fashionable attire appropriate for the place and time of day. She was also one of the new, more athletic-shaped women who could be found cycling through Central Park and was free enough from her image to the extent that she could enter the workplace. In addition to her refined beauty, she was calm, independent, confident, and sought personal fulfilment.

Camille Clifford was one: her neck was thin, and her hair piled high upon her head in the contemporary bouffant, pompadour, and chignon ("waterfall of curls") hairstyle fashions. She defined the style with her long elegant gowns that wrapped around her exaggerated S-curve torso shape - achieved by wearing a swan-bill corset. She was a woman known as the "ideal Gibson Girl" and posed for various photographers exemplifying the physical characteristics of the Gibson Girl.

Whilst the Gibson Girl took on many characteristics of the New Woman, she did so within the boundaries of feminine roles without too much transgression. She was depicted as an equal and sometimes a teasing companion to men. Next to her beauty, men often appeared as simpletons or bumblers who could not provide her with satisfaction. Most often, she appeared single and uncommitted; however, a romance always relieved her boredom. Once married, she was rarely depicted as taking part in any activity that could be seen as out of the ordinary for a woman.

Figure 16 *The Weaker Sex.* Gibson Girls examining men under a magnifying glass (adapted)

Some people argue that the Gibson Girl was the first national beauty standard for American women. Gibson's fictional images of her published in newspapers and magazines during the Belle Époque were extremely popular. Merchandise bearing her image included saucers, ashtrays, tablecloths, pillow covers, chair covers, souvenir spoons, screens, fans and umbrella stands.[11]

Yet, I hasten to add; there are many variations of and thousands of Gibson Girls in every country. The claims to that particular distinction are the result of a fine combination of the best points from many races and cultures, which all help to make up the human population!

CHAPTER TWO

1966: The Start of my Career

1966 – Easter Holidays

The pressure was on to do the exams at the college. Everyone was told to speed up to get their garments completed before the Easter holidays. We were told that after the break, we would be having continuous mock exams before the real events.

Now, as it happened, during this holiday, and as per usual, I bought a *Vogue* Magazine.

The word *Vogue* in French means "style." This magazine is full of fashion and lifestyle, and it is published monthly in 23 different national and regional editions by Condé Montrose Nast. It has been described as Fashion's Holy Book, where the elite and the ambitious alike turn for the style of the present, as well as the past.[1]

I loved looking through this top magazine; I adored the beautiful, slim models and their postures, showing off the splendid clothes. These were the days of the fawn-like model known as 'The Shrimp' and the photographer, David Bailey. Bailey is known for his advertising, celebrity and fashion photographs[2&3] and Jean Shrimpton was a notable model in the sixties and a *Vogue* cover girl.[4&5]

I looked at the picture of The Shrimp, and she stared back at me. Above her was written the name of a shop. I read the details:

'This label means quality, superb fabrics, elegance and individually designed just for you.'

I knew what this meant; it was the highest of fashion, sometimes known as haute couture.[6] I turned over more pages to read about some of the other fashion services, and then I went back to have another envious look at the photographs of the alluring models.

I started to read about the garments themselves:

'Sharon £5 9s 5d, from *Singa*, W1, is in blue and green Finnish cotton printed with a pattern of formalised flowers, the sleeve ends in tiny ruffles. It is also available in reds or brown or gold.'

I turned over the page, glanced at the next photograph and decided to read about the dress:

'This keyhole-necked dress is exclusive... at Sloane Street, S.W.1. and Baker Street, W.1. It is also available by post, from April 1. Price: 7 gns. There are other colours as well.'

As I stared at the mannequin, I mentally began to draw this model and her pose. My illustration looked different from all the other photographs, and it really stood out from the rest.

It was *this* that gave me the following idea:

To stand out from all the other advertisements, it had to appear different - not part of the same batch.

I just felt that this was the answer. This was the key to selling one garment or garments over and above the rest in this top magazine.

At this very moment, I knew that I had to act on it; I needed to write to this firm to ask them if they would like me to draw their garments for them in preference to having photographs for *Vogue* Magazine. I decided that the best way forward was to post them some of my work, so I sat down to create some elegant drawings of models with lots of feeling. They had to look sophisticated, individual, exclusive, and most of all, the detail on each fabric and style of their garments had to be meticulously accurate.

Figure 17 My first illustration published in *Vogue* Magazine: black evening dress

It was here that I soon realised that the featured shops catered for pregnant women - the garments were maternity wear. And so, on our kitchen table, I decided to draw two to three illustrations. The models needed to look calm, content and proud - almost dreamy like - because they were happy to be pregnant. I then packed up my work carefully and wrote the address on a large envelope:... Sloane Street, Knightsbridge, London, S.W.1.

I went round to our local post office to post it straight away- telling the shop assistant all about my plan into the bargain.

"Oh well, we'll wish it good luck, shall we?" She said as she smiled kindly and slipped it into the mailbag.

I felt so proud of myself to have plucked up the courage to get this far, and for the next twenty-four hours, I seemed to have plenty of energy to get on with my college work. I was pleased to have made my first independent move towards finding a job with my apprenticeship skills.

I lay in bed that night wondering when they would receive the parcel, how long would it be before they actually opened it and whether or not they would ever get back to me. After all, I suddenly thought, they must get hundreds of people asking them the same question. With this, I came back down to earth, snuggled up under the covers and fell asleep.

The next day, I was busy with my college garments. We lived in the south of England, in a modern council house in the quiet market town of Basingstoke.[7] My mother worked in a butcher's shop as their accountant, and my father was a locomotive steam train driver – he had been all his working life. That afternoon he came home from work on his bicycle. As usual, he was pot-black from the engine smoke and coal dust, which would be stuck to his face with the sweat from the heat of the engine's fiery furnace, and sometimes, of course, from the hot weather too. The first thing he would do was take his shoes off in the passageway before entering the kitchen. He would use Kiwi black boot polish, and with an oblong brush, he would rigorously clean his shoes, which he always finished off with a duster.

We were busy deep in conversation when the front doorbell rang. My father looked up and made his way out of the kitchen and into the hallway. I could hear him talking to someone.

A little later, he came back into the kitchen holding what I thought was a letter.

He held it out towards me and said, "It's for you, Janet!" His face, especially his eyes, was full of surprise as he continued, "It's a telegram! It's from London!"

I took the telegram from him and opened it up. It read:

'Mrs Grayson would like to see you as soon as possible.

Could you please telephone her on…'

I noticed that the number was a London one, and I said to my father, "What do I do?"

At first, he didn't know how to answer, and then he scratched his head and replied, "I would go round to the telephone box on Queen Mary's Avenue, duck, and ring her up!"

Figure 18 Telephone box

And that is exactly what I did!

I put on my coat and shoes and went upstairs to get the appropriate coins out of my father's coat pocket. Then I earnestly made my way around the corner, in a semi-walk/semi-run fashion, to Queen Mary's Avenue and its red telephone box.

There was someone in there - there always was - and they always seemed to be going on and on. I could also hear all of the conversation because there was a broken pane of glass in the door frame. I felt rude listening in, and so I stepped back a bit to the edge of the pavement.

Eventually, this man in the telephone booth put the phone back onto its hook. He turned himself around with a puff and a shuffle and then pushed the heavy door with his arms and his body and proceeded to manoeuvre his way out of the booth.

He turned and smiled at me, saying, "It's all yours now, love!"

And with that, he slowly walked away in his brown carpet slippers.

I went in.

I always hated this bit - a wet mouthpiece!

'Oh well, here goes,' I thought.

I wiped the mouthpiece with a spare piece of cloth that I had remembered to take and then proceeded to dial the number – trembling at the same time.

A voice at the other end answered, and as it did so, I quickly put the coins into the slot one at a time. Each one dropped with a clang.

I started speaking with a squeaky voice, cleared my throat and started again.

"My name is Janet Hann, and I posted some drawings yesterday to the... shop. I have just received a telegram from Mrs Grayson telling me to get in touch with her by telephone."

I paused. There was a quiet spell, and then I heard another voice. There were two of them, and they were talking to each other.

"Oh yes," came back the reply. "Mrs Grayson has left a message; she says to ask you if you could come here tomorrow, she would like to meet up with you. Oh, and could you bring your drawing pens and pencils etc. with you as well? Mrs Grayson will want to see some more samples of your work."

"Well, yes," I replied, "but it would have to be some time in the afternoon."

"Shall we say 2:00 pm?" the voice said.

"Well, yes!" I replied.

"Okay, we'll see you tomorrow then, at the Sloane Street shop."

"Oh yes! Oh, how do I find Sloane Street?" I asked.

"Just take the tube and get off at Knightsbridge Station."

"Okay," I said, "and thank you very much."

"You're welcome! Mrs Grayson is looking forward to meeting you!"

We both said goodbye, and I came out of the red booth.

I had only been to London once before, and that was on a day trip with the Brownies to see Buckingham Palace by coach.[8&9] Oh, and I remember on the Brownie Trip that we stopped off at the Tower of London as well.[10]

Do you know, I believe that I ran all the way home. If you were to ask me if I met anyone on the way back, I wouldn't be able to tell you. I do know that when I told my father, he was just as excited as I was - but much more cautious than me as well!

The next thing to do was to find out the times of the trains to Waterloo station, to be able to keep my appointment for 2:00 pm.

Meeting up with Evette Grayson

I don't remember sleeping very much that night in case I didn't wake up in time for my appointment! That evening, my mother had been busy pressing my clothes for me whilst my father did an extra good job of cleaning my patent shoes. Oh, and I also washed my hair, sharpened all my pencils and got my portfolio ready. I left them all by the kitchen door before I went to bed; they were all ready for the off!

I was so excited!

I finally emerged up out of the underground tube at Knightsbridge station. I wore a pink skirt, pink ribbed sweater, white stockings and freshly dyed pink patent shoes, and I had a black crotched beret on my long, straight, shiny black hair.

The time was ten minutes to two.

It was a very wide elite road, and the shops were definitely for a selected class of people, so they came across as extremely elegant. I have since learnt that Sloane Street is one of the major London streets in the Royal Borough of Kensington and Chelsea. It runs north to south, from Knightsbridge to Sloane Square, crossing Pont Street about halfway along. It appears to have long been a fashionable shopping location, especially the northern section closest to Knightsbridge, known informally as Upper Sloane Street; the shop was situated down near the end. On an international basis, Sloane Street is recognised as one of London's best addresses and has been home to many of the world's most famous designer names. Ever since the 1990s, its status has increased further and is now on an equal footing with Bond Street, which has been London's most exclusive shopping street for two centuries.

Sloane Street is also the home of many flagship stores. It has become the area for many of the world's most famous brands in fashion; for instance, Gucci, Fendi, Dior, Jimmy Choo, Yves Saint Laurent, Valentino, Chanel and Dolce & Gabbana - to name but a few. As I walked down this road, I felt extremely proud and honoured to be there. I remembered that these kinds of designers would send their fashion models, or *mannequins*, to the

Longchamp races wearing their latest inventions. They aimed to use the newspaper photographers there to get their elite creations into the press for advertising purposes.

I didn't have to walk far to get to the shop.

I was really nervous when I entered this tasteful place.

It was so large, tall and very spacious. There seemed to be just one rail of clothes, two to three dressing cubicles and a counter with two assistants behind it. Oh, and a luxurious Persian carpet throughout.

Immediately, as I entered the building, one of the assistants came over to me.

"Are you Janet Hann?" she enquired.

"Yes," I replied.

"Hello, and I'm pleased to meet you!" the middle-aged assistant said. "I've been told by Mrs Grayson to take you downstairs to the stock room."

I followed her down some stairs until we came to what appeared to be a storeroom. There were all these rails with garments on them, and each item had its own transparent plastic cover over it. Immediately, my eyes started watering as we walked through the clothes to get to the other end of the room. Once on the other side, we came to a kind of office. Inside were two women working on an oblong table; there were piles of catalogues everywhere. They seemed to be busy preparing them for posting, using sheets of paper consisting of lists of names and addresses. They had already set aside a table and chair for me in a corner, and they asked me if I would like some tea or coffee.

"Yes, please," I replied, but I was very nervous, and my eyes were watering badly.

"Mrs Grayson has asked me to show you some dresses," said one of the ladies. "She would like you to draw two or three of them for her."

I could hardly see her by now; my eyes were in a terrible state. "What's wrong with my eyes?" I asked.

"Oh," she replied, "it's the dressing in the clothes; it's really strong, isn't it?"

By now, my eyes were gushing with water.

I selected some dresses as best as I could and sat down in the corner to draw them. However, at this point, my eyes had got worse: it was as if someone was peeling onions at close range and on a permanent basis. I tried several attempts to get started, but my tears kept dripping onto my work.

"I'm really sorry," I said, "but I just can't see *anything.*"

I decided to ask for permission to move somewhere else - at a distance from the supply of clothes - and they agreed. However, this other part of the building was extremely cold and dark, and I was now rapidly beginning to lose my confidence.

I didn't know what to do.

I sipped my coffee, and I knew that it was going to be pointless.

I eventually looked up and said, "I'm truly sorry, but I just can't do anything for you today. I'm so cold. Do you think it might be possible for me to take two or three of your dresses home with me to draw? I will bring them straight back afterwards with the drawings."

The assistant went away for a while and then returned. "I've just spoken to Mrs Grayson, and she says that will be all right with her."

This member of staff started to pack up some clothing in tissue paper, and then proceeded to put them in a large dress box. She went to the cash-till, took out some money, and as she did so, she left a note in the till.

"Mrs Grayson says to give you the dresses and some money for your journeys - both here and back. She asked that you post the clothes back in the dress box when you've finished drawing them. She wants you to put the drawings in the dress box as well. She will get back to you again when she has viewed your drawings. Oh, and can you make sure that you complete the work by the end of the week?"

I agreed to do all that this kind lady had asked of me; I thanked her, said goodbye and stumbled out of the door. I knew that I was walking badly - awkwardly - as I stepped out of the shop and onto this elegant street. Plus, I found it extremely difficult to manage such a large oblong dress box, my portfolio and my handbag - even more so, on the tube and the train.

My parents were really excited when I arrived home, and more so when I told them my news. I remember my mother treating the dresses like gold; one was made of pure silk, and she couldn't get over the price of them too.

I worked really hard for the next two to three days. I became 'one' with the silhouettes; this was because I needed to breathe life into their shapes; I wanted to provide them with their rightful feelings. I further enjoyed drawing the textured fabrics; it was a challenge, plus the folds in the garments - and all in pencil! This was because pencil seemed the most appropriate media to offer a soft silky finish. On the one hand, it was a joy, but it came with a lot of pressure because I knew that this was for 'real' - it meant either a 'Yes' or a 'No!'

By the end of the week, I had carefully wrapped the garments up in dress-tissue once again, with the loving care of my mother. The drawings were the last items to go in the box. They were placed on the top whilst I wore white gloves, and it was my father who sellotaped the dress box together and prepared it for posting.

I journeyed round to the post office, and of course, I told the shop assistant about the progress of my mission. She was just as eager as we were to know what was going to happen next.

The following week, on Tuesday, another telegram arrived. Once again, it was asking me to make a further appointment to see Mrs Grayson at the shop in Sloane Street.

I eagerly ran round to the red telephone box once more, and this time it was empty, so I hurriedly opened the stiff metal door and squeezed myself inside. An appointment was fixed for the very next day, and all expenses would be paid. As I left the booth and made my way home, I felt very optimistic and, needless to say, happy. Yet, I was also well aware that I didn't actually know whether the next day would bring a Yes or a No.

I arrived at 2:00 pm. Once inside the shop, I noticed my drawings were laid out on the shop carpet and there, looking at them, was the most beautiful woman that I had ever seen.

Evette Grayson was around 5' 4" with her court shoes on, and I would say in her mid-thirties. She had the loveliest of features - high cheekbones and delicately pale skin, but it was her hair that I found stunning. It was a reddish-golden colour, swept high at the sides onto the top of her head with large curls on the crown at the top. Everything reminded me in an obscure way of the film *My Fair Lady* because Evette looked so very much like Audrey Hepburn.

Figure 19 A rendering of Audrey Hepburn

The 1964 Academy Award-winning film, *My Fair Lady*, is set in Edwardian London and is about Eliza Doolittle *(Audrey Hepburn)*, a rough Cockney girl. She meets Colonel Pickering and Professor Henry Higgins *(Rex Harrison)* in Covent Garden, where she is selling flowers. Higgins remarks that he could help Eliza speak properly and raise her status in the community, so Eliza takes him up on the offer.

Mrs Grayson wore creams, gold and browns in exquisitely subtle fabrics, and she carried a parasol.[11&12]

Figure 20 Parasols

She greeted me with a smile; she had the sweetest expression with a gap in her front teeth and the softest brown eyes that you could ever imagine. Mrs Grayson was a petite Jewess, and I liked every bit of her, complete with her surroundings - it was love at first sight for me.

She parted her lips in the way of a smile and said, "I really like your work, Janet. Shall we go for tea?"

Not actually knowing what she meant by the word 'tea,' I just said "yes" and hoped for the best.

"There's a nice little tea shop across the road; we shall go there," she said. After telling her assistants that we would be about an hour, we departed to the other side of the road.

As we walked together down this little side-road, off Sloane Street, I made sure that she walked on the inside. I glanced at Mrs Grayson, this admirable, petite lady, who was carrying her lacy parasol up high, and I felt that I was in some kind of film - only this was for real!

She asked me what tea I preferred, and, feeling a little confused about preference, I quickly said, "I will get your tea for you if you wish."

Mrs Grayson was taken aback by this but insisted that she pay.

We sat in the corner of this tea shop, and it was an 'instant like.' She asked me if I was Jewish, and I said I wasn't sure. I didn't really know what a Jew was in those days.

She replied, "I think that you are a Jew," and with this, I was glad.

Evette then said, "I want to talk to you about money; how much would you charge for producing a catalogue of approximately thirty items?"

I looked at her in amazement and then peered down at my tea. Here I was, for the first time, in the big City of London. At the same time, I was still a student at Southampton College of Art; but yet this businesswoman was willing to pay for my work!

I stirred my tea and hoped that I was doing it right.

How much money?

Of course, I hadn't got a clue.

Evette continued, "I do two catalogues a year, and they each consist of approximately thirty items. I have an agency at the moment; however, I like your work and have decided to take you on as my illustrator."

I just remember saying, "Thank you very much."

Evette sipped her tea with her lace-gloved hand, and her little finger was held high. She glanced up at me over her bone china cup. "How about seventy-five pounds for the first catalogue?" she asked.

Seventy-five pounds registered as an awful lot of money to me, and in terms of value for my work, I had no idea what this would mean.

I just remember saying, "Thank you very much," again.

With this, Evette glanced down at her watch for a few seconds, looked up at me and said, "I must go now, but if you go back to the shop, they will have packed up a box with some dresses in it for you to illustrate. They will pay you for your two-way travel fare, plus postage for you to return the first box of clothes. Once we receive the first box of garments, together with your drawings, we will send you some more; and this is how it will work."

Evette got up, and I just remember shaking her hand and saying, "Thank you very much" again; and then she was almost gone.

Nevertheless, before she did go, as she got to the door of this quaint tea-shop, she turned around, saying, "Oh, don't tell my staff what we have been discussing, will you?"

"No, I won't - but thank you!" I replied.

I sat back down at the table and sipped my tea, all of a daze.

And then I remembered that I needed to go to the shop and pick up the box of garments.

I hastily stood up, said goodbye to the tea shop's staff, and left for Sloane Street.

I really cannot remember wending my way back to the tube, nor do I know how I managed to get on the train at Waterloo station. All I recollect is the rhythmic sound of the train on the railway track:

Seventy-five pounds!

How about that!

All expenses paid!

Clickety-clack!

Clickety-clack!

Before I got off the train, I had worked out that seventy-five pounds would be enough to buy a car.

The journey from Basingstoke Railway Station was a physical struggle intertwined with mental excitement. The nearer I got to the house, the more I wanted to run to shorten the time to tell my parents the news. It had started to rain, and I worried about my portfolio and the large dress box, and I began to feel all of a dither. When I opened the side door to our home, my father was in the kitchen having a wash; he hadn't long got in from work. I could tell that he was enthusiastically impatient to see me and to hear about the account of my day. He poured me a cup of tea. As I told him about my activities, he gradually sank back in a chair.

With his head in a towel, he said, "Seventy-five pounds, duck - that's a lot of money!" But he said no more - I think he was trying to digest it all.

When my mother came in from work, I told her the same as she bustled around the kitchen trying to prepare dinner. This was the practical aspect of my mum.

At the end of my conversation and without looking up, she just said, "I wonder what we should have for dinner tomorrow!"

I think it was too much for her to take in.

I love them both very much.

Farewell to College life

It was now April 1966, and the two pressures in my life were full-on. Boxes of garments were being delivered to my house much faster than I had expected. In fact, I would be up nearly all night, most nights, trying to keep up with the illustrations. I seem to recollect that during the early hours of the morning, I would put the tip of my pencil down in one place, yet my point of focus would be two inches further to the side of it - the two functions were finding it difficult to coincide due to tiredness. At the same time, we were having mock written exams every week, whilst garments were rapidly being completed, neatened, pressed and hung up.

I remember being in the tailoring class, which was given by the professional tailor Mr Hollywell. In that class, we would sew with the garment moulded over our knees during some stages. This particular day, I had brought with me a drawing to finish in my lunch hour. I found an empty room, set-to, spread my work out and got on with it. As a commuter from Basingstoke to Southampton Terminal, I would also try to keep up with my illustrations on the train. However, the carriages would get quite crowded, and it was proving difficult this way. Nevertheless, 'some' intricate patterns on a garment were a possibility - when the train stopped at a station, that is. Every minute and all my lunch-hours, in those days, were highly calculated to get the maximum amount of time for my work out of them. I was like an acrobat, attempting to

perform great feats of dexterity and then manipulating them to
suit my purpose.

By the end of May - June, the college workload and exams were
over; yet the college itself had not come to an end, so I decided to
make the most of it and went down to the pottery and sculpture
classes. These rooms had always drawn my attention; they appeared
extremely creative; the occupants seemed so dedicated, so full of
enthusiasm and enjoyment.

I had passed these rooms many times, but it wasn't making
vessels of baked clay that I was interested in; I wanted to be a
Michelangelo and make a statue of David. This is because I used
to read on the train - and many of the times - it was my fathers'
Readers Digest books. In one of them, it told the story of the artist
and sculpture Michelangelo (1475 - 1564), who was born in
Florence, Italy.[13]

I found him so powerful and attractive that I wanted to *be
him*, so much so at times, I felt that I *was* him. So, here I was
telling the sculptor-come-pottery teacher this story, and that I had
now completed my Dress and Design Course.

"Is it possible for me to sculptor with you a statue of David,
just like the one that Michelangelo has made?"

This confused and kind teacher scratched his head and replied,
"Well, I wish we had the time to do that, but with just two weeks
left before the end of term, I'm afraid it's not possible!"

And so, I ended up doing a relief in plaster. The teacher was
really pleased with it. It was oblong, about eighteen inches in
length, and it reminded me very much of a rough sea - so rough
that I didn't bother to take it home with me at the end of the year.

Well, I hadn't achieved a statue of David. But one day,
I thought, I will fulfil my dreams.

Figure 21 An adaptation of David

N.B. Little did I realise in those days that I was waking up a gene from within. Unbeknown to me at the time, a relative in my ancestral past, my great, great grandfather (paternal), had not only been a plasterer but a freelance Master Sculptor and into such things himself! I have proof of his work too because recently, I've been given an old photograph of his house. All over the outside front walls of his home are stuck and nailed a variety of curiosities for sale: wall plaques; sculptured representations of heads; some with shoulders and chests; upper fronts, or circumferences of people's bodies. Even the garden is littered with decorative trays, furnishings and sculptured statues.

"Thank you, great, great grandfather Henry Sculptor for waking up within me because I believe that it was *you* that made me pursue the next part of my dreams – just like you did!"

Figure 22 An adaptation of Dawn

By the end of June – July, I had successfully achieved three City and Guilds of London Institute in Dressmaking, Tailoring and Dress Manufacturing, plus an extra English Literature GCE thrown into the bargain.

May - August 1966

It took me until July to complete Evette Grayson's *Autumn-Winter (1966)* catalogue. I was nineteen years of age, and this was to be the very first of many of my works being published by way of advertising for one company or another thereafter.

I had also been working hard at something else: at the end of May, I visited Basingstoke Technical College to apply for a post as a teacher in dressmaking; but at the time, there were no vacancies.[14] A few days later, I received a letter from them saying that the upholstery teacher was off sick and could I step in for the evening class. At first, I was apprehensive - after all, I hadn't been trained in upholstery and told them so. Nevertheless, they insisted that it didn't matter and that it was just for one evening. I was delighted that they had asked me and decided to accept the offer.

There were no more than a dozen mature women there that evening. I did tell them my qualifications, and if I could be of any help, I would do so. As I went around, making observations at what these people were doing, I found the craft and their skills fascinating. Surprisingly enough, it was amazing how much of my tailoring training came in useful, especially with the padding and wadding, top-stitching and blind-stitching. I really enjoyed the relaxed group; it reverberated my own courses just weeks earlier.[15]

Needless to say, I needed something much more substantial than one evening class per week for a career. It had to be of real value and solid structure, so I decided to order a *Drapers Record* magazine from the Smiths Book Shop. There were some job vacancies in there, and one of them caught my eye. *Harlee*, which was apparently part of the Lady Bird Group in London, wanted a children's coat designer. I had heard of Ladybird Children's Clothing; in fact, I remembered wearing one of their coats when I was young.

I thought about it for a while.

This would mean that I would have to commute to London every day.

I thought about the word 'Ladybird' and 'Group' and decided that it might have something to do with the Ladybird books as well, and I really liked them. It was this that made me apply.

At the same time, a friend of mine from college had also got herself a job in London and was living in a YWCA somewhere on the outskirts of the city.

Lo and behold, I got called into *Harlee* for an interview, and the next part was to find out how to get there. Once again, I took my portfolio, plus my work with Evette and headed off somewhere down the West End and from there, I went down the Clerkenwell Road. At the same time, I had set up a meeting with my college friend to join her for tea afterwards at her YWCA (Young Women's Christian Association). The interview with *Harlee* was a success, and they told me so straightaway, with a letter of confirmation to follow in the post.

I headed round to see my friend afterwards as planned, and I must admit, although it was good to see her, the place itself was very dark and dismal - a bit depressing - and even school-like. Nevertheless, my friend mentioned another YWCA that was somewhere in the West End.[16]

She said, "Why don't you live there? You will be safe, and you can travel to work from there much quicker."

As I sat on the train from Waterloo to Basingstoke, I felt like a completely different person - like I was outside of something for the first time or leaving something behind. Something was getting smaller due to something else taking over. I suppose I was beginning to sense the influence of independence - too much, or too quickly, though, because it was making me feel quite scared. Here I was with a permanent job in the pipeline; I now had everything a fashion design student could wish for. I was to be the sole designer of Children's Coats - not just with any small unknown company, but with the *Ladybird* brand that advertised in the contemporary children's magazine *Swift*.

Needless to say, I couldn't wait to tell my parents, plus the wage that had been discussed, and once again, it was a lot of money. But how was it going to work with me 'living' in London - and right in the centre of the city?

That was the scary part - and to get permission!

I was supplied with all the details necessary as to how to apply for accommodation in a YWCA in London by my college friend. Now, all that was left, was to tell the good news and the tricky aspect of staying in London to my parents.

I sat them down and told them the good news, and then I asked if I could live in a youth hostel. I think my mother thought I was talking about some kind of a drop-out centre, and she quickly got up to do something else in the kitchen. I started to explain that it was a Christian Organisation and that it was *only for women,* and with this, the atmosphere and my mother calmed down a lot. I told them I had found one, or rather, my friend had found one for me, because she was also in one whilst working in London. I would be very secure in there. It was a hostel called The Helen Graham House, which was at 57, Great Russell Street, Bloomsbury, London, WC1B 3BD.

At first, my parents declined, and then I think my father thought that they were spoiling my chances of a career, so they decided to go along with the idea.

I wrote to the hostel a few days later, and an appointment was arranged for an entry interview - one parent had to come with me.

The receptionist on the telephone told me, "You need to take the underground tube and get off at Tottenham Court Road Station. A few yards away, you will see a road called Great Russell Street, and we are just one minute's walk away, facing the entrance to the British Museum."

My mother was to be the parent to accompany me, and we were really quite excited - or I was - my mother was very nervous about London. She had only been there once or twice by coach as a sight-seer to go down the famous market in Petticoat Lane, where you get your purse stolen one end and can buy it back at the other end (so they say). Although the market at Petticoat Lane was not formally recognised and given legal trading rights until the 1930s, this location has been a market site of sorts for many centuries. However, it has to be said that this area was not always a safe place to be in. Described as "long, narrow and filthy" and a "modern Babel," many Victorians saw the market and its surrounding area as a place that respectable people avoided.

The East End of London at that time was also crowded and often unsanitary. This was a poor area with high numbers of criminals and prostitutes, and it further sat smack in the middle of Jack the Ripper's territory, the notorious women killer. It was not uncommon for police cars and fire engines to simply drive through the market with their sirens on to try to disrupt the market's activities, that is until it was made into a legal trading site.[17]

The interview at Helen Graham House was homely and wonderful. Three full meals a day consisting of not only English meals to choose from, but continental choices as well – and you could eat as much as you wanted. The bedrooms were classed as shared bedrooms with one or two others; plus, there was a television lounge. The cost was something like £4.27p per week, and you even had a cleaner - your bedroom was cleaned for you.

How heavenly is that?

Oh, and you had to be back in the house by something like 10:30 pm, except if you had a late-night pass of around 11:00 pm (I think) - but only once a week.

Now, this my mother really liked; and no guests were permitted to go upstairs.

I believe that because I had a fixed job, the interview was a success.

Once outside and down the steps, we were facing the British Museum. I had heard about this place where objects were on display illustrating antiquity, art and science. I couldn't wait to go in there; however, it was not to be on this day.

As we walked back to the tube station entrance, we passed a grand cinema. It was showing *The Sound of Music*; in fact, it was a long-standing film there with a permanent showing. We walked closer to read the posters outside to see what it was all about. The first London production of *The Sound of Music* opened in May 1961. The story is based in Austria in the 1930s and tells of a young woman named Maria (played by Julie Andrews), who is not doing very well at being a nun. Navy captain Georg Von Trapp's wife has died, and he asks the convent for a governess that can handle his seven mischievous children while he is away. Maria is given the job. The children are unhappy when Maria arrives, and she is met with hostility, but her kindness brings some much-needed joy into all their lives - including the Captain's. (N.B. The film won five Oscars in 1966 and became one of the highest money-making films in history. Fifty years on, and the fans are still talking about it.)

My mother thought this was very elaborate, and then we noticed Oxford Street. My mother had heard of Oxford Street regarding shopping and clothes, so she became very excited.

We talked a lot on the train going home, and I felt very close to my mother - perhaps one of the few times in my early days that I did.

Figure 23 Mum & me

The letter came through confirming my post with *Harlee,* and so did my residential acceptance at the YWCA. There was also another letter that dropped onto the mat. It was from Basingstoke Technical College offering me a permanent teaching post due to the upholstery teacher resigning. It was inviting me to go for an interview with the principal - the post would commence in September. Needless to say, my reply to that one was 'No,' although I did consider an odd evening class here or there.

It was only then that my parents had chimed:

"Don't be silly!"

CHAPTER THREE

London

Helen Graham House

I emerged from Tottenham Court Road Tube Station awkwardly, together with a suitcase, a large bag, various other bits and pieces and a handbag. I squinted with the brightness as I looked around and then decided the first thing to do was to telephone my mother. I walked a few yards along from the tube station entrance and stood by the two public telephone boxes. They were already occupied, but nevertheless, it gave me a chance to park myself by the booths. I fumbled with my handbag to get the necessary money out ready and was very much aware of strange people standing and watching me, albeit at a distance. This cosmopolitan setting - being free from national limitations - was something in itself that I was finding curious, even challenging. However, it was definitely one that I was going to have to get adjusted to, and as quickly as possible.

The booth was extremely hot and stuffy when I got inside it, which became even more so after I had been in there for some time with all my belongings. There was one thing that instinct had *already* warned me of - not to leave all my belongings outside a phone booth in the City of London!

I could hear the telephone ringing the other end, and then I heard my mother's voice.

"Hello Mum, I've arrived safely!" I said.

"Ah, hello, Janet. Where are you?"

"I'm at Tottenham Court Road, just around the corner from the Helen Graham House; in fact, I've got my back to *The Sound of Music*." I thought that this way, my mother would be able to visualise me better.

"Well, you take care of yourself, sweetheart, and I hope all goes well on Monday with your first day at Harlee. Let us know how you get on. We'll be thinking of you. Dad sends his love."

I said my goodbyes and put the telephone back on the hook. I managed to squeeze out of the booth backwards, which seemed to be the most sensible thing to do, and then arranged my luggage comfortably, ready for the next part of my journey.

It was a lovely sunny August day - a Saturday; what more could I wish for on the very first day of the start of my independence? My Independence Day!

I headed eastwards along New Oxford Street, with which I soon arrived at Shaftsbury Avenue. I struggled to cross over the busy junction, but eventually, I continued onwards, walking past Coptic Street, which was on my left.

Suddenly, I began to feel very lonely, like a fish out of water. Everyone was a stranger, and nobody stopped to say hello. This was to be the onset of a totally new pathway in my life, and what did my future hold? I missed my mum and dad already, and I choked back a few anxious tears. My baggage was uncomfortable, and my fingers were beginning to hurt as I turned left into Museum Street.

Another crossing and a turn to the right brought me onto Gilbert Street. I sighed with relief, for Helen Graham House was visible and now ahead on my left. I walked up the entrance steps of this pretty Victorian facade; this place, number 57 Great Russell Street, was to be my new home in the heart of Central London for how long? Well, only heaven knows!

I entered the interior-room entrance; the receptionist was kind and welcoming, and she chatted to me as she showed me around this stunning building. She told me that the home offered not only safe but comfortable accommodation as well. The first place that she took me to was a room where I would have the chance to make and meet up with new friends - the Television Lounge. I was amazed at the amount of young international women there were in there. The receptionist told me that Helen Graham House was one of the most popular accommodations for university students in London, with approximately 200 rooms.

We moved towards an enormous dining room, and from there, we walked on to some other communal areas. These were the places, she said, where you could feel comfortable and socialise. We ventured downwards to the laundry room, which of course, was quite damp and humid. Nevertheless, it served an important function as with any laundry space in any home; and we made our way back upstairs again to the ground floor. We then took the stairs to take us upwards, where we walked along the upper corridors. The assistant pointed out the shared bathrooms on each landing and proceeded to tell me about the telephones that were mid-way along each passageway. As we neared my bedroom on the second floor, she told me that each room provided for two to three people, and every room had a washbasin.

"You will have your own door key," she told me, "and there is a door security chain provided for additional safety."

The receptionist knocked on the door, and a voice from within said, "Come in!"

We entered, and sitting on her bed was a dark-haired girl reading a magazine. She was wearing dark clothes; her face was very pale but friendly, and she appeared to be about the same age as me. This young woman looked up.

"This is Janet, Kirsty; your new room-mate," the assistant said.

Kirsty smiled and got up off her bed. The receptionist told me about another room-mate, who was called Hannah and would be back in the hostel a bit later. She began to leave the room, and as she did, she turned around, saying that there was a hostel safe, should I need it, and that the reception had a twenty-four-hour policy.

"Anything you are unsure of, you can make enquiries at the twenty-four-hour reception desk." She smiled gently and asked if I had any further questions. I shook my head to say no, and as she left, she said, "Oh, we have plenty of Tourist Information leaflets in reception next time you pass."

I smiled and said thank you, and with this, she went out and closed the door.

It wasn't long before Kirsty and I got talking to each other, and the first thing I found out was that she was a trainee buyer for a well-known dress shop called *Top Shop* in Oxford Street.

Immediately we had something in common!

Harlee

Buses came and went past, but there was never the right one.

The receptionist had told me to walk to Clerkenwell and wait at the end of the road. When the right bus comes along, you need to flag it down, she had said. And that it would go down Old Street heading east.

This is where I stood at 8:15 am on the first Monday morning of work.

I stepped up onto the bus and made my way down the aisle of this motion-swaying vehicle full of cosmopolitan strangers, and then I found an empty seat and sat myself down. The journey wasn't long, and it was the bus conductor who told me where to get off.

I made my way to the building's location, and there I stood and waited by the door. Within a few minutes, a man appeared from around a corner; he was walking along the roadside between the buildings, and all the while, he was looking at me. He then crossed over the road and headed straight for me, smiling. I turned away from him a little.

"Are you our new coat designer?" A voice asked.

I turned around to face this person; he was a tall, slim, middle-aged male with spectacles, and he was wearing an ankle-length beige gabardine and carrying a briefcase. Immediately, I got the impression of a crime detective, and I had to smile a little to myself.

"Harlee," I said. "Is this the place for Harlee?"

"Yes, you've come to the right place!" he replied.

We ventured up some bare wooden stairs together until we came to a small dark room.

"Come in," said another voice from inside. "Are you Janet?"

"Yes," I said.

I began to see inside this space, and on my right, was a small, plumpish round-faced male in his mid-thirties. He was wearing a black cloth waistcoat and sat squat on a stool with elbows on a bench reading a newspaper. He turned round to face me properly and gave me a warm smile.

"Come in," He said. "Welcome to our room."

I looked around at this room, which had a kind of wooden bench running around the three walls. On it was scattered all those memorial things of my college days: pattern-cutting paper and card, a set-square, shears, pins, tape measures, rulers, pencils, rolls of fabric and a sewing machine. In the corner was a free-standing bust with a child's coat on it, which appeared half-finished with only one sleeve.

Figure 24 The workroom

The untidiness of it all was like heaven, or rather, like going from one college to another - I liked it a lot! I was told where my wall bench space was - opposite the door from whence I had just come in. But first, there was to be a tour of the whole of the building - which was really quite small.

The first place I was taken to was the administration department - a tiny office - to meet the rest of the staff. I think there were about three of them; they were very friendly and told me that I would need to use the photocopier sometimes to photocopy my work - ready to be put into their "Range" book. We, Jacob and I, stayed there for a while and then we went back to Fran in our room.

We all took a break, and as we did, Fran pulled from under the bench a chessboard, complete with chess pieces still on it in certain squares, and he and Jacob played a continuation of a game of chess together. After the break, Jacob gave me some sheets of paper and asked me to produce some coat designs for him. He told me to think of a theme - a style - that is in Vogue at the moment and then to modify it for children. He told me to continue with this one theme and adapt it in various ways for my first sheet of designs.

He said to me, "Take your time; this is what you will be doing - all the time!"

At first, I did some elaborate drawings - like my work with Mrs Grayson; but that was immediately rejected.

"It's not illustrations for publication purposes that we want from you," I was told gently. "It's the *design* of the garment that we're after. If you can design some young children's coats - say around six on a sheet - they don't even need to have heads on the sketches." I was reminded. "As long as you go into depth with the design - both the back and the front of the garment and add a description of the type of cloth, colour and trimmings - that will be it for today."

I sat there looking at the wall and went quite blank, and then it was time for lunch. I went across the road with the others to get some sandwiches - liver sausage - like the others, and brought them back - like the others - and I sat there eating my sandwiches watching the other two play chess again.

The afternoon was much better. I began to get the gist of things, and my mind cleared and went back to college days - just those few months earlier. We used to do a string of cut-out shaped garments, all the same height, width and breadth, and all in a row, as if ready to cut them out to stick onto some kind of a cardboard doll. Jacob was happy with these, and some of them were workable, he told me.

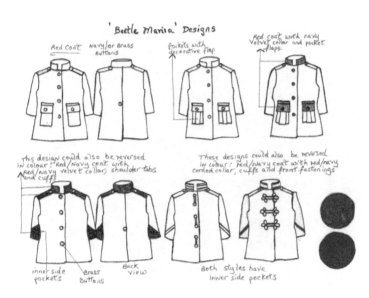

Figure 25 Coat designs

It was time to go home, and as I stepped outside the building, the first thing that hit me was the cool fresh (well, relatively speaking) air. Immediately I had a headache, and I soon realised how hot and stuffy the room had been. I sat on the bus going back to the hostel, oblivious of whom or what else was on there besides me. In one respect, I suppose I was happy - day one at work was over, but what had the rest of the day to bring?

Anyway, the first thing to do was to ring my mum - from inside my new home!

Social Life

I opened the door of my bedroom, and there, lying on her bed face down, was Hannah, my other room-mate; she had books all over her bed, and she was writing in a notebook. She looked up at me with a smile. I went over to my bed and put my bag down; we had a lot to talk about.

Hannah was in her early twenties, tall, slim, with short, fair hair and a pleasant face - she was a trainee medical doctor and extremely enthusiastic. Hannah was not like me or Kirsty, who left early in the morning and came back early evening five days a week; Hannah was unpredictable as to whether she was going to be in all the time or out most of the time. However, this wasn't a bad thing because as far as sharing a washbasin between the three of us, it worked out to be a good arrangement. Besides, we all had something different to talk about. I enjoyed the set-up in this room immensely; although I must say, I can't remember if there was ever any day where we ate together in the dining hall!

There are two young women that are really close to my heart - even now as I write this so many years later. Their names are Silky (my pseudo-name for her) and Kathy.

Silky was German, and she came across as one of the most philosophical, tender and caring persons that I think I had ever met. She had come to London to learn the English Language, and she worked in Foyles, the book shop in Charing Cross Road. Foyles was once known as London's largest educational bookseller. Silky and I met up because she was eating alone in the dining hall on my first Monday evening, and when she saw me eating on my own as well, she came over and asked if she could join me. We were both very shy and reserved, and we both liked each other for that reason. One thing that I learned almost immediately was that Silky was more of a vegetarian than a meat-eater.

After our evening meal, I went to join her in her room with her room-mates. We all chatted for a while, and then I left for my own room.

The following day, Silky and I had our evening meal together again; she talked to me as we wended our way up to our rooms and then she burst into tears. She began to tell me about a customer that had come into Foyles that day: it was a young male who had come up to her holding out a small tin. He begged her to take it off him, and she was frightened of what it might contain. She continued sobbing as she told me that as he spoke to her, his teeth kept dropping in his mouth. He wanted so much to give up his habit and this was what it was all about. Silky had gone over to her boss and told him about the young man, and he told Silky that he would deal with the customer.

Silky was very upset! She said, "Why do these people get themselves in such a mess?"

It upset her deeply, and I loved her very much for that.

My other friend Kathy is someone I also met in my early hostel days. I was waiting to use the hostel's telephone - and so was Kathy. It wasn't long before we got talking, with which Kathy poured out her life to me. She was a New-Zealander - not an Australian - she promptly corrected me, and they had similar weather to us! Kathy worked in a London Office, and she was older than me - in her early thirties. She had come to England, to London, to start a new life. Her life back home had gone pear-shaped!

As I listened to her, she told me that she had an illegitimate baby boy and had to have him adopted. She was very depressed and upset with the circumstances and decided to make a radical change in her life. As I took in what Kathy was saying to me, I could tell she was very unsettled. There were so many things that she disagreed with, and I felt that she had travelled such a long way – from New Zealand to London - when really all she needed to do was to look deeper within herself.

The three of us (Kathy, Silky and myself) began to eat together in the evenings. It wasn't long that I had been in my new home, no more than two to three days before Kathy said that she wanted to go to see Simon and Garfunkel at the Windmill Theatre near Piccadilly Circus. She asked if Silky and I would go with her.

I hardly knew anything about Paul Simon and Art Garfunkel; apparently, they started from humble beginnings as a Rock n Roll duo 'Tom and Jerry.' It was in these very days, the swinging sixties, that they were doing well with their hits including, *'Mrs Robinson,'* *'Cecilia,'* *'Bridge Over Troubled Water,'* *'Homeward Bound,'* and many more.

As for the Windmill Theatre, I had never heard of it at all. I remember sitting in this quaint theatre in the middle of my first week in my new home, watching this film and feeling very proud of myself. Here I was in the centre of London, and I hadn't needed to go on a coach trip and make a long journey to get there; or travel some long-distance home afterwards. We just had to take a few minutes to walk around the corner to where we lived.

However, I think if I had known the history of the Windmill Theatre, I do believe I would never have gone![1]

Needless to say, we thoroughly enjoyed ourselves. We had created a very close-knit bond between us, with which we decided that we would go out again – the three of us - another time!

What would my parents have said?

The first week of work was pretty much the same as the first day. I would arrive and find that Fran and Jacob would be playing chess. I would produce a few designs until lunchtime, then we would go across the road and get our liver pâté sandwiches, and I would watch the two of them playing chess whilst I ate my lunch. In the afternoon, I would complete the sheet of designs and then it would be home time.

However, as the week moved on, I began to take more and more notice of the other events that were taking place in the room. Each day, there seemed to be some kind of movement, an increment, or an increase, towards some kind of goal. Fran would be making patterns using the pattern-cutting paper or card, and Jacob would be placing Fran's pattern pieces onto cloth and cutting the shapes out using a large pair of tailoring shears. Jacob would then proceed to machine the parts together and put them onto the free-standing tailor's child bust. It was about Thursday when I noticed that the garment on the dummy was a design from my very first day's sheet of creations.

'So, this is how it works in here,' I thought.

In these particular days – that is, the '60s - Ladybird was one of the UK's best-known children's clothing brands with a long history dating back to the 18th century. Its main aim was to make children's clothing both fashionable and functional. Each garment was designed to cope with the rough and tumble of a child's life, from messy playtimes to smarter occasions. It had been the 1950s that saw the first of the famous Ladybird press adverts, depicting Ladybirds in various human-like roles, including scientists and computer boffins. Later, in the 1960s, the firm's clothing was being promoted by "The Ladybird Adventure Club," a full-colour comic strip in the children's magazine *Swift*.

During this period, Ladybird was effectively selling two ranges: one in high street stores where this clothing was cheaper and more accessible to ordinary families; the other was for the independent retailers, where the Ladybird brand name itself was used. These latter garments were generally more expensive and higher quality pieces bought for Sunday best or by better-off families.[2]

Figure 26 Ladybird (adapted)

I remember that first Friday evening, sitting on a bus on my way home from work and enjoying a great sense of satisfaction - the first week of my career was now complete!

That weekend, we (Kathy, Silky and I) decided to catch a bus to Petticoat Lane.
"We need to leave early," they had said, and that's what we did!
We had a wonderful time - the three of us - and I began to feel somehow that I was settling down quite nicely, with the City of London being my home and my new way of life.

It wasn't many days afterwards that Kathy told me she was moving out of the hostel. I was shocked. She told me that she didn't agree with all the tight rules and regulations - especially only one late-night pass per week. Kathy had got herself into a flat with five Australian young women. The cost was £27:00 per week. I found this hard to comprehend, especially as she had to buy all her own food on top of that, considering the hostel charged £4:27p per week for everything - even food, three meals per day etc. and your room cleaned for you. I just thought that she was crazy, and all because she needed more freedom. Well, I suppose she was older than me, more worldly, and perhaps I was just a young naïve woman at that stage.

However, Kathy invited me round to her flat about three weeks later to have dinner with her. We enjoyed an omelette each - because that was all she could afford. In every room, there were her flat-mates, plus a male or two or three. I remember walking back to the hostel, and I can tell you, I really slept well in my bed that night - even if we did have warm water coming out of the cold tap. One of my friends had also said that, in London, you could drink a glass of water one week, and the next week you might be drinking that same recycled water again.

Yes, I, too, had to think a bit about that one as well!

About three to four weeks later, my room-mate Kirsty said that she was going out for an evening coffee with a girlfriend of hers from work and would I like to join in. It was a café not far off Oxford Street, she said, so I decided to go along with them.

We met Kirsty's friend at the top of Oxford Street; it was around 8:00 pm, and the three of us started our walk down Oxford Street. I had no idea where we were going; they just said it wouldn't take us long.

We turned off to our left and made our way down this side road; it was now dark, and there were quite a lot of people walking in groups. Some of them were singing out loud, and I could smell alcohol. It was the kind of scene that I'd been told not to mix or mess with at home; I found it very creepy - and I really didn't seem to take to Kirsty's friend.

There was this little grubby café that looked very bare inside, just a few round tables and chairs and, I believe, a jukebox. The light in there seemed extremely bright. I didn't want to go inside, and I told them so, but it didn't seem to make any difference - they said they were going to meet up with someone else in there.

We entered this place, and the smell of stale smoke nearly knocked me over as we walked towards a table. They had chosen to sit at the centre table; yet I wanted to sit more by a wall, out of the way; but the other two were adamant they had chosen the right space. They went over to buy a coffee, and I followed them; however, there was no way that I wanted any coffee - or tea - from *this* place. I went back to join them. There they sat, just talking about nothing much and smoking their cigarettes while the time was ticking on now to gone 10:00 pm. I'd had enough and told them I wanted to go home.

I exited the café, but as I made my way onto this narrow street, I looked back at the coffee shop. It was only then that I realised that the café's window was very dirty, well smeary, and exhibited a white skull and cross-bone in its centre. I shuddered with fear. However, this was nothing compared to what was about to follow.

A male stared at me from a distance, then sauntered up to me and said, "Hello, Doll! How much do you charge?"

I glowered at him, turned my back in horror and started to walk quickly to make my way out of this dark street. A party of around three to four sailors were heading my way; they were swaying as well as walking, and they were laughing and joking. I knew they were out to do all those things that they would not normally do, and they were coming towards me, but I won't tell you what they said. I quickly ran back to the café and rushed inside, pleading with the other two to return home with me. I didn't feel safe in this horrible road.

It took a long time before they reluctantly stood up, dragging their chairs as they did so, and not before finishing their conversations with some males they had palled up with.

As a scattered procession, the three of us made our way along the street. It was noisy, many men in pairs and groups strolling along this road, seemingly friendly and flirty, lots of loud music blasting out from more grotty places. I was really tired and not amused by it all – and, by the way, what was the name of this road? We got to the end of it and came to Oxford Street once again, but before we turned off out of this road, I had a chance to glance up at its name on the wall of a building.

'Soho Street,' it said.

The Soho area has been at the heart of London's sex industry for over 200 years. From the 1930s to the early 1960s, Soho folklore states that the pubs of Soho were packed every night with drunken writers, poets and artists, many of whom never stayed sober long enough to become successful. Prostitutes packed Piccadilly Circus and the streets and alleys around Soho.

By the early 1960s, the low end of the legal sex trade generally depended upon streetwalkers picking up clients on the street and taking them back to cheap rooms. Almost every doorway in Soho had red-lit doorbells or open doors with little postcards just inside advertising "Large Chest for Sale" or "French Lessons Given." While the area was home to nearly a hundred strip clubs, it was also during this period that the Soho pub landlords established themselves.[3]

I hardly slept a wink all night, for my head was full of the evening's noises, smells and dangerous events, which came across as a nasty nightmare. When I arrived at work the next day, I was exhausted and tired. I told Fran and Jacob where my friends had taken me the evening before. They both looked at each other and chuckled and then told me to give it a miss if they asked me again - and to change my hostel room.

I decided to tell the receptionist that I wanted a change of room, and the next thing I had to do was wait until a bed became available elsewhere.

A few days later, I was given a choice of two - up on the third floor!

Nearby Attractions

I considered myself fortunate because Helen Graham House is situated in a very exclusive area of London, known as Bloomsbury - right opposite the British Museum. It wasn't long before I found out why the house's residents were keen to make the most of their stay in London.

For a start, the hostel is within walking distance of many of London's most famous landmarks and museums. For example, the London Transport Museum tells you the story of London and its transport system over the last 200 years. Furthermore, it highlights the powerful link between transport and the growth of modern London, culture and society, since 1800. The museum also offers many opportunities by way of skills development to a variety of audiences.

Once we leave this museum, and only a few minutes away, other concerts and dance exhibitions are held in the Royal Opera House.

Helen Graham House also sits very close to the busy heart of London's West End, near The Fortune Theatre and Theatre Royal in Drury Lane. There are also other theatres like the Adelphi Theatre, Cambridge Theatre and The Lyceum Theatre. Not only is there the beauty of so many choices, but you can go to any of the West End musicals, and after curtain down, you can be back in the hostel within a ten-minute walk. Or, if you want to, you can pop down to Covent Garden and enjoy listening to and watching the free performances by the buskers.

There are other exciting events as well because it doesn't stop there. If you choose to visit a restaurant for an early supper, the chances are that you will be sitting next to a cast member of a musical or play. You can even watch these rising stars in action in shows at the nearby Bloomsbury Theatre.

There is also a range of gatherings to sell varying commodities; for instance, at the old Grade II-listed Flower Market building in Covent Garden Piazza, there are various markets selling 'fruits, flowers, roots and herbs.' It became London's principal vegetable, fruit and flower market, and in the 1830s, permanent buildings replaced the traders' stalls in the central square. There are other markets - supermarkets - and restaurants of global selection; there are cafés as well as the shops on Oxford Street and Regent Street. What more could you want in the way of excitement, entertainment and choice?

Helen Graham House is located just a five-minute walk away from Holborn and Tottenham Court underground stations. This, in itself, provides yet another fascinating interest for here, you can also visit the electronic shops on Tottenham Court Road. If you are keen to become a budding pop star, you would do well to pay a visit to Denmark Street's fabulous guitar shops.

I could not get over the fact that there was so much variety and so many interesting things so near at hand. It seemed as if we had everything at our fingertips. What more could we wish for?

British Museum

Nevertheless, the real love of my life in those days was the magnificent British Museum. I could not have even dreamt that I would be living just one minute's walk from the architecture and wonderful exhibits of the British Museum. It was literally just across the road from my home. I could view all those treasures anytime I liked - and for free!

The British Museum was founded in 1753, the first national public museum in the world. From the beginning, it granted free admission to all 'studious and curious persons.' The origins of the British Museum lie in the will of the physician, naturalist and collector, Sir Hans Sloane (1660–1753). Over his lifetime, Sloane collected more than 71,000 objects that he wanted to be preserved intact after his death. So, he bequeathed the whole collection to King George II for the nation in return for a payment of £20,000 to his heirs. The gift was accepted, and on the 7th of June 1753, an Act of Parliament established the British Museum. The founding collections largely consisted of books, manuscripts, natural specimens with some antiquities (including coins and medals, prints and drawings) and ethnographic material.

The British Museum opened to the public on the 15th of January 1759. It was first housed in a seventeenth-century mansion, Montagu House, in Bloomsbury on the site of today's building. To make room for the increasing collections held by the Museum, the natural history collections were moved to a new building in South Kensington in the 1880s. This became the Natural History Museum.[4]

All those galleries! I stared up at the boards in the entrance with astonishment: *Africa, the Americas, Ancient Egypt, Ancient Greece and Rome, Asia, Europe and the Middle East.* Which way should I go? Well, to be honest, it didn't really matter, after all when it happens to be your next-door neighbour, you have plenty of time to visit them all!

It was here that I fell in love with ancient cultures, and every Sunday afternoon, I would stroll across alone to the museum to wander through those glorious galleries. The vast holdings of the British Museum come from all millennia and from all over the world. There were objects from ancient Greece and Rome; the Medieval and later periods; the Oriental and Japanese Antiquities. I would saunter through the countless galleries, completely immersed and oblivious to the people around me. I would peer inquisitively at the Roman coins and sculptures. I would stare intently at the Assyrian art and the medieval tiles and pottery. However, there was one that I had become extremely interested in, and that was the Americas - especially, for some reason, Mexico. I think they held my attention because the Maya believed that the world had been created and destroyed at least three times and that the last cycle of creation began on the 13th of August, 3114 BC.

But there was something else. It was to do with the Yaxchilan and the 'Place of the Split Sky,' which was located on the banks of the Usumacinta River, close to the present border between Mexico and Guatemala. This city had been constructed between 400 and 800 AD by successive rulers. Two buildings in Yaxchilan had contained a series of panels, and on them were scenes depicting the rituals performed to ensure success in battle and secure captives for sacrifice. Each panel formed the upper lintel of a doorway so that the participants in the ritual passed beneath them.[5] The lintels, which were in the British Museum, had been collected by a Dr Alfred Maudslay, who had journeyed from England (Herefordshire) to the ruins of the 'lost' Mayan city of Quirigua in January 1881. Alfred Maudslay's casts and moulds were displayed in the Maudslay Room, and this was the only time that a living scientist had been honoured in that way.

I really enjoyed those Sunday afternoons, but it was the Egyptian galleries that held my imagination the most.

**Figure 27 Taken from the Neskapashuty papyrus
(Third Intermediate Period)[5]**

The above papyrus tells of *Nut* at the top, that represents the sky. At the bottom, *Geb* evokes the earth. Between these two bodies sit *Shu* and *Tefenet* in a boat; they have just separated *Nut*, the sky, from *Geb*, the earth.[6] The more I stared at this remarkable work, the more I could see my work as a fashion illustrator within it: the elongated bodily forms; the expressions; the gestures; all created for a symbolic purpose - that is, that there is a deeper meaning of something 'other' within it. On the left, I could see Creation at work through the epochs (divisions of geological time). I felt that the number four represented the Earth, and with this, the shapes, the things in the picture, gradually began to come alive. The eyes, for example, were constantly watching over Creation as to what was taking place. I saw the baboons as representing, perhaps, humankind.

As I stared, fixed, on the plant-shaped items surrounding planet earth (to me, the square), they first became rockets with which they gradually changed to become comets that were seeding and shaping our planet. They seemed to be suggestive of various eras or epochs on earth. The upright snake-come-serpent too, represented to me the changing era, or cycle on earth - an end of an old era and the beginning of a new age. I felt that these illustrative symbols were talking to me, and the more I studied them, the more multi-dimensional they became. The comets were furthest away, whilst the more prominent features were items closer to us.

These ancient Egyptians had such a deep-seated belief in the afterlife - which is their way of life, their religion - that it appeared to me to be embedded in their history. I soon came to view these pictures, these hieroglyphs, as their symbols for *their* Bible, *their* Torah, *their* Koran. Why do we say that their beliefs are any different to ours? These illustrations seem to be expressing their deep-felt feelings about *our* origins and *our* way of life - so much so that it appeared to me to be not only related to *their* religion and about *their* creation but *ours* as well!

I would move in closer to the notice boards on the walls, which told many stories of this mysterious ancient land, where giant pyramids, colossal temples and huge statues still stand. These lasting monuments relate to Egypt's Greatness. They tell of the growth of this country, and as one of the oldest centres of civilisation, they tell of the many pharaohs who ruled the nation.

Figure 28 Rameses II charging into battle

Rameses II (19th dynasty) was perhaps the best-known pharaoh in all Egyptian history. Maybe his real significance lies in the fact that he built more buildings and sculptures than any other pharaoh. In 332 BC, Alexander the Great of Greece marched into Egypt and took control of the country. When Alexander died in 323 BC, the rule of Egypt was taken over by his general, Ptolemy 1. That was the end of what was called 'The Pharaonic Age' and the beginning of 'The Ptolemaic Period.' Slowly, Egypt became culturally more Greek. The native population continued to speak the ancient Egyptian language and practice their own religion, but the most educated amongst them also spoke Greek and were given Greek education. Queen Cleopatra was the last of the Ptolemaic rulers. She tried to restore the dignity and glory of ancient Egypt, but it was too late. In an effort to keep her rule, she married Anthony of Rome.[7]

Figure 29 Cleopatra and Anthony

Later, when Anthony was defeated by Octavius, Cleopatra took her own life. After her death, ancient Egypt ceased to exist as an independent kingdom.

The Egyptian Galleries also tell a story of the common people who worked and enjoyed life in ancient Egypt. They worshipped many gods and goddesses, and the museum tells of their lifestyles, regalia and precious treasures.

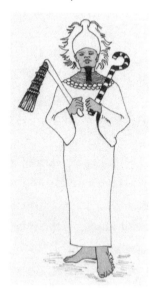

Figure 30 Osiris, King of the 'Other World'

Osiris was the god of the underworld, judge of the dead, and symbol of eternal life. He wears the *Atef* crown, similar to the 'White Crown.' He carries the royal scourge and hook. Osiris was often shown as a mummy, tightly wrapped in a linen shroud. Following tradition, his skin would be painted green.

Another god was Anubis, the jackal-headed god of the 'Other World,' whom helps prepare the burial of the corpse with embalming and glorifies the dead. An ornamental tail hangs from his belt. He holds the *was* sceptre and an *ankh*.

I also noticed that mummification, magic and ritual were being investigated in these galleries through the objects on display. It is the death and afterlife rooms containing mummies and funerary equipment that held my heart most of all, and this is where I would spend most of my time. These included coffins, mummies, funerary masks, portraits and other items designed to be buried with the deceased.[8] Death and the afterlife held particular significance and meaning for the ancient Egyptians. They would hold complex funeral preparations and rites which were thought to be needed to ensure the transition of the individual from earthly existence to immortality.[9]

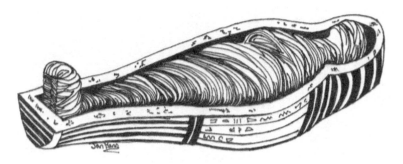

Figure 31 Mummy

It's strange, isn't it, how mummies still have the power to fascinate us? They are some of the most popular museum exhibits. After the body had been embalmed and wrapped, a mask was usually placed over the head. This not only protected the mummy's face but also provided something else for the Ba and Ka to recognise. The masks of the pharaohs were made of solid gold or silver and decorated with semi-precious stones or glass. For the less wealthy, the masks were made of cartonnage, a type of papier-mâché formed from papyrus and linen, which was cheap, light and easy to paint. Although the masks were painted with portraits of the dead, most of these were highly stylised and were barely recognisable as the real person.

I found all these things absolutely fascinating.

Figure 32 Iconography

Symbols

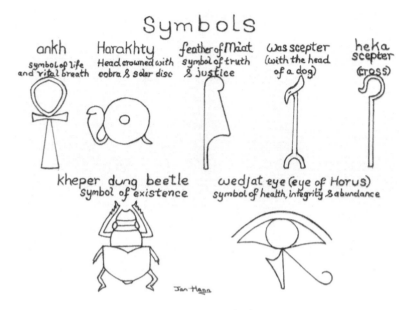

ankh
symbol of life
and vital breath

Harakhty
Head crowned with
cobra & solar disc

feather of Maat
symbol of truth
& justice

Was scepter
(with the head
of a dog)

heka scepter
(cross)

kheper dung beetle
symbol of existence

wedjat eye (eye of Horus)
symbol of health, integrity & abundance

Jan Hana

Figure 33 Symbols

It has been said that Egyptian hieroglyphs could only be read after 1822 when a French scholar called Jean-François Champollion discovered how to decipher them. It was thanks to him that such findings as the Rosetta Stone were decoded. This grey granitoid stone was discovered in 1799 AD and contained a copy of a decree written in three different texts: the Egyptian, which is written in two scripts: hieroglyphic and demotic, whilst the third text is in Greek.[10]

These artefacts had such a deep, profound and rewarding impact on me that they have affected me for the rest of my life. On reflection, they caused a fork in my pathway of life, which I later pursued further.

"Have you come up for tea again?" the security officer would say.

I would just smile a little and, without replying, head back to the hostel to be alone again. After all, I would have more work to complete; not only was my London Fashion Illustration freelance business continuing to be a success, but it was also expanding. It was during this period that I was further asked to undertake illustrating for Evette's friend and her Stacy Knitwear business in Finchley Road, London. And before long, I was to be producing illustrations for all ends of the fashion trade.

Figure 34 Fashion Jumper

Figure 35 Design Your Own Wedding Dress (advert.)

Figure 36 Two-piece outfit

Figure 37 Ciré Mac

Figure 38 Bikini (advert.)

Figure 39 Underwear (advert.)

A Dream

I tossed and turned; there is something that will not let me stay asleep, yet I'm not awake either. It's one of those strange things where you are in the midst of a vivid dream, but yet you are consciously controlling it at the same time. I decided to give in and let my lucid dream continue:

I am looking at a kind of catalogue, a photograph album, a really old one, which is oblong, as in landscape in shape, and I open it up. I begin to focus on the photographs in there until I come to a particular one. The photograph has been produced using a kind of sepia tone, which provides the viewer with an archaic scene.[11] There is a street in the City of London that I am focusing on, with several shops. It appears to be something like the Victorian days because the women show bustles on the rear of their long, beautiful dresses, and they wear brimmed hats with feathers. These people are thronging the street, crowding together as if they are waiting for a procession to pass. I suddenly notice a little girl sitting on a large stone curb, and she is looking at the photographer that is taking the picture. She has a lovely smile, and it's as if she is smiling at me too.

Suddenly, it's as if she has noticed me; she gets up off the stone slab and comes across the cobbled street. All the while, she is staring at the photographer, which makes me think that she is looking at me. She seems to be trying to get my attention and is beckoning me with her finger to come into the picture – to go in and join her. I get closer and closer, and she tells me a name and then she goes back to where she was at the beginning, but she wants me to join her.

I don't know what to do, so I wake up.

I think, 'That's a funny dream!' And I ponder over it.

After a while, I try to make sense of it. I come up with the idea that my mind has pieced together all the bits in my contemporary life: my love for the British Museum and its ancient artefacts – which takes me into the past; my drawings of fashions, lovely clothes and the catalogues that I produced. Add my work as a child's coat designer, and they were all linked together in this neat little prominent dream.

I began to feel really tired.

Something else was happening to me – I was getting very home-sick.

As I looked out of the hostel's window, I watched the various visitors coming and going into The British Museum. I could see some sitting and eating on the steps of the building, while others were having their photograph taken in a group.

I began to think, 'What is my profession doing for me?'

I thought about it for a while . . . and then I knew.

'I had acquired the ability to see patterns in things and to link them together. And more importantly, to change pieces around, which allowed for a whole host of themes. But most of all, I believe that I had learnt the silent quality of being able to think for myself!'

CHAPTER FOUR

Meeting up with Dave

October 1966:
Something important is missing in my life

It had been when I turned 20 years of age that I began to feel more and more alone. It was time for me to find a companion, so it seemed, and to settle down. I was hearing a greater degree of others coupling up and going places with their boyfriends. I was also discovering that my lifestyle seemed to be attempting to allow extra time for finding a companion, but how and where should I start?

One day, my friends said they were going to Leicester Square to the Mecca Ballroom dance hall there and asked whether I would like to join them. I thought about it for a while - the ins and outs of what to wear, of meeting someone, and whether I *really* had the time to spare - and with this, I decided not to go.

My life in those days, as always, consisted of work; Harlee, Evette Grayson's Catalogue, and her friend's knitwear shop; Helen Graham House and oh, not forgetting the British Museum. What I mean with the latter is that I had now not only got into making regular saunters across to the museum, but I had also become curious as to why certain people would be sitting near objects and artefacts etc. They appeared to be arduously making notes or creating sketches and were normally students doing research. This is what was to sow a seed (or thought) and provide me with a desire for my own later lifestyle - I wanted to be like them - I wanted to be a researcher. Nevertheless, in those days, it was just a wishful dream.

On this particular day, something different happened. I overheard a young woman in the hostel's dining hall saying that she had an evening job at a café that was in the next side street to the hostel. However, she was stating that she wasn't able to work that evening and asked if someone would be willing to take her place. I sat there and listened to what she was saying, and I remember thinking that she looked respectable, so I offered to stand in for her that evening.

I walked my way around the corner to the café, which only took me three to four minutes, with which I was there for 7:00 pm. It was a lovely, small, cosy, relaxed coffee house that catered for no more than about five to six tables, which would seat three to four people around each table. The owner was Greek, and the decor was smart black and white Grecian-style. My job was to serve the customers with coffee and perhaps some of the owner's homemade apple pie and wash up in between. The coffee house closed at 11:00 pm. At this point, we, the owner and me, finished washing any cups and dirty plates etc., and then sat down and had some apple pie and a chat. By this time, it was 11:30-11:45 pm. I got paid and went back home to the hostel - just minutes away.

I was very tired the next morning when I set off for work, yet it had been a different experience as well as enjoyable. The next evening the young woman asked how I got on, and I told her that it was good. It wasn't long after this that she asked if I could take her place again - and so I did. It appeared that she worked there three times a week, and she wanted to leave; she asked if I would take her place. I thought about it for a while and decided that it was refreshing, plus a change from my other work, so I told her - and the Greek - that I would work there temporarily until he found someone more permanent.

One of the things that I found out whilst working there was that there were a lot of educational institutions around the area. Just a short distance away was the University College of London; the School of Oriental and African Studies; the London Business School and School of Economics. The University of the Arts and the London School of Hygiene & Tropical Medicine were also nearby, and so was the King's College and Regents College, plus the University of Westminster campuses. There were also several language schools in central London. Therefore, it wasn't surprising that such students regularly visited the coffee shop.

One month later, I am still working there; and although I enjoyed the atmosphere and the extra money, I was suffering badly from tiredness.

One evening, the Greek asked me if I would work for him on Saturday as he desperately needed help on that particular day. I accepted his offer, but just for this Saturday only.

At the end of Saturday's shift, the Greek closed the café saying, "I want to show you something."

He took me across the road and unlocked a door; he showed me into this other place that was just like the café, only this room had Greek sculptures and carvings in it - all his own collection. I was amazed and in awe of these items of beauty. As you know, I loved everything about the formation and modelling of sculptured statues. He was very happy - excited - whilst he showed me his treasures. It was then that he told me he was divorced and was looking for a partner with the same interests as himself - artwork. I began to feel very vulnerable and frightened because I was alone in this building with this middle-aged man; plus, I had already noticed that he could easily become fiery-spirited. I stayed cool, calm and in control of myself and continued with our conversations.

I eventually told him that I had to get back to the hostel as I had work to do. He was very reluctant to let me leave, but eventually, he unlocked the door and, we walked back to the café so that I could receive my day's pay.

As I walked back to the Helen Graham House, I decided that it was time to give that part-time job a miss from then onwards - and that's what I did.

All Alone

More and more, I was finding London a very lonely place. So many of the young women in the hostel were foreigners, and a lot of them were homesick too - just like me. All I can say is that if you are looking for excitement and the jet-set and to be up front with the latest in England, of course, London is the place to be. You will also need plenty of money to visit and experience the variety and choices of interesting places, but that is what the City of London is all about. However, it was here in the very heart of London that I learnt of another side to life - relationships. It seems that we are not only built on relativity, but we also *need* friends and people who care about us and with who we would like to share our lives and interests. This is what I was missing most of all – close bonds!

As a person who was dedicated to getting a career in her life, I had not been bothered with boyfriends, as such, but there had been one in my life. It had all started at the school dance when a local band came to play. It had a lead singer, and during the interval, the curtains closed, and a record was put on. It wasn't long before a hand touched my shoulder. I turned around and much to my surprise it was the lead singer of the band.

"Would you like to dance with me?" He had asked.

I was very self-conscious in company. Even though I was sixteen, I had never been kissed.

He was extremely good-looking and wore a brown tweed jacket. He was very caring and tender and danced extremely well.

At the end, he said, "I must go for the second half now."

With this, he proceeded to put his hand in his pocket and pulled out some car keys saying, "Can I take you home tonight?"

Extremely shy, I had replied something like, "But I came with my school friends, and I can't let them down!"

He smiled and said, "Well, I can take them home as well!"

And he did! But *I* was the last one that he dropped off home that night!

As I say, I was sixteen, and it was later that I discovered he was twenty-six years old. Needless to say, I always had exams on my mind plus a career to create, and this was the brunt of our arguments. You see, this male wanted a permanent settlement together with me.

It had been sometime in July 1963 when I told him that I had been accepted at Southampton College of Art for a two-year Fashion Design course, and it was to be the end of our relationship.

"Why?" he had asked.

"It's because, well, I won't be able to cope with both you and a career!" I replied.

He had shaken his index finger violently at me, and attempting to stifle his tears, he said, "Just you remember, when you get to the top of your pinnacle, I will look across at you from mine (he was a first-class and excellent builder with his own business), and I will say to you, 'Do you remember *me* in those earlier days?'"

I remember I had silently got out of his car, walked into my parents' home and closed the door without looking back. 'Would I regret it?' I had thought to myself in those days.

Well, here I was in London, feeling very lonely, even though I was doing well with my career. I was already beginning to wonder if I had done the right thing!

There is something *deep* about 'Love' and 'Bonding,' and sharing one's life and feelings, isn't there? It seems to be the most powerful and natural thing. And that's where I was with my thoughts - all alone at the age of twenty.

Dave

There came a knock on the door from one of my hostel friends; she had come to say that the three of them were planning to go back to the Mecca Ballroom dance hall again at Leicester Square tomorrow, and would I like to go along with them? I declined at first because I didn't feel like it, and I had too much to do.

But she was persistent, saying, "It will do you good to do something different for a change!"

It was nearly the end of October 1966. and I had been working hard with Harlee for a while now.

"It's only around the corner!" she had said, "and we don't have to stay late!"

Eventually, I gave in and started sorting something out to wear for the next evening.

We made our way round to Leicester Square in the West End of London, which is a pedestrianised square with a small park at its centre. It lies within the City of Westminster and is located north of Trafalgar Square, east of Piccadilly Circus, west of Covent Garden and south of Cambridge Circus.

In the 19th century, Leicester Square became known as an entertainment venue, with many amusements that were peculiar to the era.[1] By the start of the 21st century (2010), a major redevelopment took place. As part of a Great Outdoors scheme, there were concerns that the square was too dangerous at night. Certain sections were to be demolished to encourage the growth of theatres and cinemas and to reduce the popularity of nightclubs.[2]

When we reached the ballroom, it was massive. I had never known anything to parallel it - not even my old school hall. This ballroom had originally been known as The Empire Theatre of Varieties and was opened in 1881 on the former site of Savile House, but it had a troubled start. It was originally a Victorian Music Hall, but it had a notorious reputation for high-class prostitutes frequenting the theatre. In 1894, the London County Council ordered the promenade on the upper balcony to be remodelled.

The first moving pictures in Britain were shown here by the Lumiere Brothers in 1896. The theatre was eventually replaced by today's building in 1928 and updated to provide multi-screen use in the 1960s, with its stalls becoming the Mecca Ballroom.[3]

The Mecca Leisure Group (also known as Mecca Leisure Ltd., Mecca Ltd, and Mecca Dance Ltd) was a British business that ran nightclubs, hotels, theme parks, bingo parlours and hard rock cafes. During the 1960s, they were the centre of entertainment throughout major UK towns and cities. Mecca ballrooms were used for such entertainments as the BBC TV show *Come Dancing* and the Miss World competitions.[4]

We (the four of us) sat around a table in a corner near the band, but even that seemed a long way away. There didn't appear to be many people in there, but it was like looking out at a vast ocean - surely there must have been others out there somewhere! We sat there with our drinks, and to be honest, I felt like a fish out of water. I seemed to have matured since those days or grown out of that sort of thing, and I just wanted to return to the hostel and go to bed - something that I had always reverted to once I had eaten my evening meal.

The television room was usually full of foreign students, and once again, this always emphasised my loneliness. In bed, I could settle down to thinking of more designs for tomorrow's work - and it was warm and cosier too.

The ballroom consisted of darkish, low-lighting, and I could see this lone figure standing there with a brown suit on. He was, I would say, a few feet away from me, but he was concentrating on us. I noticed that he had dark, wavy hair, and I've always liked dark-haired men, which probably stems from having a dark-haired father. The four of us young women started talking about something, and then this male was now asking me to dance with him. I got up, and he ushered me onto the dance floor. He was very nervous, and I knew that it wasn't something that he did very often. Immediately afterwards, he asked me if he could take me home.

I said, "Well, maybe, but we only live just around the corner."

He smiled and replied, "That's fine; I will take you there."

To be truthful, I just wanted to go home straight away anyway - I was so tired. I asked my friends if they would like to leave too, and with this, they discussed it between them, and they all agreed it was time to go back to the hostel. The four of us got up, and together with this male, whom I shall call Dave, we all left the ballroom together.

Once outside the ballroom, there were two men dressed as Egyptians doing a soft-shoe-shuffle in a long box of sand; they were dancing to the sound of eerie snake-charming music. They had a hat with money in it, but it wasn't for that reason that I wanted to hang around. It was so different and strange to me that, to be truthful, it really was the highlight of the evening. These funny street entertainers, or buskers, as they are commonly known, are everywhere in the City of London. Some of them are so talented; it makes you wonder why they are still performing on the street and not in a theatre. However, perhaps they are just waiting for someone in the right profession to notice their skills and give them their big break, that is - to move them further up the scale to make a lot of money.

The original Sand Dancers, Jack Wilson and Joe Keppel with Betty Knox, formed a popular British music hall and vaudeville act in the middle decades of the 20th century. They capitalised on the fashion for Ancient Egyptian imagery following the discovery of the tomb of Tutankhamun. The eccentric "sand dance" that formed the highlight of their act was a parody of postures from Egyptian tomb paintings, combined with references to Arabic costumes. The flexible and extremely lanky Wilson and Keppel wore long moustaches and make-up to emphasise the sharp angularity of their features, making them appear almost identical. They demonstrated their impressive suppleness in adopting wild gestures and dancing in identical "stereo" movements whilst Betty watched their antics. The dance itself was a soft-shoe routine performed on a layer of sand spread on the stage to create a rhythmic scratching with their shuffling feet. The act was usually performed to the familiar *Egyptian Ballet* (1875), by Alexandre Luigini.[5]

It was amazing, so unusual, and I loved it! Eventually, we all started to move around the corner, and as we did so, Dave went up to a car and unlocked the door. This was a surprise, but I insisted that my friends get in it too. After all, he was a stranger, and I had already noticed, being a country mouse girl, how many strange people there were in London!

We drove the two-minute trip back to the hostel, and my friends went in. I stood on the steps with this male, and he asked if we could meet up again. I thought about it. I remember looking at his face and thinking it looked as if he had a bit of a tan. He was taller than me, which was a good point, and besides that, he had dark hair, which was equally important.

Eventually, I decided I would say yes, but I was really quite scared at the same time. I think it was the fact that he was softly spoken that perhaps this made a difference – enough, anyway, for me to say yes.

Our Relationship

We were to meet up again at the hostel in a couple of days, in the evening, but I was very wary about meeting up with a complete stranger, so I decided to tell the receptionist in the hostel about my fear.

"Why don't you invite him into the television room? You are permitted to bring friends into there," she replied.

And so, that's what I did.

After a while, this male got restless, and so did I. It was very noisy in there, and so many different foreign languages were being spoken. He decided that it was time for him to leave, but before he did, he set a date for a couple of days later. With that meet up, he wanted me to meet him *outside* the hostel on the steps.

Two days later, Dave arrived early. I knew this was because I was outside before the set time, and he was already there waiting for me. But, before I had time to ask him in again, he told me that he was going to take me for a special meal.

Pakistani Restaurant

We wended our way through the streets of London until, eventually, we arrived at a Pakistani abode. It was not a restaurant as such, but a place of eating for the Pakistanis themselves.

Once we had chosen our table, Dave took me over to the selection of foods that were truly exotic and appeared extremely appetising. Pakistani cuisine, I was told, is a refined blend of the various regional cooking traditions of South Asia. Most of the food preparations are renowned for their aromatic and sometimes very spicy flavours. Some dishes, quite often, contain generous amounts of oil that help contribute to a richer, fuller, tastier flavour. Cinnamon, mace, cloves, brown and green cardamom, nutmeg and black pepper are the most commonly used spices, while turmeric, as well as bay leaves, cumin seeds and chilli powder, are also very popular.[6]

Dave seemed very shy and quiet, yet intelligent at the same time; he further appeared as an introvert and as if something was bothering him. It was in this place that I learnt that he was thirty years old and an Anglo-Pakistani. We continued with our fascinating evening.

Dinner, for the Pakistanis, is considered their main meal of the day, and it appears that kebabs seem to be one of those items regularly prepared. The main courses are usually served with wheat bread (either roti or naan) or rice, plus a salad, in these kinds of places.[7]

I sat there engrossed with this enormous variety of foreign delights. Dave chose the food one item at a time and with long pauses in between - which was good because it allowed us time to talk and get to know each other better. Soon, it was time for me to choose a drink of some kind. Apparently, Pakistanis drink a great deal of tea, which is locally called "chai." Both black (without milk) and green teas are popular, and they have many different varieties. Besides tea, there are other drinks that they may want to include as part of the Pakistani meal. All of them, though, will be non-alcoholic. It was also very common, however, to have soft drinks in those days, and I remember asking for a milky drink with herbs and sesame seeds and pistachio nuts in it. It was very fulfilling and thirst-quenching, and I found it amazing - so different! Yet there were others as well, for instance: Almond

Sherbet, which is sherbet made with almonds; and then there is
Gola_Ganda, which consists of different types of flavours over
crushed ice. *Kashmiri Chai/Gulabi Chai* is a milky tea known for
its pink colour, with either a sweet or salty taste. There is also lassi,
which is milk with yoghurt, and this too has either a sweet or salty
taste. If you like lemonade (Limu pani), they will serve you this as
well, plus *Sikanjabeen*, which is lemonade where mint is further
added - and many more. So many luscious choices, where do I go
from here?[8]

Well, after all the savoury dishes and drinks to choose from,
there were even *more* varieties to come next!

'So many different deserts, gosh, which one should I select?'
I thought.

This is because popular desserts in Pakistani cuisine might
include an assortment of ice-creams – which I really love; but
there are other sweet dishes as well, such as *Kheer*, which is made
of roasted *seviyaan* (vermicelli) instead of rice. Another sweet is
Gajraila which is made from grated carrots, boiled in milk, sugar,
and green cardamom, topped with nuts and dried fruit. The latter
is eaten a lot in Pakistan as well as in other parts of Southern Asia,
including Afghanistan.[9] I sipped and spooned at the remains of
my milky drink; it really was a very interesting and enjoyable
evening, cultural-wise. Dave was so different, so homely, quiet,
but friendly. Dave's character really suited me!

When he took me back to the hostel, he spoke quietly; yet he
was definitely the leader out of the two of us - and I liked that. It
was this father figure that I had been missing. There were no kisses
at the end, but another meeting was fixed for a few days' time.

This one was to be on a Saturday - and for the 'Day!'

I was really excited and couldn't wait!

Dave met me at the hostel on Saturday. It was a nice bright sunny day; we couldn't have wished for more. We were going to have a wonderful time. We were going to be sightseers for the day – and on foot!

At first, we decided to head towards Leicester Square and then straight on to Trafalgar Square, which has been a significant landmark since the 13th century. This public square in the City of Westminster is built around the area formerly known as Charing Cross. Its name commemorates the Battle of Trafalgar, a British naval victory in the Napoleonic Wars with France and Spain. Nelson's Column is in the centre of the square, flanked by fountains and guarded by four monumental bronze lions. At the top of the column is a statue of Horatio Nelson, who commanded the British Navy at the Battle of Trafalgar. The square has been used for community gatherings and political demonstrations. Surrounding the area are the National Gallery on the north side and St Martin-in-the-Fields Church to the east. To the south-west is The Mall leading towards Buckingham Palace via Admiralty Arch, while Whitehall is to the south and the Strand to the east. Charing Cross Road passes between the National Gallery and the church.[10]

We continued our walk down the Strand, which is a major thoroughfare in Central London. It runs just over $\frac{3}{4}$ mile (1,200 metres) from Trafalgar Square eastwards to Temple Bar, where the road becomes Fleet Street inside the City of London and is part of the A4, the main road running west from inner London. The road's name comes from the Old English word *strond*, meaning the edge of a river because it historically ran alongside the north bank of the River Thames. The street was popular among the British upper-classes from the 12th to the 17th century, with many historically important mansions being built between the Strand and the river. The aristocracy moved to the West End during the 17th century, following which the Strand became well known for coffee shops, restaurants and taverns. The street was a centre point for theatre and music hall during the 19th century, and several venues remain on the Strand. Several authors, poets and philosophers have lived on or near the Strand, including Charles Dickens and Virginia Woolf. The street has been commemorated in the song, "Let's all go down the Strand," now recognised as a typical piece of Cockney music hall.[11]

We both felt like we were on holiday, so we acted as if we *were*. We were being tourists for the day, and there were other places that we visited as well - one of them being a kind of a pop-in-bar to have something to eat. We both chose an omelette and salad, and I knew that Dave was very happy because he smiled a lot. However, I could also tell that he was very tired and really quite quiet. We were like two reserved people getting used to each other. I had also by now begun to notice something strange: whenever I brought up the subject of my work, he would play it down and even cut me short. In fact, he didn't want me to talk about my career at all!

When it was evening and time for us to part, Dave told me that he would get in touch with me shortly. He wanted to take me back to his place, but he needed permission to do so first; he said he would be back in contact with me soon.

A few days went by, and I was missing him; this lovely warm homely figure had disappeared into the City of London. Two or three more days went by, and it was Saturday again, this time in the afternoon. There was a knock on my bedroom door; I went to open it and there in front of me was a young woman.

"Are you Janet Hann?" she enquired.

"Yes," I answered.

"There's someone on the telephone for you. You need to pick up the telephone extension on this floor level, and you can speak to him from there."

I ran along the landing and picked up the telephone. It was Dave. I was ecstatic!

He told me that he had got permission for me to be taken to his home and that he would come and pick me up the following Saturday, in the afternoon.

I couldn't wait!

Over the next few days, I was really happy; I seemed to be floating around on air all the time! Even down in the dreaded steam-filled laundry room, the very chore of washing my clothes appeared much lighter, better and quicker.

The point of the matter was that 'I was not alone!'

The next Saturday, as planned, Dave came to the hostel to greet me, and it wasn't long before he was driving us down the West End. Our journey took us about thirty minutes before we arrived at our destination. It was so lovely to be sitting next to him, and as he drove the vehicle, it was as if he was in control of me, and I really 'did' feel in a kind of a comfy zone.

The nearer we got to our destination, the roads widened, and the houses became neat and tidy. They were large houses and of a semi-detached style.

When we arrived, Dave got out of the car first, walked up this small driveway to the front door and rang the bell. Almost immediately, a pleasant-faced Asian male stood in the doorway. He greeted us with a smile and welcomed us in. I was taken into a sitting room and told to take a seat on a sofa. It was clean and immaculate, and for some reason, this made me feel very happy. Dave's friend decided to put on some Asian music. Pakistani music, I was told, receives its influences from many countries, including Arabia, Persia and even Turkey. The sounds that are produced with the musical instruments are a combination of both melody and rhythm, which make up their delightful compositions.[12]

I sat there and enjoyed the rhythmic music, and it wasn't long before I could smell some truly foreign aromas again. Soon, they both came out of the kitchen carrying oval dishes, which contained a variety of hot and spicy Indian foods with which they placed them on a *takht* in front of me. A takht is a raised platform where people eat their food sitting cross-legged after taking off their shoes. Many Pakistanis, I was told, tended to eat on a takht. However, large Pakistani families, particularly when guests are too many to fit at a table, eat sitting around a cloth known as *Dastarkhān*, spread out on the floor. Nothing here was for tourism; I can tell you, nor artificial. Everything was natural and with ease - well, of course, it was their cultural home!

Dave's friend, Taz, proceeded to sit cross-legged on the floor while Dave sat next to me on the sofa. They told me that Pakistani cuisines generally differ from home to home, and apparently, they can be quite different from the mainstream Pakistani style of cooking. But a typical Pakistani lunch might consist of meat curry along with rice or a kind of bread. *Daal chawal* is one of the most commonly taken dishes at lunch, they said, but other popular dishes included *aloo gosht* (which is a meat and potato curry) or any vegetable with mutton. Chicken dishes like chicken karahi are also popular. Some varieties of bread, too, they said, such as roti or naan, have become more common during the day, being served with yoghurt, pickle and salad.[13]

Dave and Taz spoke a lot in their own language, and sometimes, I felt a little uneasy. They ate this scrumptious food with their hands, scooping up the solid parts plus the sauce with a piece of baked bread. I was pleased with the set-up: it was decent, polite, respectful towards me, and exciting at the same time, for I had never been in such a setting before!

In fact, in Basingstoke, everyone seemed white and British-Basingstoke born. I don't think that I had ever met a person from a different country or another culture before I came to London. I knew that if I had told my mother that I was going out with an Asian male, she would have automatically thought that he was African - because she had seen 'these people' on the television, and she wouldn't have known any different.

After we had eaten, Taz put on some classical music. Pakistan's classical music is based on the traditional music of South Asia, which was patronised by various empires that gave birth to several genres, including the Klasik and Hindustani classical music. The classical music of Pakistan has two main principles, 'sur' (musical note) and 'lai' (rhythm). The performance of musical notes into a scale is known as a raag. The arrangement of rhythm (lai) in a cycle is known as taal. While the major genres of classical music in Pakistan are dhrupad and khayal, dhrupad is approaching extinction, with which khayal is the most popular genre and is also enjoyed with much enthusiasm in Afghanistan.[14] The varying instruments that are used, for example, are the sitar, tabla, harmonium, sarangi and santoor.[15]

Suddenly, Dave disappeared from the room, and he seemed to be gone for a long while. I decided to get up and asked if I could help with the clearing away and the washing up, which appeared to please Taz. We gathered the plates etc., from the takht and transported them out into the kitchen where Taz washed the items, and I dried them; then he put them away in a cupboard. All the while, we were chatting, and then out of the blue, he asked if he could take me out - he wanted a date with me. I was shocked and dismayed at what he had said. I didn't answer but kept my head down low. Taz left the room, and then it seemed as if they both came back together - both Taz and Dave.

Eventually, it was time to go home. Once outside, I felt at ease; we got into the car, and I felt extremely happy with our relationship. It was then that I told Dave what Taz had said to me - that he wanted to have a date with me. Dave was very quiet and didn't attempt to make any comment.

We stopped down a side road by the British Museum. Dave switched off the ignition and told me there was something important that I needed to know. He proceeded to tell me something that just bowled me over – that he was married! I was horrified. He then added that it was an estranged marriage - this meant, he said, that he was separated from his wife. When I asked where his wife was staying, he said that she was living with her parents as they always had done.

He then lowered his head and told me that he had three little children.

I felt terrible. Here I was, enjoying myself with someone else's husband, and he also had three children.

I was so upset; something that was feeling so wonderful to me - so mature - was now turning into something very corrupt.

I swallowed hard; I felt too uneasy to speak, and I just wanted to get out of the car.

However, Dave insisted that we talk for a little longer, and it turned out that being in the same house as the in-laws, he said, meant that he was never in control of his own family. His wife was British and white, just like me, not Asian, and thus, the household was not of Asian culture.

One thing I was becoming consciously aware of was how much Dave was concerned about his age. He was constantly worrying about showing signs of ageing, and he thought that he was getting old. To keep proving his point, he would tell me how many more grey hairs he had noticed on his head, and it seemed to make him fret a lot.

I wanted to go; I was feeling confused, but he insisted that we see each other again. We made another date, but I needed a gap to think things over - a lot. I got out of his vehicle and left, and up to this point, there had been no kisses, no physical contact - except to hold hands!

For the next few days, I was very depressed, and I didn't know what to do for the best. I had really enjoyed Dave's company and his friend's, and more than anything, I had fallen in love with the Asian culture. I felt so guilty being happy in the company of someone else's husband, but yet, he was separated from his wife and children - should that make a difference? I really didn't know what to do or how to feel, so much so that I felt like I was on a roller-coaster full of emotions that were activating in opposition with one another. One thing for sure was that I definitely wasn't going to tell my parents! That would be like adding salt to my wounds.

I missed Dave, I had experienced a mature male's company, which was just what I needed, and I was enjoying it. I further loved his culture, and I could see how beautiful Asian women were. They were so soft-looking, with beautiful eyes and teeth and skin; they appeared so cuddly. Most of all, it was their womanly femininity that I adored, and their exotic clothes - bright colours and delicate, silky fabrics. This brought me back to Dave. He wanted to be in charge of his own family - like a 'proper' male should be, but yet, he was undermined by the circumstances. With this in mind, I gave in and decided to give him another chance. It gradually appeared unquestionable that I should continue to see him; after all, I could understand his point of view. But I was mixed-up about whether I felt right about our meetings - after all, he still belonged to somebody else!

Another date was arranged, and we went to the pictures. This was the start of many meetings; we were relaxing and enjoying each other's company, and the set-up seemed well – comfortable! We started to travel out into the countryside, and Dave seemed blissfully happy; he would lie down on the edge of a field and look up at the sky, and he would tell me to do the same.

One really hot day, the sun beamed down and touched our skin. Everything felt precious… and on this particular day, we actually kissed!

It was as if we were allowed to - as if we somehow felt 'free' in this setting!

But is it for companionship, procreation or something more that makes us so willing to become targets for Cupid's arrow?

I believe that Love is a feeling that immerses a being (an existence) in a sense of Hope. It seems to me it is a sensation that creates some kind of value for happiness or worthiness - whether that is to know or understand something better to move on better in one's life or, perhaps, lift one up out of the mire. I have heard it said in psychology that Love and Hate are not far apart - that Love can slip into Hate. I reasoned with this one for a moment. It's as if the state of Love places us in a protective bubble of happiness, free from the pain and suffering caused by the external world, and then sometime, one day, it might pop, and it's gone. This engulfed state of bliss is now felt as an error, and thus, all the expectations that came with it become worthless, without value. All the feelings of the so-called love become shattered somehow, and all the sensations of protection with it. The person feels duped; they are now a victim of deception.

But perhaps I ought to leave this to an expert to explain it better.

What is LOVE?

At the most basic level, love is about survival of the individual and the species. Humans are highly cooperative; we have to cooperate to subsist, gain knowledge and raise our highly dependent off-springs. But cooperation isn't easy. In an ideal world, we would live in blissful solitude, doing what we wanted when we wanted and not having to consider the needs of, or the threats from, others. However, we need to live in groups which mean that we have to compete for resources, coordinate our movements, exist within a hierarchy and make sure that we keep an eye out for those who might lie, cheat or steal. So, what has evolution come up with to ensure that we start and then invest in these survival-critical relationships, despite their costs? Well, the answer comes up with LOVE.

Love evolved to bribe us to commence and maintain those relationships with lovers, children, family and friends, which we require simply to stay alive and perpetuate our genes. And this biological bribery comes in the form of a set of four neurochemicals that underpin attraction and love. They are oxytocin, dopamine, serotonin and beta-endorphin.

Oxytocin is really important when you want to attract because it lowers your inhibitions to enable you to start new relationships. Oxytocin quietens the amygdala, the fear centre of your brain, which means that you feel confident when approaching a new acquaintance. Dopamine is always released at the same time as oxytocin. It is your body's reward chemical and is released whenever you do something you enjoy. In this case, it rewards you for your confidence, as well as works with oxytocin to make your brain more plastic – i.e., capable of change. This enables you to learn and memorise new facts about this new person – and, as the hormone of vigour, it motivates you to get out of your chair and make the approach.

These chemicals act mainly in the limbic area of the brain, which is its unconscious core. This is because attraction (or lust) is initially a purely instinctive and unconscious sensation. Lowered serotonin unleashes the obsessive element of love. Unlike the other chemicals, serotonin drops at the start of a relationship, which is why your mind tends to be overwhelmed with thoughts about your new love. And finally, we have beta-endorphin - the hormone of long-term love. Humans can be in relationships for decades, and oxytocin, in particular, is not powerful enough to underpin love in the long term. Moreover, oxytocin is mainly only released in significant amounts in situations related to sexual and reproductive love. This means that it is not capable of underpinning (i.e., strengthening) friendships, which is key for survival and critical for human bonds.

However, beta-endorphin can, and it does so because it is an opiate, like heroin or morphine, and as such, it's addictive. It works because we become addicted to those we love as the source of our opiate high, and when we are apart, we go cold turkey, motivating us to return to them for another euphoric hit. Due to beta-endorphin's capacity to underpin love rather than lust, both the unconscious and conscious areas of our brain (respectively the limbic area and cortex) are recruited. This means humans can experience love as an instinctive drive or emotion involving lust, euphoria or delight, plus a conscious process involving reflection, trust, empathy, attention and planning.[16]

Needless to say, on this particular day, I too was learning to be one of those people who, in this special kind of a setting, was releasing those chemicals so that I might just learn how to let go. I was disregarding anything else that might spoil my feelings. I was beginning to take off my protective suit of armour - and I felt good!

Sunny Brighton

One day, Dave said to me, "Shall we go on holiday together?"
I thought about it for a while, and then I eventually agreed, and he said that we would go to the sea.

We went to sunny Brighton - and it *was* sunny too - for a long weekend. Dave drove us there, and it was wonderful; I actually felt *part* of him, bonded to him. However, I mustn't allow myself to feel that I was his wife - that would be too risky!

Brighton has a fascinating history, so I am going to tell you a little bit about it.

It had been a small place until the Saxons landed in Sussex in the 5th century AD. They founded the kingdom of Sussex - including the village of Brighton. Fishermen lived in Brighton as well as farmers. The farmers lived in a village above a cliff, and the fishermen lived under this cliff on the foreshore. In 1313, Brighton was given a charter (a document granting the people certain rights), and afterwards, it became a busy little market town. There was a daily fish market on the beach, weekly pig and corn markets, plus a general market where goods of all kinds were sold, and Brighton also had annual fairs.

In medieval times, Brighton was a small town with only four streets: North Street, West Street, East Street and South Street. A fifth street, Middle Street, had been added by 1500. At this time, there were also fishermen's huts along the shore. However, the French came and burned the little town of Brighton in 1514, which was an easy task since most buildings in the town were wooden and had thatched roofs. Yet, by 1580, the town was rebuilt, and once again, it became a flourishing little place.

In the late 17th century, Brighton declined due to England's series of wars with France and Holland. In 1703, a terrible storm struck England, and it further devastated Brighton. Another storm in 1705 demolished houses below the cliff, along the foreshore; however, its recovery started in 1750 when a doctor named Richard Russell claimed that bathing in seawater was good for a person's health. Gradually, wealthy people began to visit the area, for they believed that bathing in seawater would cure their illnesses.

The population of Brighton grew rapidly in the late 18th century. Prior to this time, ships had simply moored off the shore, but in 1823, the chain pier was built. During the following year, a steamship began carrying passengers between Brighton and northern France.

In 1841 a railway from London to Brighten opened, and as a result, the population rose rapidly from 40,000 in 1841 to 65,000 in 1861. Meanwhile, in the 19th century, amenities continued to improve. Between 1901 and 1939, electric trams ran in Brighton, and in 1904, the first motor buses began running. In 1939, the trams were replaced with trolleybuses that ran on electricity from overhead wires, while they also ran on rails. In 1939, when World War II started, many schoolchildren from London were evacuated to Brighton.

In the 1950s and early 1960s, a new industrial estate and council estate were built, and the university was founded in 1962.

Brighton continued to flourish as a seaside resort, with today's population being 156,000.[17]

And so here we were in Brighton in 1967, walking along the beach hand-in-hand. It was beginning to feel as if we were not only physically linked together – but we were mentally connected as well - we were enjoying the same things and values!

I felt that I had found someone, at last, to share my life with, out of lonely London.

We strolled along the pier, and it was here we learnt that Brighton has a history of three piers: the Chain Pier (1823-1896), the West Pier (1866-1975) and Brighton Pier (1899-ongoing). However today, Brighton has just the one pier: Brighton Palace Pier, which is on the east side of the seafront and is in good working order, attracting approximately 3 million visitors each year.

In its original form, Brighton's first pier was the Old Chain Pier which was primarily used as a landing stage for passenger ships that sailed from Dieppe in France. Realising its commercial value, the owners began charging an entry fee of 2d and introduced kiosks selling souvenirs and confectionary as well as entertainment stalls with fortune-tellers and silhouettists. The Chain Pier was struck by many storms in a ten-year period between 1824 and 1834, causing irreparable damage. The pier was eventually bought out in 1889 by the Marine Palace & Pier Company. In December that same year, the pier was destroyed in its entirety by an almighty storm.

The West Pier, on the west side of the seafront, is a scene of dereliction. All that remains of this building is its blackened, charred iron skeleton.[18] It is Britain's only Grade I listed pier and was built to the designs of Eugenius Birch, the most celebrated of all pier architects. The pier was originally built with two toll houses at the landward end, twin kiosks for shelter in the centre and ladies and gentlemen's retiring rooms at the pier head. It was only later that the landing stage and theatre pavilion were added. The pier closed to the public in 1975 and has been the subject of a long-running campaign to restore it to its full glory.[19]

Brighton Pier was taken over by the Marine Palace & Pier Company and was finally opened on the 20th of May 1899, costing £27,000 to build. On the opening night, a series of eight iron and steel arches were spectacularly illuminated by 3,000 light bulbs. Today there are 67,000 lights illuminating Brighton Pier, the majority of which have been converted to long-life energy-saving bulbs.

In 1905, a collection of amusement machines were installed on the Palace Pier, including The Lady Palmist and Punch Ball machines. It wasn't until the 1980s when traditional machines started to be replaced with the new style arcade machines, including Space Invaders and virtual reality machines. There was also a concert hall, and by 1911, this had become a theatre. The Palace Pier continued to develop, introducing more entertainment facilities, including a bandstand. Today, the Palace Pier (Brighton Pier) employs over 500 people from around the world and plays a major part in Brighton's economy.[20]

Gosh! All that history about the piers, but it becomes really interesting to learn about the past regarding these well-trodden monuments and the many changes that have happened to them.

As we walked along the pier - just as thousands of others had done in the past - we bought some popcorn and sat and ate it, enjoying the view and the fresh air at the same time. We had several attempts at the amusement machines and found ourselves laughing wholeheartedly all the while. It really was beginning to feel very pleasurable to be part of this mature male's life. I felt that he was looking after me, caring about me and sharing his existence with me. I had never had this before – well, only when I was sixteen, and then I think I was far too young to understand what it all meant.

We went into a café and enjoyed a seafood meal. Dave was a non-drinker, and so was I; he was also a non-smoker, and so was I.

We decided to have a moon-lit walk in a leisurely way along the beach. There was a slight, gentle breeze, which caressed our face and hair, and in turn, it enhanced the smell of the potent sea. The water's edge lapped its way over the stones, resting motionlessly for a short while until it was pulled and sucked back once more by the moon. The sea's beating heart - its ebb and flow was truly heavenly!

Eventually, we resurfaced onto the promenade in front of the hotels and guest houses; it was time to find somewhere to sleep! Dave selected a few bed and breakfasts, and he asked my opinion of which one looked the best - I liked that! I asked if I could pay or share the cost, but he refused. After a brief period of contemplation, he made his way closer to the one of his choice. It was a bed and breakfast that gave the impression of a large bungalow. We walked up to the door, and it was very dark save for a little glowing porch light. As we stood there, Dave pondered, hesitated for a minute, and then he pressed the doorbell. At the same time, he said to me, "Do I ask for two bedrooms or one?"

Guilt flooded in on my behalf. What should I say?

Someone was coming to the door, and I had to make my mind up quickly.

I had already contemplated this one to myself on the beach earlier. I had decided that it was to be two bedrooms, even though I knew that it would cost Dave twice as much. I had overcome that prospect in my mind because I was going to pay for my own bedroom. My answer was to be that we were to sleep in separate rooms.

I stood there frozen to the spot as the door opened. A burly male in his mid-fifties filled the doorway.

He smiled and said, "Hello, can I help you?"

Dave looked at me longingly to give an answer - and probably the right one.

I stared at this stranger; he was a homely man; this was his home, and I immediately thought of my mother and father and felt very sinful.

I carefully cupped one hand over my mouth to soften my voice. "Can we have two bedrooms, please, Dave?" I said earnestly.

Dave looked at the man sheepishly. "Have you got two bedrooms for the night, please? he asked quietly.

The man looked at Dave, and then he looked at me and seemed to be assessing the situation.

He glanced down at the ground and hummed a bit, and then with a sigh and a shake of his head, he said, "I'm sorry, I don't have two bedrooms vacant tonight, but I have a really nice en-suite double bedroom facing the front!"

I just wished the ground would swallow me up!

Both males were now looking at me earnestly. What should I say?

I cupped my hand over my mouth once more. "Ask him if we can have two single beds!"

"Does it come with single beds or just a double?" Dave asked.

"Oh, it's a double bed in that one!"

Both sets of eyes were once more on me.

It was late, and I knew that it was going to be too late to go searching for another guesthouse to suit my needs.

I looked down at the ground and started thinking of various ways to try and get out of this awkward situation.

At last, I eventually gave up.

Most probably, Dave would be very cross with me for messing about in front of this man; and so, with my eyes still down on the ground, I said, "I'll leave it with you."

So, that's where we stayed.

Well, that's not the end, because he said that he would sleep on the floor.

And that's where HE stayed.

All night!

All night, I was very frightened: What would my parents think if they knew? And even being in the same bedroom with the opposite sex was wrong for me. I had been brought up in a household with no brothers. I had gone to a school that was for girls only. I had a shy father, so much so that if a couple of people on the television started to kiss, he would hide his face behind a newspaper and tell my mother to switch it off. When I would ask why, the answer would be, "It's a load of mush!"

In the morning, I wouldn't go down for breakfast; it would have been too embarrassing. Instead, I told Dave to go down; after all, it was part of the deal: 'Bed plus Breakfast!' However, he refused to go without me, and so I crept downstairs. We could smell the aroma of breakfast cooking – crispy bacon, mushrooms, tomatoes and a fried egg, laced with a slice of fried bread. I felt so guilty, but I just needed to get out of there. Dave came outside with me to open the car door; he said that he needed to go back and tell them that we had left. I felt really mean, but there was no way that my guilt would change its mind. We'd had a really happy time here in Brighton, and I now knew – or felt – that it was going to end as a complete disaster.

I would say that Dave was gone for around ten minutes before he returned. There was no need to talk at that point, and besides, I don't think that he had slept very well on the floor. I had offered to be the one on the floor, but he had refused; I suppose that was something else about him that I admired.

We started to discuss our following moves - what we should do next. He turned on the ignition and switched the car heater on; it really was very cold that morning. Suddenly, there was the sound of clattering bottles filling our ears. Dave stretched his neck to see what was happening, and there, down the road, was a milk-float - a milkman was delivering milk. Dave got out of the car and walked over to the milkman, and shortly after, he returned with two bottles of milk. He gave one to me, but I refused, so he drank out of one bottle and persuaded me to have a sip of it. He then decided to keep the other bottle of milk until later.

I began to feel depressed. Not only had I probably spoiled a wonderful weekend, but it might mean that this was to be the end of our relationship as well.

We started to drive around the streets and then along the coastline, but to be honest, I think that we were both very cold and tired - and hungry.

Eventually, he said, "I think it's best if we forget a second night here and go back home."

We *did* talk on the way home, but things were very strained, tense to be precise; I don't think he wanted to argue with me, and neither did I.

It was better that way!

Back at the hostel steps, he dropped me off and said that he would be in touch in a few days' time. There were no kisses, and I really thought that this was to be the end.

No Phone Call?

As I have already mentioned, I found London a very isolating place. It was an environment where companionships could easily be wrenched apart, and although Dave and myself would meet up around once a week, I would have liked to have seen him more often. The other downside was that the YWCA had only approximately two telephones in the reception area, and they would receive phone calls for some three hundred young women - especially in the evening. You would hear the loudspeaker announcing a name, and you would hope that it was for you; but many a time, callers would tell you that they had tried to get through on an evening, but to no avail, because the lines were *always* engaged.

One evening, I received a message on the loudspeaker, saying that I had a visitor waiting for me in reception. Of course, it was Dave, and he seemed very annoyed. He told me that he had been trying for several days to telephone me and could not seem to get through, as always, and so, he thought that driving to the YWCA was the best way to go about it. I put on my coat, and we went out. We went to the delightful Pakistani food house again, and when I got back to the hostel, I was made to sign in to a 'late' book. I looked at the time on the clock on the wall, which was around 10:35 pm, and I was told to expect a warning the next day for overstepping the mark. I had never received one of these before, and so it seemed to me to be a very odd thing at the age of twenty.

A few days later, Dave had planned for us to spend a whole day together. It was a Saturday again, it was springtime, and we had a wonderful day in the countryside. We found somewhere nice to eat our picnic: we had cheese and ham sandwiches with crisps, some cake and apples and bananas with bottles of flavoured milk, and then we decided to make our way back to Dave's lodgings.

In his room, he had laid out some delicate Danish pastries – they were horn-shapes filled with jam and cream. Apparently, they were one of his favourites, and he treated himself now and again. And there we were, huddled together again, eating and talking. The time was ticking on, and I needed to get a move on if I was to be back for 10:30 pm.

This was to be the day that I broke the rule.

"Why go back?" He had said. "You can stay here with me!"

I thought this was awful - I never liked to break the rules. What if they found out, or my room-mates worried?

I tried to get hold of them on the hostel telephone, but to no avail.

Dave went downstairs, and a few minutes later, he came back saying that his friend didn't mind if I stayed the night.

Well, that was the beginning of a chain of similar events!

Work: August 1966 - May 1967

My freelance work with Evette was ongoing - the first catalogue had been a huge success.

Figure 40 Catalogue Illustrations

Around October 1966, I had started my second catalogue with Evette: the *Spring-Summer (1967)* one. Sometimes I took some illustrations to show Dave, but he really wasn't interested. I used to ask to see the pictures that he carried around with him - of his three children. They were very sweet, and I felt so guilty somehow - but yet, not so much now.

I also worked hard with *Harlee* on a full-time basis. Sometimes, Dave would drop me off in the morning whilst he drove on to his workplace. He was a foreman at a well-known garage. However, on other occasions, he would get me to phone the garage in the morning and say I was his wife and that he was not well enough to go to work that day. This only happened twice, though, and then we would go out to our special retreat in the countryside. Dave wanted so much to leave London, to have a cleaner, healthier life - as he put it.

I worked with *Harlee* producing many, many designs. Days, weeks and even months were going by; various designs were being selected regularly from my sheets of work, and the lucky ones were made up in cloth by both Fran and Jacob. The completed coats were put onto a rail, and when the rail got full, it was moved out into another room. This other room was the Buyers' Room. Some items were regularly being taken out to be modified or rejected altogether, but only to be replaced by more. Eventually, the necessary number of selected garments made up the complete season's collection.

We worked twelve months ahead, so my designs were for the Autumn-Winter 1967-8 Collection. Shop buyers would come in to place their orders, which would be either via the rail of coats or the Range Book and occasionally, using a real live child model. As the orders were placed, the sample pattern was graded into various sizes on pattern card, which were sent out to the factory, complete with the sample coat. From there, they would be made in their various sizes - in their hundreds.

Ah! So this is how it worked!

When it came to the next season's collection - Spring-Summer, 1968, work took on a change. I was being told to take regular trips down to Oxford Street to get ideas as to how the latest fashion trends were moving. I was instructed to sketch what was in the main shops' windows, plus ask the assistants inside what could be classified as their best sellers, etc. These would be helpful clues or perhaps good predictions for my next collection – I was told.

And so, I would sketch what the major stores and departments had on their models in their windows, and then I would go back to the hostel and modify those styles for a range of children's coats.

Another new item was introduced - *The Draper's Record*. This was to provide further useful information as to how the trends were moving.

At the same time, I was busy with Mrs Grayson's catalogue of two per year.

I had been with *Harlee* for approximately nine months, and it was May 1967 when something happened on this particular day.

As we all left the workshop, Fran said cheerio to Jacob and started heading *my* way. He said that he needed to go home via a different route. As we walked along the street together, he broke away from what we had been discussing and started to break out into a different tone.

"There's something that I need to tell you," he said. "To be quite blunt, you are about to lose your job!"

I couldn't believe what I was hearing. "What makes you say that?" I asked.

"Because I've been working in the trade for around four years now, and I know how things work." He continued, "Designers tend to stay for an average of twelve months, and then there is a change."

"Why is that?" I asked, getting upset.

"Well," Fran said, looking down as he spoke, "designers tend to have fixed patterns, set ideas with their work, and firms like to keep their 'look' fresh and the way they do it is to keep renewing their designer."

Fran looked at me, and in a serious tone, he said, "I'm only telling you this for your own good; I would start looking for another job. There is an agency down Oxford Street that deals specifically for employment in the rag trade. If I were you, I would pop in there and see what they have to offer."

With this, he said that he needed to take the next road off, which was different to me.

He smiled and said, "I will see you tomorrow, but don't mention a word to anyone at work as to what I've just told you."

"No, I won't," I said.

I sat on the bus feeling sad and dejected, but I didn't tell anyone - not even in the hostel.

The next day, I had planned to go down Oxford Street to see how the shops front windows had changed. It was a good way to see what was selling or not by looking at which garments had changed, and which stayed in the windows from the week before.

I also planned to pop into the agency, as Fran had said, at the same time.

The agency's assistant made a few telephone calls, with which she found a particular Fashion House that needed an In-house Illustrator and managed to get me an interview.

"It is with the *House of Rhona Roy*," she told me. "They are looking for a Fashion Illustrator."

"What type of clothes do they make?" I asked.

"Women's dresses, skirts, suits, etc. It's a Women's Fashion House," she said. "Are you interested?"

"Yes, please," I said.

She gave them a ring, and an appointment was made – straight away!

The director of *Rhona Roy* said to me, "When can you start?"

A date was fixed, and I walked out of there feeling quite dizzy.

As I sat on my bed back in the hostel, I felt quite sad. However, at the same time, I was pleased with myself because the starting date that I had given *Rhona Roy* was going to allow me a few days break between the two jobs.

The first thing to do was to think of where I would like to go for a rest!

I enjoyed the first few weeks that I worked at *Rhona Roy* - even though the owner's son was urging me to be one of their three designers as well as their sole illustrator. My illustrations were being shown to such buyers as Marks and Spencer, C&A, Debenhams etc., and the sales department would arrange for the selected garments to be worn and paraded by the House Model for potential orders to be placed.

For some reason, I was beginning to feel very tired. I began to feel listless and unwell. Even so, I had been working hard to complete my third catalogue with Evette: *Autumn-Winter (1967)*.

Figure 41 Catalogue Illustrations

CHAPTER FIVE

Sickness

Feeling Strange

Almost ten months into my relationship with Dave (around July 1967), I began to feel strange. Dave was always most adamant that he couldn't have any more children, so I accepted that. I had no reason not to trust him and went along with it. After all, there was no such thing in these days as a contraceptive pill that I could have taken; well, not that I was aware of anyway. Besides, surely it was for the man to take the leading role in such matters - the situation seemed most definitely under *his* control... wasn't it?

Birth control has actually existed for quite some time, but the accessibility to it is what is so new. Condoms have been around for ages, becoming prevalent in the 16th century in response to syphilis. They were originally fashioned from sheep gut or fish bladder, and sometimes linen was used with ointments and medicinal solutions. The change in rubber processing in the mid-nineteenth century revolutionised condoms into slowly evolving to those we know today.

Apart from condoms, there grew a wide variety of contraceptive options available, but with mixed reliability, including douches, spermicides, cervical caps, diaphragms and sponges. Most of these were acquired through a visit to your local doctor. However, women not only found this a difficult topic to pursue with their doctor, but this subject was also restricted to 'married women only.'

The contraceptive pill did not arrive in England until the 1960s, and that too was not available to unmarried women until 1968. Needless to say, even if young men could acquire condoms through local chemists, there was no 'real' birth control in those days. The euphemisms for condoms were 'johnnies' or 'French Letters,' but for the most part, men relied on their beau's knowledge of the withdrawal method.

Parents did not discuss sex with their offspring, and besides, they were only equipped with antiquated terms such as 'taking the kettle off before it boils' (withdrawal) or 'driving a car without petrol' (non-coital forms of lovemaking). There was no such thing as sex education in the schools, and contraception was not included in midwifery texts until the 1960s. However, the sexual revolution was drawing young men and women much closer together before they entered into marriage; yet, it was failing to provide them with little more information than the generations before. A girl's ignorance around sex was thought of as 'moral purity, innocence and respectability;' and yet, it was doing very little to protect them from the very real dangers of unprotected sex.[1]

Needless to say, it was tiredness and sensitivity, plus swelling of my breasts, that worried me, and I was late with my period. I guessed I was just getting over-concerned, and it was this that was bringing on all these weird feelings. I decided it might be a good idea to have a hot bath to help me relax; it might work to bring on my period, and that's what I did. Afterwards, I lay in bed thinking about how I felt: it was like a burst of extra hormones; I felt super sensitive - a tendency to want to cry all the time or to be quite irritable. Nevertheless, it was definitely due to the pressures at work, so I shrugged everything off and went to sleep.

The days went on, and the feelings became more severe. What worried me the most was the tingling and swelling sensations of my breasts, plus they felt so bruised. I began to notice further that I had started an urge to want to pass water more frequently, and then came another horrible feeling. It would build up from a slight dizziness or giddiness, which eventually became faintness - and then came nausea. It was as if I couldn't move from A to B without feeling sick!

I decided to go off sick from work for a couple of days and stop worrying - just stay in bed - and this is what I did.

It was late on the first morning, and I was deep in sleep when the bedroom door scratched and clanked and woke me up. With a rattling and a scratching sound of a key in the lock, the door creaked open, and a small slim woman in her fifties stood there with her cleaning overall on.

She looked across at me sharply and muttered, "What's wrong with you?"

I turned over properly to face her, and then I answered meekly, "Oh, I'm not feeling too well . . . I seem to have picked up a bug or something."

She replied, "Have yer let them know at work?"

"No, not yet!" I said.

"Well, you'd better get on the telephone and tell them."

And with this, she turned around and went out again, slamming the door shut.

I sat up, and as I did so, the room was spinning around. Nevertheless, I managed to get to my bag on the chair and get out the work's telephone number.

In my pyjamas, I made my way onto the landing. I was on the third floor and went to the telephone on the windowsill. I picked it up and asked the downstairs receptionist if she could give me an outside line. I dialled *Rhona Roy* and told them that I was feeling unwell and would be away for a couple of days. The voice on the other end of the telephone sounded very sympathetic, so I felt more relaxed about it. I put the telephone down and made my way back to my room, where I immediately got back into bed and went straight to sleep.

Two days later and I am back at work again. We had a walk-through open plan office with just two office girls in there.

They asked me how I felt, and I just said, "Listless!"

However, in reality, I felt worse than that. I had noticed that my breasts were leaking with fluid, and I mentioned this to one of the office girls in private in the ladies toilet - silly me!

My 21st Birthday Party

It was going to be my 21st birthday, and I was going home to celebrate. Really, I had nothing to honour or praise publicly and was more worried than anything else.

My mother had asked me what I wanted for my special birthday, and to be honest, I had so much on my mind that I couldn't think straight.

However, one day, I had been walking around in the busy streets of London when suddenly I became aware of just how noisy it was and how much the varying noises (sounds) would change. There would be the jostling and bustle of the underground travellers and the rhythmic rattle of the downward and upward escalators. Straight on would be the globally known, tired and well-worn angry monsters - the underground trains - with their carriage doors *hissing* and crashing open, then slamming shut. Next, there were the market stalls and the babble and bartering of the traders; the sound of excited bee-activity from the buyers from within their individual hives (stalls) their buzzing, murmurings, shouts and their chatter. There was the noise of buskers in the open streets in competition with other music blasting out of the main shops; the traffic and the honking horns and the police car sirens and ambulances. It was such a highly audible environment, which appeared to be unbelievably magnified, whilst clearly perpetual in this materialistic land. So much so that I knew without question what I wanted for my birthday - an audio-tape-recording machine. I wanted one that I could put in my pocket so that when I walked around, it would be recording all these sounds. I would then be able to play it back to my family - especially my grandmother, who lived all alone - and my friends whenever I went home.

Meanwhile, back in Basingstoke, my mother wanted me to have a party, but I flatly refused, so she arranged for me to go out for a meal with a girlfriend of mine that I had met at Southampton College. I found this fortunate in one respect. At least they - my parents, that is - wouldn't be able to realise how ill I really felt.

My girlfriend and I chatted a lot, but I never told her why I didn't really want anything much to eat; I just said that I was under a lot of pressure at work. And all in all, one of the most fantastic days in a 'grown-up' teenager's life turned out to be quite quiet for me - luckily. However, my parents had planned for us to go to Portsmouth to see my Nan, my paternal grandmother, the following day.

Portsmouth had been established about 1180 when a merchant called Jean De Gisors founded a little town in the southwest corner of Portsea Island. De Gisors divided up the land into plots for building houses, and he started a market. Craftsmen and merchants came to live in the new settlement, and in 1185, a parish church was built, which, in the 20th century it became Portsmouth Cathedral. In 1194, the king gave Portsmouth a charter (a document granting the townspeople certain rights).[2]

My grandmother lived next door to the famous Portsmouth Temple of Spiritualism. This is because she was very spiritual herself; yet, the rest of the family, apart from me, were sceptical. I went to a meeting for the first time in the Temple when I was barely sixteen with my Nan and my parents, and the visiting medium came in late because he had travelled all the way from London. I remember it well: he was called Joe Benjamin, and we sat near the back.

I was amazed at what he was saying to people in the audience, who were verifying that what he was saying was absolutely true. All of a sudden, he pointed to me in the audience, and he gave me a message. He told me that he could see all these drawings around me and that I was going to have two shops.

At that particular time in my life, I had no idea what I wanted to do when I was to leave school some twelve months later.

All I would like to add here, for now, is, 'I take my hat off to you, Mr Benjamin. You were absolutely correct!'

The Portsmouth Temple of Spiritualism is the largest Spiritualist Church in Portsmouth. It has been at its existing site now since 1905, although the present two-storey building was opened in 1940. The Temple is open at various times on nearly every day of the week. Services consist of Prayers, Hymns and Absent Healing, as well as a Reading and Address on some aspects of the Philosophy of Spiritualism. This is normally followed by the Visiting Medium linking to the Spirit World for Communication.[3]

Figure 42 The largest Spiritualist Church in Portsmouth Established in 1905 73A Victoria Road South, Southsea, Hampshire, PO5 2BU

Spiritualism is an officially recognised religious movement with its own churches and Ministers. It embodies the main ideas of all religions: that there is a life after death, immortality and the existence of a God. However, the difference between Spiritualism and other religions is the ability through mediumship to prove that humans survive the grave. They say that Mediums are highly sensitive people who have developed their natural psychic abilities to communicate with those who have passed over, thus providing conclusive evidence of continued existence in another world. Even so, Mediums cannot just call up these people; they come to us, but only when they are ready, willing and able to do so.

The philosophy of Spiritualism is based on seven fundamental principles, with the first principle recognising that God is our Father. However, He is not regarded as a nebulous person sitting on a throne, but an *Infinite Power* embodied in all that is good and beautiful in our world. It is the greatest factor in the universe and the controlling force of all nature.[4]

The seven fundamental principles are:

1.   The Fatherhood of God
2.   The Brotherhood of Man
3.   The Communion of Spirits and the Ministry of Angels
4.   The Continuous Existence of the Human Soul
5.   Personal Responsibility
6.   Compensation and Retribution Hereafter for all the Good and Evil Deeds done on Earth
7.   Eternal Progress Open to every Human Soul.[5]

In 1880, Portsmouth came into prominence in psychical matters through the experiments of Major General Drayson and Arch Deacon Colley, together with the mediumship of Mrs Maggs. In 1890, Dr Arthur Conan Doyle (1859-1930), a practising doctor in Elm Grove, became interested in the subject. Thus, the foundation stones of the work that he did for Spiritualism were laid in Portsmouth.

It was in 1898 that a physical society was started, which held regular, weekly night-meetings for the discussion of psychic matters. The membership grew to nearly 100 but quickly dwindled. They had no mediums, so most of the meetings were occupied with discussing phenomena that they had only read about, and in the spring of 1900, it came to an end. Following this was an attempt to start a Spiritualist Society; the organisation held their meetings on Sundays in a small room and paid 2s.6d a week for the rent of the room. The young society had to draw all its mediums from London, and as the attendance was seldom twenty, it was struggling.

In the spring of 1901, the society was reformed, calling itself the Portsmouth Spiritualist Society with about twenty members. They now made a move towards better speakers and mediums. The society soon needed a bigger hall and subsequently gravitated to the larger Albert hall, with a capacity of some 750 people. The expense was found to be too great, and so they moved to the lesser Victoria hall. As the hall was only used on Sundays, development circles were started in members' homes, under the supervision of the church. There were over a dozen of these, and a Mr Oaten attended every circle once a month to mark progress and to give advice.

In 1918, Sir Arthur Conan Doyle proclaimed his belief in Spiritualism and on the 22nd of October 1926, he spoke at the old schoolhouse. In 1938, the old schoolhouse was demolished in preparation for a new Temple building. A library was later added, and two large houses next door were bought, which were rented for years to the Temple members and officers at peppercorn charges. However, they became such a financial responsibility that selling was enforced in the 1970s.[6]

N.B. Sir Arthur Conan Doyle (1859 –1930) was a British author, born in Edinburgh, and originally a doctor until his creation of private detective Sherlock Holmes and his companion Dr Watson in *A Study in Scarlet* 1887 led him to full-time authorship. He penned several volumes of short stories (first published in the *Strand Magazine*) and novels, including *The Hound of the Baskervilles* 1902. He also wrote historical romances, e.g. *The White Company* in 1891 and science fiction - *The Lost World* in 1912, with an irascible hero, Professor Challenger. In his later years, Doyle became a spiritualist.[7]

My paternal grandmother was into Spiritual Healing herself, and her home was set out for the purpose of healing performances. The patients would go in through the side door and down the steps. There, in front of them, was a small room which housed a kind of hospital bed, complete with an oblong rail above it and running around it, which held up a pull-around curtain via rings, for privacy. But it was the beautiful picture of Jesus on the wall that I always fell in love with - just His head and shoulders with one hand beckoning people towards Him. I adored His eyes and His beard and long hair for some reason, and I must be honest, it has permanently stayed with me for the rest of my life.

To the left of the entrance door was my grandmother's enormous lounge, with at least two sofas in it and many armchairs which were set out as a patients' waiting room. There was also a coffee table in there with Church Magazines and newsletters neatly placed on its top, but it was the notices on the wall that interested me. They were a kind of command to the patients to take off any metal objects before visiting the doctor - something to do with the power of electromagnetism, I believe.

When we arrived for the day, my grandmother greeted us, and it wasn't long before my mother mentioned to her that I wasn't feeling too well.

"Oh!" my grandmother said sympathetically. "Lie on the couch, Janet; we will give you some hands-on healing."

Which she did - with the help of a Doctor Baden, who lives in the Spirit World!

Spiritual Healing comes from the Spirit, they say, through the Healer's Spirit to the Patient's Spirit. Its aim is to balance the Physical, Emotional, Mental and Spiritual parts of the patient. No promises are made as to the results, although most people feel better in some way. Spiritual Healing is not Faith Healing as such. All that is required is for the patient to have an open mind and a desire to be well. Patients are normally asked to remove their glasses and hearing aids – for comfort and safety reasons. The healer may either place their hands on the patient, that is, if they are agreeable to that, although the healer will avoid any 'sensitive' areas; or, they may put their hands within three inches of the body. Absent Healing is where the patient is not present; however, even so, this can be just as effective as Contact Healing.[8]

After a while, I eventually sat up, and my mother said, "Do you feel better now, Janet?"

"Yes!" I replied.

But I didn't really. I stepped down from the couch and silently put on my shoes; I straightened up my clothes and steadily passed through the passageway to get to the kitchen.

My grandmother was in there snipping and pruning some sweet peas. This was one of her favourite flowers, and I always remember that she would put them in a jam-jar full of water and place them on the kitchen windowsill.

She turned and strode over to the kettle to make some tea and passed me a cup.

She looked me in the eye and said quietly, "You know that you are pregnant, my sweet – don't you? But I won't say anything!"

And she didn't.

Back to work

A few days later, and I'm back at work and being violently sick. Nothing seemed to stay down - only if I laid down and went to sleep.

I'm back off work again and asleep in the hostel. It is in the afternoon, and the others are at work and college. Suddenly, the door began to clank and rattle, and then it scratched with which it swung open, hitting a long chain attached to a bunch of keys. I lay there, all of a shake, when suddenly this 'cigarette breath' was heading straight towards me.

"What's wrong with yer today?" the voice said sharply.

Sheepishly, I replied, "I'm being sick a lot." I spoke quietly, covering my face with my hand so that I wouldn't keep swallowing her breath.

"You're not pregnant, are yer?" she asked.

My stomach came up and met my mouth, there was an almighty gush, and with one hand over my mouth, I rushed to the washbasin. I could hear the rustling of paper, but I hadn't any energy to care or to even look round. Besides, I was petrified of this woman.

She thrust a piece of paper in my hand, saying, "Have yer got yerself a doctor yet?"

"No!" I said.

"This is the hostel's doctor; get yerself down there today!" With that, she walked towards the door.

She was just about to leave when she turned around and said, "Yer know that if yer pregnant, yer can't stay here! We don't have pregnant women in this place!"

With this parting comment, she slammed the door shut!

I didn't phone the doctor; I phoned Dave instead. It was his friend that answered the phone.

"Can I speak to Dave, please?" I asked.

"Oh, hello, Janet. He's at work," he said.

Well, of course, I knew that he would be - but still, I just wanted to talk to him.

"Can you ask him to give me a ring, please, when he gets home?" I said.

The reply came back, "Well, of course! Are you okay?"

"Oh, yes. Nothing to worry about."

"Goodbye!"

I didn't go to the doctors, I listened out for the loudspeaker all evening, and I didn't hear from Dave either.

The next day, I phoned *Rhona Roy*, and they weren't very happy on the other end. It was a very busy period.

Two days later, I returned to work. No-one spoke much to me, only my boss, who seemed sympathetic - another father figure to me.

He asked if my sickness had gone, and I said, "Not really, but I'm okay - just tired!"

He said no more, but I knew that he was thinking a lot and seemed very quiet.

That evening, I couldn't eat my meal, I told my friend how bad I felt, and she said that it was best to visit the doctors to give me peace of mind.

At the Doctors

The following day, I made up my mind that after work, I would go to the hostel's doctor. As I left the hostel's entrance steps, I turned right onto Great Russell Street and then right again into Bury Place. From here, I turned first left onto the A40, which led to Theobalds Road (A401). I walked along this road for a few minutes until I noticed King's Mews on my left. Just a short distance further on, I could see a cross-road. I turned left here onto the A5200 of Grays-Inn Road (W.C.1). It was here that I turned left for the Doctor's surgery.

I was very pale, felt really tired and listless, and I was extremely worried. This was my first time visiting a doctor in London, and when I opened the door, I was surprised to find that I had stepped straight into the surgery. Well, it was just a small dark square room with a very high ceiling. There were three small windows in the outer walls that had been placed right up near the ceiling to let some light into this otherwise very dark room. There was a bench-type seat attached to all the walls that went all around the room, and on the bench seats, patients sat waiting to see the doctor - and there was *only* one. Everyone looked pale and miserable. It was like something out of a Charles Dickens book - even the room itself!

Charles Dickens (1812-1870) was a novelist whose works are especially associated with London, as it is the setting for many of his novels. Dickens described London as a Magic Lantern because it fired his imagination and made him write. So much so that he doesn't just use London as the backdrop or setting for his works; instead, his writings are concerned with the city itself - with its character.

I sat down by the entrance door. Every now and then, the doctor would peer out from a side room and call out, "Next!"

The patient nearest the doctor's room would get up and disappear under the doorway's lintel into the dark of the unknown. The rest of us would just keep shifting our position, shuffling along, to keep the space filled in front of the doctor's doorway.

It was my turn, and I was shaking like a fragile leaf.

I went into a type of office with a desk and two chairs. The doctor sat down, and he told me to do the same.

"What can I do for you?" he asked, looking at me over the top of his glasses.

I just looked at my hands on my lap as my fingers twiddled with each other. "I'm not very well!" I said.

"Oh dear!" he replied sympathetically as he wrote something on a sheet of paper.

"In what way do you not feel well?" he asked casually.

"I keep being sick!"

He stopped writing. "Do you have any other symptoms?"

"Yes, I feel queasy and tired . . . and hmmh . . . my breasts hurt!"

He stopped writing altogether, but he didn't look up. "Do you think you are pregnant?" he said.

"No!" I replied. I looked down at my fingers and started playing with them again.

"Have you a boyfriend?" he asked.

"Yes!" I replied.

"Does he think you are pregnant?"

"No! Well, I haven't said anything to him yet."

"How long is it since you had your last period?"

"About nine weeks."

He sat back in his chair, and it creaked as he did so. He looked at me - straight in the eyes. "I need to examine you, but I will have to do it at the end of surgery."

He stood up. "If you take a seat back in the surgery for a while, I won't be long."

We walked through the doorway together, and as we did so, he told the next person to go into his office. As the patient stood up, the doctor told me to sit in the empty space nearest his door. This was obviously so that he could keep an eye on me. But I didn't mind; I felt safe - well sort of - another father figure to me, you see.

Surgery came to an end - about forty-five minutes later. There was just me sitting there playing with my fingers. I was positive that I wasn't pregnant – because Dave had said so.

The doctor came out into the doorway again and said, "I won't be a minute."

With this, he walked across to the outside door and locked it. He strolled back towards me and told me to follow him. We went through the doorway, but not into his office this time - to the right, into another small room with a single bed in it.

He asked me to take my knickers off and lie on the bed, which I did. He opened a drawer, pulled out a pair of rubber gloves and proceeded to put them on, after which he dipped them in some kind of jelly. He told me that it would be cold, but to spread my legs. He continued with his series of actions by giving me an internal (vaginal) examination to see if he could find a soft enlarged uterus (so he told me), and as he did so, he was looking up at the ceiling.

I knew that he had found something because he said, "Ahha - there it is!"

He was sort of clutching at something, and it felt like a lump.

He turned around with his back to me, took off his gloves and said, "I want you to get dressed and then come back into my office."

When I arrived in his office, he asked me to sit down. He got out a packet of cigarettes, and he offered me one.

"No, thank you," I said.

"Do you smoke?"

"No!" I said.

He lit his cigarette and puffed the smoke out away from me, and said, "You're about ten weeks pregnant."

"No," I said. "No, I'm not!"

There was a pause…

"What do you both plan to do about the baby?"

I shook my head. "I'm not pregnant!"

"What makes you say that?" He asked with a surprised tone in his voice.

"Because Dave told me that he couldn't have any more children!"

"Is he married?" he asked.

"Yes, but separated."

He puffed hard on his cigarette. "How do you know?"

And so, this is where I told him the situation.

He was silent.

"So, do you plan to keep the baby?"

I was silent - horrified, in fact. "I'm not pregnant!" I said.

"Do you want an abortion?"

"No!" I said. "I'm not pregnant."

"If you don't want an abortion, would you consider an adoption - for your baby to be adopted - or fostered?"

"I'm not pregnant!"

He began to write something down on a piece of paper and then offered it to me, saying, "Here is an appointment for you to take to this hospital. We'll get a second opinion, shall we? Just to see if 'they think' you are pregnant."

He looked up at me and smiled a little; then, with a gentle nod, he continued, "I think this is the best way forward."

I took the piece of paper from him, turned around and walked out of the door.

I strolled back to the hostel in a daze.

But the worst was yet to come!

Telling Dave

I decided to phone Dave that evening. I was able to get an outside line, and I did manage to speak to Dave. I told him that

I needed to see him, that it was important and could he come round to the hostel that evening.

"Okay!" he said. "Give me an hour to get there!"

Things seemed better now - I wasn't going to be alone with my concern!

And then, all of a sudden, I changed and began to worry about what he would say to me.

Would he be angry with me?

Should I feel guilty?

I became very tense and filled with emotional dread - I think it was the fear of rejection, of being left on my own to face the consequences.

I stood outside on the steps of the hostel all of a shake and a tremble, and it seemed ages before he arrived. At last, I spotted him. He was down the road a bit, so I ran over to his car, and he opened the door for me from the inside. He didn't look very happy, and it looked as if he had just dropped everything and had left in a hurry. I do believe that he still had on his slippers.

I didn't know how to start, really, and so I just took hold of his hand and kissed it. I think that he was probably as nervous as I was. Then, there I was, pouring out my story of what the doctor had said.

He was very quiet!

"But, I can't be pregnant, can I?" I urged. "You said that you can't have any more children, didn't you?" And with this, I am desperately looking closely at him in the eyes.

He nodded his head in agreement.

"Then I can't be pregnant, can I?"

He kept his head down.

"You told me that you can't have any more children, and so I don't need to worry, do I?"

Dave nodded his head.

There was silence.

"When do you have to go to the hospital?" he asked.

"Thursday, will you come with me?"

"I can't!" he said.

"Why can't you come with me?" I asked earnestly.

"I've got to go to work, haven't I?"

I looked at him hard, but he wasn't going to change his mind.

I picked up his hand again and kissed it, and he just said, "I'd better go!"

I got out of the car, and as I went to shut the door, I asked, "You won't leave me, will you? You will come back again, won't you?"

He was staring straight ahead at this time, paused, then turned and looked at me, and answered, "Yes."

He turned around to face frontwards again and switched on the ignition, saying, "You'd better go in now, or they'll give you a warning."

I felt so lonely, and I didn't go to work the next day or the rest of the week, in fact. I just felt very depressed - and sick.

The Hospital Appointment

It seemed to be a specific hospital for trainee or student doctors.

I felt so alone.

When I turned up, I showed the receptionist my appointment card, and she pointed me in the right direction.

I found the room. It was a fairly small type of ward with approximately four separate compartments, with curtains around each one to screen for privacy. I stood there and wondered what was going to happen next. It wasn't long before a nurse came in; she smiled at me and drew the curtain open a little from around one of these cubicles, and there was a bed in there.

"If you go inside," she said, "take your shoes and knickers off and pop yourself on the bed. The doctors won't be long!"

"What are they going to do to me?" I asked. But I never got a reply because she was gone.

I lay there on the bed feeling quite rude and sensitive.

It wasn't long before I heard the voices of a group of young males. Shortly afterwards, the cubicle curtain was ripped open, and I was faced with a group of at least six young men in their early twenties - not much older than me. They were wearing white coats and had stethoscopes around their necks.

One of them spoke to me, "Can you pull your skirt up for us, please?"

"Why?" I asked. "What are you going to do to me?"

I heard some murmuring from the group. This first male proceeded to put on some plastic gloves, and then he told me to spread my legs. Everyone was quiet now, and all you could hear was their breathing. This first male was quite roughly fishing around inside me.

After a short time, he stopped, stood upright, and said, "Hmmh! I'd say it's around ten weeks!"

There was some mumbling and chattering from the group, and then came the words, "Spread your legs again."

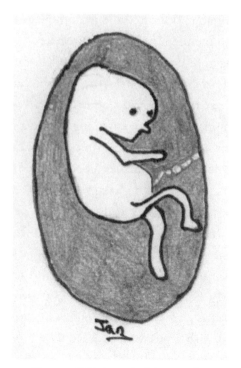

Figure 43 Fetus at eight weeks

This male was worse than the first one - really rough! "I disagree!" he said. "I think it's more like eight weeks!"

There were some chuckles from the others at the rear end of the bed, and they all began to swop places. They were mumbling and muttering amongst themselves with their backs turned towards me, and then I felt someone force my legs open again and push his hand up inside me.

I was so humiliated, and then I heard this one say, "I think it's more like twelve weeks myself!"

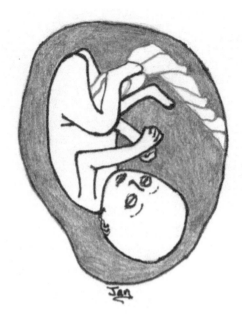

Figure 44 Fetus at fourteen weeks

Another voice quickly added, "No! It's definitely less than that!"

With this, the group all started chuckling, and at the same time, they were trying hard to suppress their laughter.

I felt a hot tear gush down my face.

This herd of savage males, with their primitive paws, started to move off with their clipboards; and I just lay there with the after-effects - the aftermath of their presence.

Suddenly, a lone male student looked down upon me smiling, and I said, "Please, I don't want any more."

He put on some gloves.

"I'm afraid it's all part of the training!" He said. "Just turn your head and look at the wall!"

He gave me his examination and then wrote something on his clipboard. He looked down at me, smiled, which turned into a grin, and then he scooted off to catch up with the others.

I lay there in a flood of tears; they had treated me like an object without any feeling - and without talking directly to me. Then they had just slithered off to another cubicle to supposedly use some other human being as bait to acquire their status.

I sat up. I was confused. I was shocked and appalled!

I guess, looking back now, that it was some kind of a shock tactic laid on by the doctor. In other words, "You don't want to take my word for it, so I will put you before several others to convince you that you are definitely pregnant!"

Canada

The following day, the extension telephone rang on the landing. I rushed along the corridor and picked it up.

"Hello!" I said.

A female's voice echoed out at me, "Can you ask a Janet Hann to come to reception, please?"

I replied, "I am Janet Hann!"

The receptionist said, "There is someone here to see you; can you come downstairs to reception?"

I rushed along the corridor and down the stairs.

Dave was waiting there by the door. When he saw me, he beckoned me to go outside with him, and we went and sat in his car.

I told him all about the day before at the hospital, and he was extremely silent. After all, he had been adamant that he couldn't have any more children.

He looked pale, and we had a coffee in a café not far from the hostel down a side street. He muttered something strange. He told me that, when the baby was born, he would send it to Pakistan to be looked after by his parents. I couldn't accept what I was hearing, and he didn't repeat it. That was *never* going to happen – not in *my* lifetime – this baby was *ours*! However, he didn't want me to talk about it anymore, and he walked me back to the hostel after an hour.

A few days later, we met up again. Dave told me to sit in his car. He was very serious. He told me that he had thought about the situation for a long time and in great depth, and then he said, "*I've* decided that we are going to Canada to live!"

I couldn't believe what I was listening to, so I asked him to repeat it.

He looked at me sternly, saying, "I've decided that we are going to Canada to live!"

"But why choose Canada?" I asked.

He replied, "I've chosen Canada because it's a very healthy place to live. London is so unhealthy!"

I dropped my glance to my hands on my lap.

So many things were going through my mind right then.

"But that's such a long way to go; can't we be somewhere nearer to home?"

Dave looked at me strictly to enforce his discipline, and then he said something that I'd never heard of before.

He said: "I am a Muslim!"

I just looked at him; I didn't know about these sorts of things.

He continued, "As a Muslim, I can have four wives, so long as there is a certain distance between them!"

Apparently, there are some circumstances in which it is advantageous to society to allow men to marry multiple wives. For this reason, polygamy is practised by many religions and cultures. Polygamy is also permitted in the Bible. However, the Qur'an gives permission to only a restricted and limited form of that practice; the Qur'an permits but does not command a man to have four wives. Furthermore, the Qur'an stipulates that a man is responsible for the maintenance of his wife or wives. If a man has more than one wife, he has to provide separate living accommodation for each of his wives. If a man chooses to have multiple marriages, it will create a heavy responsibility on him because he must divide his time equally among his wives. He may, for example, spend one night with each wife on a rotating schedule. Furthermore, if a man cannot maintain justice in the treatment of his wives, the Qur'an stipulates that he is to have no more than one wife.[9]

I felt like I was in deep waters and had lost my bearings - all these things didn't seem to make sense to me.

Wife Number Two

Everything was echoing in my head; I seemed to have lost *who* I was. Dave had a sense of values so different to what I had been used to; it all appeared so alien to me. One thing for sure was that I definitely didn't want to be Wife Number Two. I had been brought up as a Christian, and this just didn't feel right.

I began to think about wife number one; how would she take to this? I put myself in her shoes, and I found it very upsetting. I began to think about Dave's other three children; they wouldn't see their daddy very often and vice versa, and I found this extremely stressful. Canada would be too far away for Dave to be in constant contact with his children – and his other wife. I thought of myself. My roots were in England, and my parents and relatives would be so upset - I would miss them all very much.

It was here that I began to realise what it meant by different cultures; sometimes they can be, well, it seemed, *Worlds Apart!*

I was also seeing Dave in a different light because, not only had he told me that he could not have any more children and now my pregnancy had proven this to be untrue; but, at the same time, he had not done anything to protect me in case he had got it wrong.

I sat there in a daze as to what to do next.

CHAPTER SIX

Time to Tell my Parents

The Awful Part

It was time to go home and break the news to my parents.

I sat on the train attempting all sorts of ways to tell them, but whatever I thought of just didn't seem to be right. What I mean is, the way I told them had to make some kind of positive sense. It would not be as bad as it first seemed; it was another event that was going to happen in my life that was going to be a good one that made them proud of me and that everything would fall into place as it always did.

As my mother had said to me many times before, "Everything seems meant for you, Janet!"

With which I would say, "Well, not everything!"

And my mother would reply, "Well, not everything at first then, but it always seems that these things work out for the best in the end!"

Well, this was going to be one of those cases where it will work out in the end – that is all!

The train stopped at Basingstoke railway station, and my heart seemed to be getting heavier. I daren't think of their first reaction in too much detail – that would be too painful!

I held my breath!

I just wished that I wasn't going home on my own!

As I passed the red telephone box, I kept my head down in shame.

'Things have changed now,' I said to myself. 'My news is not going to make them proud of me at all!'

I passed the booth silently, crossed over to the other side of the road, and headed upwards towards home. All seemed to be so quiet everywhere. There were no children or people about, and it was as if all the trees, bushes, plants, blades of grass and even the houses were bowing their heads in shame of me.

And then, I had almost reached their door.

I opened it and went inside.

My parents seemed quite normal. In fact, they were delighted to see me and very happy for me to be with them. We had our first meal together, but to be truthful, I can't remember what it was - nor even what happened just after it had been eaten. We cleared everything away, and then we moved into the living room to sit down.

My mother said casually, "I'm glad you're feeling better now, Janet!"

I just went quiet.

"What's the matter?" she said, preparing to sit down with her knitting.

"Well," I said.

"You're not pregnant, are you?" she asked half-heartedly as she picked up her wool.

I just bowed my head.

My mother's face dropped, "You're not – are you?"

I said, "Yes."

"Janet, you're NOT pregnant, are you?"

"Yes," I repeated again.

My father, by now, was sitting in his armchair, and he had not long picked up his newspaper. He didn't look up; instead, he seemed, well, motionless, like a frozen statue that was beginning to wilt and melt.

I don't think he wanted to believe what he was listening to - he was, so it seemed, playing deaf.

In fact, my mother said, "I'm dreaming, aren't I?"

"No," I said, looking down at my feet.

Her face shrunk to half its normal size as she screwed it up in anger.

"Whose is it? What's his name? Does he know? Is he married? It would have to be someone we don't know! How did it happen? Was it in a bedroom?"

The interrogation was awful. She wanted to know every single little bit of detail.

I just sat and stared at her. That was private! That was my business!

And then she said, "Is he Black?"

I just looked at her in surprise. And then I answered, "He's not Black; he's Anglo Pakistani!"

My mother's lower jaw just fell open, and her eyes were like saucers.

She stared at me, "Is that Black?"

"No," I said.

My father's newspaper began to tremble and shake, then it dropped onto the floor, and my dad started sobbing.

This was the first time that I had ever seen my father cry. In fact, it was the first time I'd ever seen him so sad.

He had been so proud of me.

I had done so well in his eyes.

I guess he also thought that this was the end of my career too!

After a while, he spoke, "Do they know back at the hostel?"

"No, not yet," I whispered.

The rest of the evening we all spent crying and then we went to bed.

I just felt safe...

They knew!

Back to the Hostel

My mother and I both decided that I needed to go back to the hostel to tell them my news. I was still on sick leave from work as well, and I'd left their telephone number in the hostel.

We travelled on the train to Waterloo station, and to be honest, I cannot remember what we spoke about. Probably not a lot; however, I do remember her asking me lots of intimate questions like, "What did you have on?" And, "Did he ask you first? Were you outside at the time - were you in a park? Were you in a car? Where were you?"

All the while, my mother was clutching her handbag on her lap, and all the time, I had my head turned away from her, looking out of the carriage window.

I had no reason or need to answer her.

I just felt like a little girl being spoken to by another little girl.

I felt so confused and mixed up inside.

Eventually, we made our way up the hostel steps, and we proceeded to walk inside. The receptionist gave me a smile and asked me to sign in.

My mother looked down and put her hand up to her mouth, saying quietly, "Do you think that we should tell them now?"

"Might as well," I said with a wince.

And so, at the reception desk, we asked to speak to the office staff.

We had to wait a few minutes, and as we stood there, we watched the students going out of the building, some coming back in with their bags, signing in, then moving off in different directions to their rooms. I felt so odd standing there with my mother - like a little girl. I had not only become socially recognised as an adult on my twenty-first birthday but in the past few months, I had been allowed to grow up - I had both mentally and physically matured. I knew what it meant to become an adult woman and be independent; to earn money and pay for my living and keep; to work and hear about and move alongside people that had made a mark using their lives in society. My life, too, had been feeling that it was worthwhile; it had felt that I had something to offer, to give back to the world.

What had gone wrong?

At last, a member of the office staff came out of a side door and asked us to go in and take a seat. She asked me my name and started looking in a ledger book and then she found me. I think that she was looking to see if I was in arrears with my rent. She asked me if I liked it at the hostel, or did I want to change my room – did I get on with the girls I shared the bedroom with?

"Oh yes," I said. "There's no problem there!"

"Oh, that's good to hear," she replied.

My mother cleared her throat. "Janet…" - and then she found it difficult to continue!

"I'm pregnant!" I butted in.

The woman looked up at me sharply. "Well, you can't stay here! We don't have pregnant girls here!"

"No, I know," I said.

"That's right!" she continued. "You'll have to leave by the end of the week!"

She hurriedly asked for the money and told me that I must return my key at the end of the week.

"Yes," I replied.

My mother and I got up silently like two naughty girls and started walking out of the office.

We walked through the entrance hall and proceeded to make our way up to my bedroom on the third floor.

I opened the heavy creaking door; it was dark inside, so I switched on the light. My heart sank; it was really depressing in there - murky. I had spent so many days and nights worrying in this place and in a state of extreme dejection, and then I suddenly realised - I hadn't been sick for at least twenty-four hours. In fact, I didn't feel sick at all.

I walked over to my bed, and so did my mother. She casually looked around, and I wondered what she was thinking about.

Then she said, "You might as well come home now rather than stay here for a few more days."

"What do you mean?" I asked.

"Well, you might as well pack up and leave now; you've still got your suitcases under the bed. I can help carry your suitcases for you - save you carrying them all by yourself!"

Suddenly, there was a knock on the door, and I opened it.

A young woman stood there, and she said, "One of our office staff, Sarah, said to give this to you."

I glanced down at the letter that she held in her hand. I said, "Thank you" and took it off her. It was a London postmark, and as I opened it, out fell my cards.

Rhona Roy had given me the sack!

"Oh well," my mother said. "It's just as well you're coming home now and be done with it!"

We started to pack everything up, and as we did so, I looked around the room. It was gloomy; I hadn't enjoyed the shared bedroom at all, and besides, I'd had so many tears in there over the last few days. I wasn't upset about leaving it.

My mother pulled up her coat sleeve and looked at her watch, saying, "If we can get a move on, we can catch the 3:00 o'clock train from Waterloo!"

We gathered the last few things together and locked up the suitcases.

'Why is there always more things to take back – much more than when you arrive?' I thought.

We moved out of the bedroom, and I locked the door. I suddenly thought of my two room-mates and felt sad that I hadn't said cheerio to them – I hadn't even written them a note to say that I'd left.

I quickly looked up to ask my mother if I had time to write them a note – but she had gone!

I walked along the long corridor and down the flights of steps. I gave the receptionist my keys and said cheerio – I didn't want to make a big thing about it.

As we stood on the steps, I looked over at the British Museum. This place, an institution that is totally devoted to displaying objects of lasting value and interests. It instantly reminded me of the many joyous trips I had made over there and the treasures held within it. I loved that place – I was really going to miss it! In fact, it had left a huge impression on me, enough to affect my future life - though little did I realise it at the time.

"Come on, Janet," my mother said. "We will miss our train, and then we'll get caught up in the rush hour!"

The Train Journey

The train was quite empty considering – well, at least our compartment was empty, and I do believe that my mother had quietly planned it that way.

As we sat on the train together, I began to feel more at ease with my situation. However, it seemed that my mother was doing the very opposite; she must have been sat there just firing herself up. I suddenly thought of Dave, and I panicked. I hadn't told him that I had left the hostel; he wouldn't know where I was!

"I haven't told Dave that I have left the hostel!" I said.

"Well, that doesn't matter!" she said.

"What do you mean?" I replied, horrified.

"Well, you're not going to see him again anyway!"

I looked at her in shock. "Why not?" I asked.

"You're going to have an abortion!"

It was as if my whole world had come crashing down around me. Well, I knew that it had – but my inner 'me' had now become void as well.

"No, No, No," I said. "That is definitely out of the question!"

"What are you talking about?" she protested.

"No, No," I said, shaking my head firmly. "I've started this little life, and there's no way that I'm going to end it!"

In fact, I had been silently sitting there on the train, preparing to give my baby a very happy, healthy upbringing.

N.B. Abortion was definitely out of the question for me. What is more, is that it was against the law and destined to remain so until 2019. I had heard that it would not be too difficult to find a back street abortionist, providing that one had money and well-connected friends. As a common expression of the time put it: 'Somebody always knew somebody who knew somebody' to arrange the abortion.

Before the legalisation of abortion, women were known to have tried various herbs, poisons, pushing of foreign objects into the cervix and even beatings to cause an abortion or miscarriage. In the 1960s, it is estimated that thousands of people attempted to abort with these unsafe methods. Hospitals regularly saw women in 'septic abortion wards,' where they would die of haemorrhage or infection after an incomplete attempt to self-abort. Seeing the danger of these methods, some small groups of people learned how to provide safe and successful *illegal* abortions.[1] The Abortion Act (sponsored by David Steel, MP) became law, only legalising abortion under certain conditions. It came into effect on the 27 of April 1968. However, since its passage that had started in 1967, the Abortion Act has been unsuccessfully challenged several times by anti-choice ("pro-life") organisations that aim to restrict access to abortion.[2]

Then there came another blow. This time my mother was insisting that the baby was going to be adopted! To me, this was far too much to take in. After all, I had only just begun to accept that I was actually pregnant! To be having my own baby was one thing, but to be told, at that point, that I was going to have it for somebody else; that it had to be given away as a gift to some stranger – that was far too extreme and painful.

I knew that my mother was working herself up for something awful because she was fidgety; she couldn't look at me. The worst part about it was that I couldn't get away either. We were in one of those railway carriages which are self-contained: they have their own entrance-exit doors on each side of the compartment to accommodate for platforms on either side of the carriage. They contain two long bench seats so that the passengers may face each other – with enough room to seat around four people on each bench.

Suddenly, my mother looked at me in horror; she was about to deliver another stab!

"What will all the neighbours say? What will the relatives think? What will your nan do? There is *no way* she must find out! We must keep all of this a secret!"

Now I knew that this was all true; I loved my nan. I had lost my granddad at around the age of six years. His death had been a big blow to the family. My mother was an only child, and so my nan was dependant on my mother and us. I had grown very close to my nan.

As you already know, my nan lived in Eastleigh and whilst at Southampton College, I had participated in the fashion illustration classes which had been held in the evening, and my nan had kindly permitted me to stay with her at those times – to save travelling all the way back to Basingstoke on those evenings. I would travel from Southampton to Eastleigh, which was around twenty to thirty minutes away by train. She really enjoyed my stays, my mother had said – and so did I. I had got to know my nan as a mother and daughter relationship. Sometimes we had laughed so much we would be in stitches - especially when I found a romantic novel by the side of her bed!

I began to feel extremely unhappy.

I had let them all down!

I had now not only lost my job, my career and my hostel accommodation, but my parents and possibly my extended family's love as well! I definitely wasn't going to lose my baby too, and I must get in touch with Dave as well when I get off the train.

I sat on the train wishing for the journey to end. I felt cornered. I looked down at my belongings around me, and I thought, 'that's about all I've got now.' I secretly cuddled my tummy, and as I did so, I knew I was not alone – there were two of us in this situation, and it was *always* going to be this way.

I began to realise that my mother was brewing up for something more, and I fidgeted. The knife was beginning to twist.

My mother's voice echoed with hate and bitterness this time! "Well, you can't live at home! You're a disgrace to the family! You must go and hide somewhere, *anywhere,* and that's my final word!"

We got off the train at Basingstoke railway station like two bookends facing in opposite directions.

The suitcases were really heavy, yet we managed them together. We struggled down many steps to get to the ticket collector, and finally, with stops and starts, we made our way out of the exit. Once outside, we turned left and went under the subway. Getting these suitcases up some steps this time and across the yard-piece was not easy, but we somehow coped between us. Then we came to another set of steps which took us up onto a mound. This was the route that I had travelled for many years on my way backwards and forwards to school.

My mother was puffing a lot, and I knew that I was a burden to her. I felt so lonely, so different; it was so quiet compared to London. I felt all alone, rejected by London and dejected by my mother, and probably my father too. To tell you the truth, I felt like a whore! A relationship that had been so lovely was now starting to feel so dirty.

We both made great efforts under the circumstances, and these suitcases and bags were getting heavier and more awkward as we struggled up the rise to reach Queen Mary's Avenue. We decided to put our luggage down for a bit, to give ourselves a rest once we arose up on the flat of this long avenue. We looked all around as we gathered our breath, and then we headed straight on; not far to go now, for there in the distance was a familiar landmark - the lofty red telephone box.

It was here when I began to realise how much that telephone booth had swept me off my feet; it had lifted me off the ground into an unbelievable world of adulthood, of excitement and lights. I had got to know of interesting places, exotic food, different cultures, entertainment and most of all, chances of success. And now here we were, my Mother and I, throwing our body and limbs about in a violent effort to return my sole belongings back home again. I started to think of my contrasting childhood and the 'only' daily delight of wondering what we were going to have for dinner tomorrow. I suppose that you could say, in one respect, that this was what was making me feel so close to my little bump - we 'both' knew the truth - we had been part of a Wondrous Land that had brought forth such a beautiful relationship!

September: 1967

I was undecided as to what to do next. For the first few days, I needed to settle back down into my childhood surroundings. The home seemed so small compared to what I had just come from, and I couldn't go off anywhere in the building and be on my own. We all seemed to keep bumping into each other; we were smothering each other, and it was back to, "What are you thinking about, Janet?"

This was something that my mother had always found annoying - for me to drift off and have a world of my own!

I did not keep in touch with Dave. We didn't have a telephone at home for a start. I would have to explain my every move, and probably, my mother would have come with me to the telephone box to tell me what to say.

I was suffocating, really. In fact, I felt that I had even less freedom now than I'd had at home before my sojourn in London. Besides, there seemed to be too many obstacles down the route of keeping in touch with Dave at that moment. Things were being sorted out for me by my mother. She had control now, and this seemed to keep the situation calmer. I must admit that for now, it also began to make more sense - plus another good factor, I wasn't being sick anymore.

A Commuter Again

Once things seemed to be in some kind of mentally stable order, I began to think things through. If I went round to the telephone box to phone Dave, what would I say? At our last meeting, he had been adamant that I was to be wife number two. I began to think about it sensibly. How could he *really* look after two wives and their sets of children? After all, he didn't seem interested in my career. It was as if I would be at home looking after the child/children as a housewife. Would he plan that I live with *my* parents and then he could move to and fro between the two sets of families? I really didn't understand this way of life, this other culture, and I don't think my father would have agreed with these things either.

I began to wonder if Dave had previously planned to find a second wife. Had the time come in his life to look for another wife? After all, he was now thirty-one. Had he been searching for wife number two? Why was he temporarily living with his Asian friend and his family?

I thought of wife number one again; would she find it upsetting to know that she was going to be one of a chain of wives? I felt very sorry for her, though I was also aware by now of non-Muslim husbands having mistresses too. I thought of Canada again, too, but that was definitely out of the question for me.

It was here that I stood when suddenly, I remembered that I was due to illustrate Evette's fourth catalogue, *Spring-Summer (1968),* so I decided to contact her via the Queen Mary's Avenue red telephone box.

Evette and I fixed an appointment for the beginning of the following week. I felt well at this point and began to feel somewhat settled that I still had managed to keep 'part' of my life in London. But there was another reason why I needed to go to the city - the London doctor had sent me an antenatal clinic appointment to be held in Bloomsbury, not far from the Y.W.C.A.

Over the weekend, I began to reminisce over such things, as when I used to commute backwards and forwards to Southampton College from Basingstoke. At this particular time, we were watching Sunday Night at the London Palladium. That night, I had a dream: I was working in the *Box Office* at the London Palladium, and it was really vivid!

I also had another dream, and it was similar to the one that I'd had weeks earlier.

A Dream

I keep turning over and cannot get comfy. Something appears to be shaking me and wanting me to wake up; however, I'm too tired to rouse from sleep. I decide to give in and let my lucid dream continue.

I am looking once again at a kind of catalogue; a photograph album, a really old one, which is landscape in shape. I begin to skim through the photographs until I get to the same one I found before. It's a photograph that was produced using a kind of sepia tone, providing a soft hue. I am in this old street in London once again, with many shops around, and I begin to notice the quaint signs on the buildings' walls. I see that there are no buses as such;

instead, there are horse-driven coaches with one, sometimes two and even four horses.

People are sitting on these open-top coaches looking very gentry, with men wearing top hats or bowlers and suits with matching waistcoats and tall, stiff collars. Once again, it seems to be set in the Victorian days because the women look trim with their nipped-in waists and long trailing garments decorated with large buttons and braids with rear bustles - and wearing neat gloves. They show off their Gibson Girl hairstyle and broad-brimmed hats with deep crowns, trimmed with lavish nets and feathers.

These people are filling the scene because everywhere, there are groups crowding together as if they are waiting for a procession to pass. I scan around to see if I can find the little girl again, and there she is, once again sitting on the curb, but this time she is looking directly at me. She has a lovely smile, and she is smiling at me.

Suddenly, this young child gets up from the curb and walks across the uneven cobbled road. All the while, she is looking and smiling at me. She begins to beckon me once again with her finger to come into the picture; she wants me to join her. As I get closer, she whispers a name.

I wake up, and I am disturbed by this dream.

The Next Day

The following day, my first stop in London was to keep my antenatal appointment in Bloomsbury. These appointments, I was told, were designed to detect any problems of the unborn baby before the symptoms occur - so that more help can be given. The clinic was a little impersonal and, to me, a bit frightening.

However, the staff were very friendly and receptive towards me, so I was not overly embarrassed to ask them my queries.

A nurse asked me some questions about my past medical history, and a doctor examined me by checking my heart and lungs, spine, stomach and pelvis. These were all vital tests, I was told, to ensure that I had no diseases. At the same time, my urine was checked for protein (to exclude kidney disease) and sugar (to exclude diabetes). They took a small blood sample from my arm to be examined for iron content and to check my blood group and Rhesus group. The hospital will need to know this, they said, in case a transfusion is needed in an emergency.

I came out of the clinic feeling somewhat refreshed - these people seemed to care about us, and everything seemed good for me and my baby. I felt happy.

From here, I left for my appointment with Evette in Knightsbridge, and this was the start of the fourth Catalogue. I had also planned to look for some maternity wear before I left for home in Basingstoke, and this is where I headed by tube to the West End.

I got off the tube at Oxford Street Station, and as I rose up from the underground station, I realised that I was not far from Liberty - a department store on Regent Street in the West End of London. This department store sells such things as luxury goods including women's, men's and children's fashion, cosmetics and fragrances, jewellery, accessories, home-ware, furniture, stationery and gifts. It is also well known for its floral and graphic prints and its beautiful collection of Indian fabrics.

I had learnt that Liberty gets its name from Arthur Lasenby Liberty, who was born in Chesham, Buckinghamshire, in 1843.

He was employed by Messrs Farmer and Rogers in Regent Street in 1862. By 1874, Liberty decided to start a business of his own, which he did the following year. He accepted the lease of half a shop at 218a Regent Street with only three staff members.

The shop opened in 1875, selling ornaments, fabric and *objets d'art* from Japan and the East. As the business grew, neighbouring properties were bought and added. The store became the most fashionable place to shop in London, and Liberty fabrics were used for both clothing and furnishings. Some of its clientele was exotic and included famous Pre-Raphaelite artists.

During the 1890s, Liberty built strong relationships with many English designers. Many of these designers, including Archibald Knox, practised the artistic styles known as Arts and Crafts and Art Nouveau. Liberty helped develop Art Nouveau through his encouragement of such designers. The company became associated with this new style, to the extent that in Italy, Art Nouveau became known as the *Stile Liberty*, after the London shop. The store became one of the most prestigious in London. During the 1960s, extravagant and Eastern influences once again became fashionable, as well as the Art Deco style.[3]

As I gazed at all of those exotic Liberty fabrics, I decided that I had to make at least one maternity garment for myself out of such prints. I touched, fondled and ran my fingers through the materials until, at last, I chose a beautiful soft brushed cotton one. It would be soft and delicate to wear; I thought, yet warm but not bulky. I fancied a dark cherry red colour with a warm pale green small Indian print, and that's what I settled for.

As I stepped out of Liberty's, I began to feel that I was coming to terms with my situation. I also knew that the London Palladium was not far away because it was in Argyll Street across the road, and so guess what I did? I just walked into the London Palladium's main entrance and into the Box Office. I asked straight out, and with a smile, if they had any job vacancies to work in the Box Office for a few weeks.

A member of staff said, "Just one moment, please."

With this, she went to have a word with the woman in charge.

A woman who introduced herself as Betty came over to me. We had a little chat, and she said, "If you like, you can come and help us on the telephones; it's shift work: 10:00 am to 4:00 pm, and 4:00 pm to 10:00 pm."

I didn't hesitate; I just agreed. I liked this homely woman, and a deal was struck to start the following week.

I took a form home with me, and as I sat on the train, I started to fill it in.

'Oh dear,' I thought as I looked out of the train window. 'What will my parents think?'

The London Palladium

The London Palladium is a 2,286-seat Grade II West End theatre located on Argyll Street in the City of Westminster. From the roster of stars that have played there and many televised performances, it is arguably the most famous theatre in London and the United Kingdom, especially for musical variety shows.

It opened on Boxing Day in 1910 with the first 'grand variety bill' featuring acts as diverse as Nellie Wallace and classical actor Martin Harvey. The Frank Matcham-designed building occupies a site that was previously home to a Corinthian Bazaar, Hengler's Grand Cirque and the National Ice-Skating Palace. By the 1950s, the theatre was known as the 'Ace Variety Theatre of the World,' a reputation enhanced by the enormous worldwide popularity of ATV's Sunday Night at the London Palladium. For many years, it played host to the annual *Royal Variety Performance*, a record 40 times, most recently in 2014 and was the home of London's most spectacular pantomimes. The annual pantomimes featured the biggest stars of the day, including Cliff Richard and the Shadows in 1964 and 1966. In 1968, Sammy Davis Jr. starred in *Golden Boy*, the Palladium's first proper musical show (as opposed to pantomime or revue). Meanwhile, variety was kept alive with seasons such as Ken Dodd, Russ Abbott and Bruce Forsyth, not to mention regular Sunday concerts.[4]

Figure 45 Statue

I turned up the following week on the 10:00 am to 4:00 pm shift. Ken Dodd and his Diddy Men were on, and it was proving very popular. In fact, Ken, with his wild mop of black hair and magnificent teeth, would come in and chat to Betty quite a lot. This is because he would eat at the restaurant next door, then pop in to see how the bookings were going and find out if it was going to be a full house that day.

Ken Dodd was born in the East Liverpool suburb of Knotty Ash in 1927. Dodd has made his birthplace famous more for what *isn't* there than what *actually* is. Although famous for his multi-million selling ballads, Dodd assembled an army of tiny high-pitched treacle miners that brought Diddy Men marching into the homes of children everywhere.[5]

The Diddy Men (diddy is northern slang for "little") existed in the earlier act of Liverpool comedian Arthur Askey. When Dodd began playing seaside resorts, he made famous his home area of Knotty Ash in Liverpool and popularised the miniature race of people who inhabited it. The Diddy Men began to appear on stage with Dodd, delighting children in the audience, where they got up to all sorts of adventures. They tended to wear slightly oversized adult clothes in flamboyant style, including tall furry hats. They were about 3 feet tall and said to work in the Jam Butty mines of Knotty Ash.

On stage, the Diddy Men are normally played by children or adults with dwarfism, whereas in Dodd's BBC television programs in the 1960s, they appeared as string-operated puppets. The stories involve the inhabitants of the small village of Knotty Ash and The Diddy Men who work there in the Jam Butty Mines, The Snuff Quarries, the Broken Biscuit Repair Works, The Treacle Wells, and the Moggy Ranch. Nigel Ponsonby-Smallpiece is the owner of the Jam Butty Mines, and Dickie Mint is the foreman. The Diddy Men's song, titled "The Song of the Diddy Men," is sung in a high pitched, chipmunk style voice. It includes the chorus: "We are the Diddy Men, Doddy's little Diddy Men. We are the Diddy Men who come from Knotty Ash."

Notable Diddy Men include Dicky Mint, Mick the Marmaliser, Stephen "Titch" Doyle, Little Evan, Wee Hamish McDiddy, Nigel Ponsonby-Smallpiece, Nicky Nugget, Sid Short, Smarty Arty, Harry Cott and Weany Wally.[6]

Figure 46 Diddy Men

There were three of us on the theatre's telephones. They didn't ring as such (thank goodness); instead, there was a glass dome on the top of each phone, which would flash when a call was incoming. We all had two telephones each, and I sat next to this interesting young lady called Pat, who was always crocheting or knitting, or such things like that. This was all permitted, making it a wonderful, stress-free place of employment really; a sit-down job involving lovely company.

Opposite myself and Pat was Maud, a middle-aged, middle-class ex-actress - so they told me. Maud would smoke a cigarette using a long cigarette holder. I found this fascinating. Plus, her word for "Yes!" was "Yah!"

The staff in the Box Office got to know a little more about me and my artistic background. One day, I spoke of Walt Disney and how much I would have loved to work with Disney and make those wonderful cartoon characters that moved with animation.

A few days later, Maud puffed on her cigarette in its elegant holder and then, looking at me, she said, "I've been talking to a very good friend of mine - Bart, who is a Director of the Walt Disney Productions in London not far from here. I've been telling him about you, Jan. He says that if you are truly serious about working with Walt Disney and the Animated Films, he can get you a five-year *serious* apprenticeship with Disney. However, you will have to go to America for the training!"

I was stunned!

'Is it possible to be as easy as that?' I thought.

I worked on it *seriously* for a few days. I didn't dare tell my parents; I felt I was in no place to think about such a thing right then - nor after the baby was born.

I could just hear them saying, "America - that would be too far away!"

I declined the offer gratefully, saying that I may change my mind in later life, and I *did* take Bart's details down and telephone number into the bargain!

Figure 47 Disney Land (adapted)

Pat, the other telephonist, was very spiritual, and I got on extremely well with her. She 'knew' that I was expecting a baby and she was wonderful! She taught me how to crochet, and she showed me how to turn the circles into a shawl. We talked about babies, and for the first time, I was really enjoying my pregnancy.

It was special; I marvelled at the fact that I was growing another human being inside me. It was God's miracle. I treated my bump with special care; I ate all the foods I felt like eating because I knew it was what my baby wanted me to eat - we were joined, and we were one! I wouldn't walk too close to anyone in case they hurt my bump or passed any infections onto us. I began to feel little movements, and I was getting really excited.

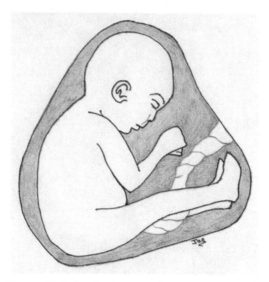

Figure 48 Baby in the womb at twenty weeks

At this time, I was working hard on Evette's fourth catalogue. Evette's shop assistants had further told me that my work had been put into *Vogue* and *Harper's* magazines again. It was also during this period that I was asked to undertake more work for Stacy Knitwear business in Finchley Road. Of course, I agreed - cautiously - but with joy at the same time!

Figure 49 Knitwear illustrations

It was just before Christmas, and I had been working at the London Palladium for around eight weeks and was about to leave. Pat gave me a surprise gift.

"These are for you both; open it!" she said.

I unfolded the tissue paper carefully, and inside was a beautiful white pair of knitted bootees for my baby. I was overwhelmed with joy, plus the reality of what was happening in this scene.

My bump was becoming a real living being - a baby!

Dave

It was about now that I truly missed Dave. After all, this was not to do with two of us, but three of us. Dave was missing out on the 'glory.'

A plan had been struck by my mother: I had to move up to Lincoln to live for the last part of my pregnancy - from January until March. But, if I showed too much before that time, I was to go up there earlier than that - before Christmas!

The baby had to stay a BIG SECRET!

I decided to phone Dave and see if we could meet up.

I dialled his friend's number, but once again Taz said that Dave was not at home, though he expected him to be there the following evening. He told me to ring the following day after 7:00 pm - Dave was sure to be there!

And so I did!

Dave and I arranged to meet in London the following week.

It was just what I wanted because I was shortly to finish with the London Palladium.

And so, after my 10:00 am - 4:00 pm shift, we arranged to meet at a particular railway station at around 6:00 pm - after Dave had finished work.

I remember sitting in the train station's waiting room, as planned, and the time seemed to go very slowly.

At last, he arrived; he still had his working clothes on. I was *so* pleased to see him, but not so Dave. He was very cold towards me and no kiss either. We stopped off at a place to have something to eat - nothing special, but I was so happy to be with him. I told him what had been happening to me and that I was to have the baby in Lincoln.

He didn't say anything at first, and then he said, "I thought that we would go to the pictures - it's not far from here!"

"Yes, that will be fine!" I said.

It was a comedy, and he sat there and really enjoyed it and laughed a lot.

I could feel our baby moving, and I put Dave's hand on my bump so that he could feel it too. As he did so, he just smiled. I think I must have done this two, or three times whilst we were in there, and he just repeated the same smile.

I felt depressed.

The film came to an end, and we got up from our seats, a bit like strangers really, although he was very careful that no one should bump into me. We walked back to the car, with which he drove to the railway station. Dave was very cold towards me, and I didn't know what he was thinking. He waited for the train to arrive; he found a compartment for me and opened the door. I stepped up, and he saw me safely get on the train.

Dave closed the door, turned around and, just walked away.

He was gone - and he didn't look back.

Well, I suppose, after all, I had been missing for some three months, and I didn't know what he was thinking.

I felt extremely depressed.

I seemed to be losing everything - things seemed to be being stripped away from me.

One thing though that I can tell you for sure, "My bump and me - we were one! My baby was listening to everything, and we had definitely formed a bond!"

CHAPTER SEVEN

Lincoln 1968: The Two of Us

Christmas: 1967

It was coming up to Christmas, and it looked like my bump and I were going to be able to stay around. However, as always, my maternal grandmother arrived from Eastleigh to join us.

This was the person that my mother had referred to when she had said, "What will your nan do? There is no way that she must find out! We must keep all of this a *secret!*"

I decided to settle down and make myself a fashionable maternity dress. It was going to be similar to one of those that I had illustrated for Evette's catalogue, but in brushed cotton. This particular material was very soft and consisted of the small Liberty print in dark cherry red with a warm, pale green Indian print. I didn't intend to design it so that it was gathered with fullness under the bust – oh no - that would have created too much suspicion. Instead, it was going to be A-line, which means it becomes slightly more flared as it lowers down to the hem. Luckily, I just seemed to have only lost my waistline, and so, this design was a perfect 'hide-the-secret' style.

I also made another good move - I had put lots of emphasis on the sleeves: they were straight and tight down to the elbow, and from there onwards, I attached a long, gathered frill that ended at the wrist. It was really pretty and had a pale green lining inside so that as I lifted up my arm, the frill would drop open like an upside-down umbrella to reveal the plain inner green material.

My grandmother liked clothes, and she really loved my dress. "Oh please, Nan, don't cuddle me!"

This was what I prayed for all over Christmas, and although she didn't, we did kiss each other a lot. I had grown very fond of my nan from when I stayed with her so much when I was at Southampton College as a student.

During Christmas, things seemed to go much more smoothly than usual. I think my father was on his very best behaviour towards my nan, not to cause too much friction.

You see, my nan suffered from a hiatus hernia.

Hiatus Hernia

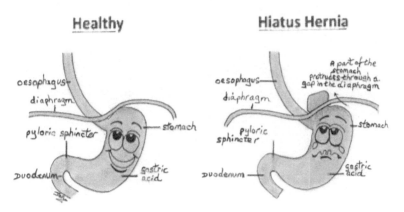

Figure 50 Hiatus Hernia

The hiatus is an opening in the diaphragm, which is the muscular wall separating the chest cavity from the abdomen. Normally, the oesophagus, the food pipe, goes through a hiatus and becomes attached to the stomach. In a hiatus hernia (which is also called a hiatal hernia), the stomach bulges up into the chest cavity through that hiatus opening.

N.B. When any internal body part pushes itself into an area where it doesn't really belong, it is called a hernia.[1]

My nan would eat her meals, and the lower end of her food pipe (the oesophagus) would fill with acid from her stomach, which eventually would rise up through her oesophagus. She would get these terrible symptoms of a burning sensation high up in her stomach that would gradually reach her throat. It would get worse as she swallowed, and particularly when she had eaten hot, spicy or acid foods. What followed was this almighty dash, as she would make a rush to the outside toilet to be sick. You could hear what was happening, and then you would hear the toilet being flushed.

We would all still be eating, or my father might be washing up when he would say, "Here we go again! I don't know why she bothers to eat so much!"

My mother would look at him angrily and say, "Don! She's got to eat something!"

My father would look confused and then bite his lip, being very careful as to what he said next.

But this year, things were very different!

My father didn't wince at all, let out any intimidating jokes, or utter any naughty words!

As always, when my poor nan re-surfaced from the toilet, she would be wiping her wet red-ringed eyes with her handkerchief.

However, *this year*, she was able to walk through the kitchen in peace!

This time, she was able to stroll into the main room, and once inside, she was safe from the cutting atmosphere.

She was careful, though, not to bend forwards, since this didn't help the matter - especially after meals. She would then sit down on the high chair, or rather, my father's favourite armchair, because this eased her stomach - she would say. She got out her knitting, and, as always, she would stretch over to get a caramel chocolate out of the sweet dish. Unfortunately for her, these were also my dad's favourites; she would pop it into her mouth and proceed to knit.

This was our Christmases, and this year, things seemed to continue relatively normally!

Thank goodness!

The Journey to Lincoln

It was just as planned: as soon as the end of the year arrived, I, or rather 'we,' that is me and Bump, were to pack 'our' bags ready for the off at the beginning of January 1968. We needed two suitcases because we were to be gone for more than three months.

In my suitcase, there were my dresses, nightwear and toiletries. In Bump's was the half-finished crocheted shawl; the bootees from Pat; some books 'we' might want to read, knitting to be done, and music to listen to. Oh, and some Christmas chocolates and sweets. 'We' also took some brochures and books on dos and don'ts when you are expecting a baby and 'how to keep baby calm' exercises. Oh, and of course, my catalogue work for Evette had to be completed.

We set off on the 2nd of January. It was just 'us' and my mother because my father had to go to work. We went by car, and I must admit that 'we' felt very relaxed; it was a bit like going on a long holiday for two reasons. Firstly, because 'we' weren't sure how things were going to work out; and secondly, because 'we' had made it through Christmas and the New Year without any hitches and my mother and 'us' were very happy about that.

We left Basingstoke by car in the morning, heading for North Hykeham near Lincoln. We travelled northwards up to Oxford, and from there, we passed Peterborough on our right and carried on bearing round to our right, passing Nottingham on our left. We had gone via the A1 route, and it had taken us several hours; but, it didn't matter because we had plenty of provisions - food - to eat on the way, and we made lots of stops. The weather, too, was mild and kind for the time of the year. All in all, our journey was around 176 miles (284 kilometres).

When we arrived at our destination, the couple were really wonderful, and we couldn't have wished for a better place. Our home was a detached house located on a new housing estate on the outskirts of Lincoln. It was immaculately clean, neat and tidy. Our bedroom (mine and Bumps) was to be the one downstairs, with a toilet and washbasin nearby.

My mother stayed for two nights, and then she made her way back to Basingstoke again. Everything was as planned: Janet was suffering from depression and living up north for a while.

North Hykeham, I was told, is in the district of North Kesteven in the county of Lincolnshire, the East Midlands of

England and geographically, it forms the southern outer part of a greater Lincoln urban sprawl. North Hykeham, both as a village and, since 1973, as a town, is independent from Lincoln. The old village dates back to the Angles, Germanic invaders who occupied much of Britain after the Romans left in 4 AD. The Danes and Vikings arrived in Lincolnshire in 9 AD, hence places with names ending in – 'by,' 'thorpe' and 'ham,' meaning 'village.'

The Domesday Book (1087) records that North Hykeham had 15 households and a 52-acre meadow. The Newark Road is built directly on top of the old Roman road, Fosse Way. It is now the A1434 road, although, until December 1985, it was the A46. North of the road is Hykeham railway station on the Nottingham to Lincoln Line, with a few trains stopping on a daily basis. Farther along Mill Lane, to the south, is South Hykeham.[2]

Life in Lincoln

An appointment had been set up locally for Bump and me to see a General Practitioner – this was so that we could keep the ball rolling for our medical conditions. The doctor was very nice, and when I asked if we could attend some antenatal classes, he seemed, well, quite surprised. We had already decided that this was what we wanted to do, that it would be good for both of us, so a date was arranged for us to join a group a few days later.

There were several mums-to-be there, and we were very happy. The younger ones, like myself, the first-timers, seemed really excited about their new venture. Of course, the first thing that I did was to scan their left hands - albeit discretely - to see if they were married. It wasn't long before we discovered that we were the odd ones out - I was the only one without a ring on my finger! Nevertheless, we resolved ourselves to the fact that there may be - just by chance - one or two of them in there that had put a ring on, as a cover-up!

As a group, we were all very chatty, and I must admit that 'we' were feeling extremely fit and healthy by now and intended to keep ourselves that way: we aimed to be happy and content!

At the first meeting, there were so many questions being asked by the mums-to-be, amongst themselves, that Bump and I just knew that it was some kind of assessment time. But we were very brave and admitted to them all that, in Lincoln at least, there was just the two of us. Gentle exercises were prescribed at the meeting to help prevent any unpleasant side effects of our pregnancy, such as backache. The nurse also gave us advice on problems caused by hormonal changes, such as constipation, varicose veins, indigestion and piles. The staff further placed great emphasis on relaxation and breathing techniques which would be very helpful during the labour period.

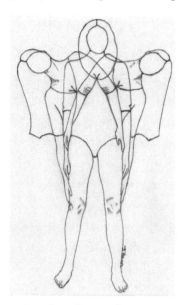

Figure 51 3 in 1 figure doing exercises

The welfare worker further indicated that for many first-time mothers, labour could be a period of stress; however, this is largely due to a lack of knowledge about exactly what will happen, and in some cases, by perhaps listening to old wives tales and stories that are quite untrue. The staff also told us that apprehension might lead to muscle tension and an alteration in breathing, and this can cause exhaustion in the early stages of labour. Expectant mothers who learn how to relax and control their breathing, they said, will be able to conserve their energy for the moment of birth. They further taught us that breathing should be easy and comfortable during labour, with a need for emphasis on the outward rather than the inward breath. When the contractions become more severe, they told us, breathing tends to become more rapid and much shallower, and as the contractions build up to their peak, the mother sometimes reacts by over-breathing. They told us that this might impair the contractions, and so they taught us how to do a gentle sighing technique to control this tendency – again - with the emphasis on the outward breath.[3]

When it came to the second class, things seemed a little bit, well, different. This is because the fathers had been invited to participate so that their involvement would encourage them to be more understanding and helpful to their wives during pregnancy. The session began with a physiotherapist who explained the physical and emotional aspects of pregnancy. This was followed by a health visitor who discussed the practical aspects of both antenatal and postnatal care (for example, bathing the baby). Afterwards, a dietician took over and advised us on our weight and nutrition, and then we were told to take a break.

Two or three mums-to-be were full of chatter together with their husbands - the fathers-to-be. They were pointing out just how busy they had been since our last meeting, 'decorating the spare rooms,' they said, 'for the long-awaited baby.'

I, or rather we, just listened and smiled; it would have been nice if we could have joined in, but that was not going to happen. I wondered if we should stay for the second half or not. Needless to say, we decided that the class was increasing our confidence about the pregnancy and the birth. *We* were just special - we were *unique* - that was *all* that was different about us. And so we braced ourselves and went along with the flow as before.

During the latter half of the session, a doctor explained the medical management of pregnancy and childbirth. A midwife followed by describing the three stages of labour and the methods available for relief of pain - this was to be done using the techniques of relaxation and perhaps by drugs.

As we walked home, we felt quite refreshed; because these entirely professional people were willing to guide us over our next few weeks, yet, on the other hand, we had mixed feelings.

As the sessions continued, things began to change; there was this one meeting where the group chose the topic of the husband's loving care and protection towards them. One or two would glance over at me as they spoke.

I bowed my head with a smile and thought, 'We're not ashamed; we had all of that too, all the love and caring and sharing!'

We walked sadly home and thought, 'No! We're not alone! We've got each other and *always* will have!'

Nursery Rhymes

In these days when we (Bump and me) visited the local shops, we had noticed that, in one small shop, they had some second-hand books for sale. We went in and fingered through a few of them when suddenly, I noticed a pile of children's books. I picked them up one at a time and found there were some children's nursery rhyme books amongst them - and so, I bought them.

'That's what *we* are going to do starting from the following day,' I thought. 'We are going to sit in the pivotal armchair that rotates from left to right, whilst I read out loud the rhythmic, poetic nursery rhymes whilst we sway slowly from left to right. *We* are going to have some fun!'

The next day we did just this.

At first, Bump would be moving or tossing and turning; but after a while, I could tell that baby was listening because all types of tummy movement would stop, and everything would stay calm.

After a while, I would stop the rhythmic sounds for a bit. At first, everything was quiet, and then, once more, all movement inside me would start up again. I gave it two or three minutes, and then I started chanting rhythmically again. Sure enough, it appeared as if baby was listening - because my bump would become motionless once more. I continued for two to three minutes again, and then I was silent. Sure enough, it wasn't long before baby would move and roll over. I was so excited; I had learnt that not only could my baby hear me, but he/she was seemingly listening to me as well. And secondly, baby seemed to find the rhythmic lull of the nursery rhymes soothing - they seemed to be sending bump to sleep!

Other times, I would tap my tummy gently, and I could definitely see a knee or an elbow kick out in response. 'Had I just woken baby up?'

These little sessions progressed into me singing lullabies. You know, those soothing melodies that put children's consciousness into suspension - inoperative for a while, and much to my astonishment, my baby would stop moving and appeared to be listening, or had he or she just fallen asleep? Once again, after a short pause of silence, baby would start moving again. I found this truly wonderful: we had worked out our own way of interacting with each other before baby had been born!

There were other times, too, when I would play music softly and hum along to the tune. I noticed that baby didn't particularly like fast music; baby preferred musical tones that rose slowly up the scale then back down the scale again. Baby would slumber quietly, and I imagined that he or she was sucking his or her thumb. I found this so comforting for some reason; it was as if my or our heart rates would slow down and our threshold of aches or pains would be lowered.

It was then that I bought a book on how a baby grows in the mother's womb. One of the photographs actually showed a baby sucking its thumb whilst in the womb. I was amazed!

'Could it be that *my* baby was doing the same?' I thought.

Time to Crochet

During these periods, I would take breaks and get on with crocheting the shawl, and I adored every minute of it. I had discovered that there are several ways of crocheting what is known as a 'round,' and one of those ways is called the magic circle.

The beauty of the magic circle is that it allows for the hole to be closed for a more complete look.

It said:[4]

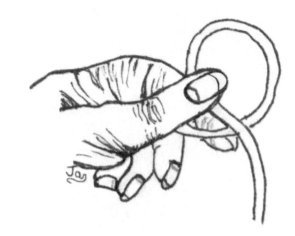

Figure 52 Make a loop

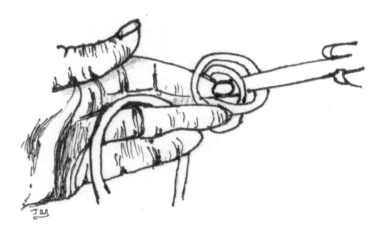

Figure 53 Pick up the yarn

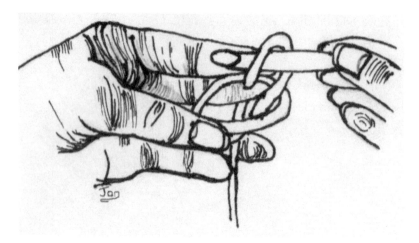

Figure 54 Pull through the first loop

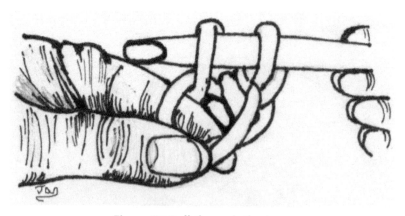

Figure 55 Pull through the loop

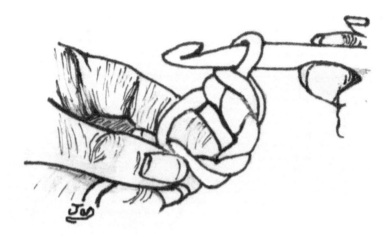

Figure 56 Pick up the yarn again and finish the single crochet stitch.

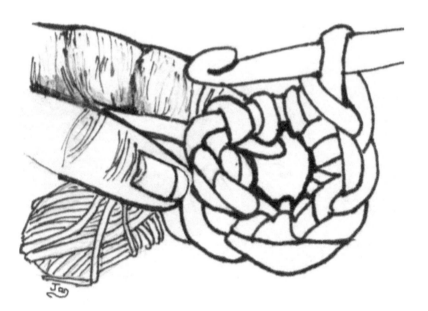

Figure 57 Continue to make single crochet stitches in the main loop.

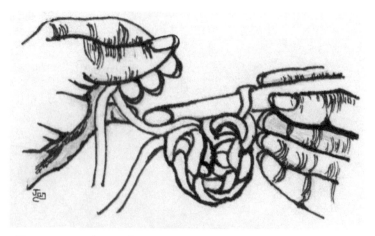

Figure 58 At the end of the round of single crochet stitches,
pull on the yarn end to gather the hole closed, and continue with
your pattern.

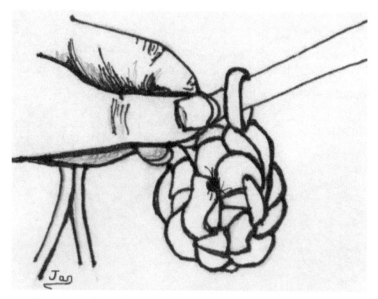

Figure 59 This diagram shows the magic circle finished,
with the hole gathered closed.

As I crocheted these circles, it was during one of these occasions that I had cried out to God. I knew that I had His presence around me; this is because I believed that my baby and I were not only interacting with each other, 'we' had now also learnt to bond on a *Spiritual* level!

I further felt that:

There was something important that I needed to know.
And the shawl was to play a part in its role.
It was a garment, a warm covering, and a form of protection.
It was full of love and thoughts of affection.

I began to see it as gladness for my baby.
The sun streamed in at this point and bathed me.
It made me warm and relaxed and to worry no more.
Everything had been scribed and was being cared for.

My crocheted circles lay there, each on their own.
Each one bore a message, all of its own.
Each message - our time - spent through all types of weather.
As I gazed at these circles, they seemed bonded together.

And then, I saw myself Knock on a Door.

My crochet hook then dropped to the floor.

We both fell asleep.

The Adoption Set-up

We had around two, if not three, appointments with an adoption organisation. I can't remember too well how I came to have these meetings, but perhaps it was the doctor who I had first seen in London that had arranged them. Doctors in those days always seemed to be the first voice of authority, and I do believe that after all the pokes and prods I received in the London Hospital, I had to go back and see the General Practitioner again in Grays-Inn Road.

I perhaps vaguely remember him saying something like, "Well, it seems that seeing as you are around twelve weeks pregnant, it's too late now for you to have an abortion!"

However, I *do* remember distinctly replying that I wouldn't have an abortion anyway!

I just remember him asking me so many questions about our future lives. What I said in response to these questions I can't remember exactly! I guess I was in too much of a daze.

(N.B. In those days, it was a legal requirement that unmarried mothers gave their approval to have their child adopted; but at the same time, if they are being told that there is no financial support for them, can it really be said that their consent is being given by free choice?)

But now, things were different, I seemed very comfortable with my pregnancy, and I felt really well. What is more, I had begun to realise that my baby was very happy too.

It was time for my first appointment to see the adoption officer. I had been sent a letter to go to Lincoln City at a certain location for 2:00 pm. I wanted to make a good impression. I dressed in smart, colourful maternity clothes, washed my long, straight, black hair and brushed it until it was extremely shiny. I had to look clean and well-groomed - I wasn't a tart!

I found out that the location was in an old part of Lincoln called Steep Hill. Lincoln is a cathedral city and the county town of Lincolnshire within the East Midlands of England. The earliest origins of Lincoln can be traced to the remains of an Iron Age settlement, dating from the 1st century BC. The Romans conquered this part of Britain in 48 AD and, shortly afterwards, built a legionary fortress high on the hill. Construction of the first Lincoln Cathedral, within its close or walled precinct facing the castle, was completed in 1092. The bishops of Lincoln were among the magnates of medieval England: the diocese of Lincoln was the largest in England. It had more monasteries than the rest of England put together.

By 1150, Lincoln was among the wealthiest towns in England, with the basis of the economy coming from cloth and wool. During the 13th century, Lincoln was the third-largest city in England; however, between November 1904 and August 1905, it was hit by a major typhoid epidemic caused by polluted drinking water. The Lincoln chlorination episode was one of the first uses of the chemical to disinfect a water supply.

Today, Lincoln is situated in a gap in the Lincoln Cliff, a major escarpment that runs north-south through Lindsey and Kesteven in central Lincolnshire and rises to 200 feet (61 metres in height). The River Witham flows through this gap, and thus Lincoln is divided informally into two zones, known locally as 'uphill' and 'downhill.' The aptly named street 'Steep Hill' connects the two.[5]

Besides being an extremely high slope, the ground here was just stones that were cobbled. I didn't want to fall over, and so I took each step carefully. Bump and I were rising steadily to the top. I looked up, and outside the precincts of the cathedral and castle, this old quarter was clustered around what is known as the Bailgate and down Steep Hill to the High Bridge. All of a sudden, I noticed these part-timbered houses with their upper storeys jutting out over the river. On our left was what seemed like another very old wooden and stone building. As I gazed at this structure, it appeared somewhat crooked, and yes, that was where we had to go.

Its old wooden door had an iron latch with a ringed handle; I grasped the ring and twisted it, and it gave out a loud, groaning creak. With great effort, it slowly moved inwards. I carefully walked up some old wooden steps which took me to another door, and this time, I cautiously opened it a little. A real musty smell spiralled towards my nostrils, and I wanted to sneeze. It was one of those things that had come with pregnancy - a very sensitive smell!

I peered inside through the half-opened doorway, and I could see a large square room with a timbered roof. I don't think there was a ceiling as such. It seemed completely empty. There appeared to be small windows letting in a bit of light; however, all in all, this room was really quite dark.

Suddenly, a bird-like voice came from out of this place.

"Come in and shut the door!" it said.

I squinted to where the voice had come from, and way down yonder, over on the far side, was a raised platform with a desk on it.

I stepped inside. It really was very musty in there, and again, I began to sneeze. The old wooden floorboards creaked and groaned as I walked over them, and I shaded my eyes as I passed through a dusty shaft of light from one of the windows. A bodily shape began to emerge from the shadows; it was hunched over a large ledger book on the desk.

(N.B. During this period, most adoption of babies born to unmarried mothers was overseen by voluntary organisations, the majority of which were religious. Church social workers were also known as moral welfare officers. The professionals (General Practitioners, Social Workers and Moral Welfare Officers) involved in the adoption process had a duty of care to ensure these women knew they had the right to choose other options available that would enable them to keep their baby - if that is what they wanted.)

I walked towards the desk and could just make out that the figure was writing. I stood there for a bit, trying to adjust my eyes to the darkness.

Eventually, the figure looked up. I would say that she was in her fifties, but more like seventies; her hair was grey and straight, unkempt, and just covered her ears. With a parting on one side, she had a hair-grip on the other side, which dragged her hair straight over her forehead. This was to stop the hair from falling over her face.

"Are you Janet?" she asked.

"Yes," I said with a smile.

However, the smile was not returned; instead, her chair gave out a dragging sound as she pushed it back to get up.

She was short and rounded. Today, she wore a grey cardigan over her soft off-white blouse; but normally, I felt she would have worn a crocheted black shawl.

She moved towards another old wooden chair and dragged it towards the table. As she bent over this chair, I noticed her full black skirt was almost down to the ankles of her thin little legs. She shuffled her way around this chair to get it into a correct position, and I was curious as to her very thick stockings that were wrinkled and ruffled over her brown brogue laced shoes.

"Sit there!" she said. "I won't be long."

She shuffled towards another door at the back of this room and disappeared.

I looked around this dismal space and immediately felt very depressed - empty in fact, pointless - and alone.

A few minutes later, a door creaked, and the figure appeared; she reminded me very much of a teacher that we had at the college. She would come into our lessons with bags of sheep's fleece that she had collected off the fences and gates of fields. I think she had something to do with farming too. And we, the students, would be given bags of this greasy wool from sheep and taught how to card and tease the fleece. The idea was to clean and entangle the strands ready to spin into a yarn. Once on spindles, we would be taught how to make our own cloth with a weaving loom. I flashed back to those days...

After the sheep's wool has been washed, the spinner must open the wool to remove all the left-over bits of dirt, twigs and plant matter. If this isn't done, these bits may be trapped in the finished yarn, making the yarn spin unevenly, causing it to be weak in some parts. These weak areas might fray, pill, or even break when used, and so, to open the wool, it is teased by hand. A lock of wool is taken and held between the teaser's hands. This piece of wool is then pulled apart with quick side-to-side movements until the wool is fluffed thoroughly like a cloud. Lots of little bits of dirt will drop out this way from the wool, although some pieces have to be picked out. Once the wool is cleaned by teasing, it gets carded, which is the last stage in preparing the fleece for spinning; it cleans, separates, and straightens the wool fibres – we were told. The hand-cards looked like a pair of wooden paddles with wire teeth, which are held in each hand. A small amount of wool is charged on one card while the empty card is pulled across the wool, being careful not to catch the teeth. This is repeated several times until the wool fibres start to straighten and half the wool is on each card. At this point, the second card is dragged backwards across the first card so that all the wool is back on the first card. The process is repeated until all the fibres are straight and fluffy. This finished batt (or rolag) of soft, fluffy wool will now make spinning easier.[6]

I really enjoyed these lessons. It's funny, isn't it, how something in the present can conjure up a reminder of something in the past?

And so, this stranger to me was not so bad after all!

But this was soon to be shattered because I was here for a purpose, and an unpleasant one at that, so it seemed, which was shortly to unfold.

This woman looked up at me sternly and said, "You know why you are here today, don't you?"

I looked back at her and wondered how I should answer such a question.

"You know that this is an adoption organisation, don't you, Janet?"

I thought for a moment and then bowed my head.

"I know what this is all about, but I haven't made my mind up yet," I replied.

She looked down at her ledger intently; her long rheumatic finger pointed down to something written in her book.

This index finger tapped the page as she spoke, "It distinctly says down here, Janet, that you *want* to have an adoption!"

I lowered my head again. "I'm not really sure!" I said.

She didn't move, and the silence was cutting.

Eventually, she decided to go through a format of questions, like: 'name, address, date of birth,' etc.

I asked, "This doesn't mean that my baby is going to be adopted, does it?"

She looked at me curiously. "No," she said with a long pause, "but we need to ask these questions in the first place as part of the protocol - the official formality."

I guess I was in there around thirty minutes. At the end, another appointment was set up for two weeks' time. I got up and said thank you and started to walk away.

I knew that this woman was watching me go to the door.

"Oh! Janet?"

I heard her voice say.

"Next time, it will take about an hour, so make sure you allow enough time!"

"Oh! Alright! Goodbye, errh, Mrs…?"

She looked at me sternly. "It's Miss!" she said. "Miss Hardwick!"

"Oh, right, thank you, Miss err Hardwick," I replied meekly.

"Oh, and don't be late! I've got another appointment to see to straight after you!" she said sharply.

"Okay, goodbye," I answered quietly.

I clunked my way down the well-worn stairway stopping at the bottom. I pinged down the latch, and the door moved inwards.

The sky seemed so bright outside. I turned around to shut the door and moved out into the street. Although it was cold, it was very fresh and inviting, with people casually walking about.

'Do I feel odd?' I thought. 'Well, yes, I do! Do you feel like a naughty child?' I thought.

'Well, no, of course not, I'm twenty-one years of age...'

But deep inside... I did!

Second Appointment

The time came for my second appointment to see Miss Hardwick, the Adoption Officer. I tread carefully over the cobbled road once more, and I was not late for my appointment.

I moved up close to the old wooden door, grasped the ring handle and gave it a twist. Once again, it gave out a loud disapproving creak with which it reluctantly opened slowly. Carefully, I made my way up the sloping stairway until I reached the top.

I knocked on the door in front of me and then gently pushed it open. I squinted once more to see in the darkness, and there in the distance, I spotted Miss Hardwick bent over her ledger on her desk. I walked across this dimly lit room and waited for Miss Hardwick to speak first.

She continued with her writing for a while, then peered up at me over the top of her half-rimmed glasses and told me to take a seat. This time, the chair was ready for me - right next to Miss Hardwick. I sat there waiting whilst she continued with her writing. It wasn't long before she turned over a page, got up and went through the other door again - just like the last time.

It was here when it suddenly struck me that the type of environment you spend your time in really does have an effect on your mood. This woman obviously liked to work alone - or rather one to one. Thinking about it, I suppose the unmarried mother-to-be is able to relax better in uncluttered circumstances - less stressful. But perhaps better lighting and lighter walls would help the matter - and maybe someone dealing with your case that wasn't quite so stern, so strict, and not so much like a child's teacher, would help one to feel more relaxed and humane. Nevertheless, who was I to dream and think about such things? After all, I seem to have a penalty to pay for my sins.

Miss Hardwick came back and sat in her chair; she seemed to have a cold and kept blowing her nose. That was not a problem, though; the problem was what came next!

This time, the questions were not objective as such. This time, the questions were more 'subjective.' The first questions started off okay, such as, "What is the father's name? What is the father's address? What is his occupation?"

Miss Hardwick then came to the question of nationality; and I knew that, in these days, outside Cosmopolitan London (which means belonging to all parts of the world), and especially with me now residing nearer the north of England, this question was going to be an awkward one to answer.

"He's, hmmh, in part, Asian."

Miss Hardwick immediately stopped writing, and I could tell that she was horrified.

"What do you mean by Asian?" she said slowly as she peered over her half-rimmed glasses at me.

"Well, he's not white, but part-Asian!"

"What country was he born in?" she asked with a sneer.

"Oh, this country - he was born here!"

"How do you know?" she said sharply.

"Well, because he told me so."

"So, is he Indian, Pakistani, African?"

"No, no, no, he's not black," I stuttered quickly, "just pale brown - pale coffee colour. In fact, you could say, he was white British, with a bit of a suntan."

Miss Hardwick seemed frozen to the spot for some reason. I think she was trying to take it all in. Without looking at me, her arthritic hand moved across the page with jerky movements as she spoke and wrote, "Anglo-Pakistani."

"Yes," I said. "That sounds correct; he is both white and Pakistani - and he has the loveliest of brown eyes, and his smile shows the sweet gap in his front tee…"

"AGE," she sounded out loudly.

"Pardon?" I said.

"What age is he?" she said sharply.

"Oh, err… He was thirty years old when I met him, but now, he is thirty-one, going on for thirty-two."

She looked up sternly. "Married - is he?" she asked viciously.

"Oh, well-"

"YES!" she shouted as she wrote it down.

"Well, no, er, not really!"

She bent her head down, moved in closer to my face and said, "Well, he either is, or he isn't, isn't he?"

"Well, he is married but separated!"

Miss Hardwick fell back limply in her chair! "What does that mean?" she said cuttingly.

"Well, he is still married but lives with his friend and his family."

"Is that what he told you?"

"Oh, yes, and I know that it's true!"

"How?" she asked intently.

"Well, because I used to visit him there.

She didn't bother to look up on that one. "Has he any other children?"

"Three," I said.

She gasped and looked up at me, horrified. "How do you know that?" she said.

"Oh, well, because he told me so."

And this is where the interrogation got more and more intimate. So much so that by answering her questions, I was basically telling her how many times, how long each time, where we were, whether we enjoyed each other's company, where we met, what places had we gone to, etc. Until I decided that I'd had enough! I just felt so humiliated that enough was enough!

I said quietly, "We were going to live in Canada!"

She turned quickly and looked at me with a frown. "Why Canada?" she said.

"Well, apparently, he can have four wives - as long as they are so many miles apart!" I continued, "And, I was to be wife number two!"

Miss Hardwick dropped back listlessly in her chair.

"But I didn't want to be wife number two," I said hurriedly.

She looked up at the rafters and scratched her throat.

She took a sip of her tea and proceeded with such side-tracked questions as, "Did I go to church? What religion was I? How often did I go to church? What were my favourite hobbies? What programmes did I view on the television?"

And this was all repeated with Dave's interests and character.

All in all, I think we were covered.

Ah, but what seemed something of great interest to her was our occupations – she curiously wanted to know how much we were both earning.

I remember leaving the room as if I were a piece of glass - she could see and 'knew' everything about me - all three of us. I felt extremely vulnerable and, in fact, quite humiliated.

As I walked back home, I went through all of the questions that she had asked me in my mind again. I remember thinking that this Miss Hardwick had probably never known what it is like to be in love with a man, and these intimate conversations with myself and other young women were something perhaps of a delight for her!

Lucid Dream

That night, I was very tired and depressed; I felt really mixed up inside; in fact, we both did. I also had another potent dream, and it was similar to the one that I'd had before.

I keep turning over and cannot get comfy; something appears to be shaking me and wanting me to wake up; however, as before, I'm too tired to wake up. I decide to lay there and let my lucid dream take control:

I am looking once again at a kind of catalogue, a photograph album, a really old one, and I open it up. I begin to skim through the photographs in there until I get to the same one as before.

I am in this old street in London once again; but, with not so many shops this time and, as before, it appears to be set in the Victorian days because of the people's style of clothing. I peer in at them more closely this time and notice how heavy their clothes appear to be. The scene seems different this time.

There are men pulling carts with large wheels, and they are carrying goods in hessian sacks inside their carts. There are several clothes laid out flat and piled high on the cobbled street – though some appear in large wicker baskets. Women are wandering around carrying babies and children, while men use walking sticks to move about. I spot a washing line with clothes hanging from it; it is strewn across this cobbled street way up high off the ground and seemingly coming from the upper windows of these houses. Suddenly, I become amused by the gas street lamps that have caught my attention. Apparently, the light from these types of lamps was said to be greenish and eerie and would keep flashing, creating flickering shadows. They were further known to give out just a small circle of light, which didn't spread out very far. This meant that anything located between each lamp post would be in a very dark patch.

Figure 60 Picture of a gas lamp[7]

I felt myself shudder.

'But where was the little girl in this scene?' I wondered. As I scanned my dream, I picked out some children lined up against a wall, playing games with a skipping rope. I search the scene once more to see if I can find the familiar little face, and there she is.

She appears to have been waiting some time because she is longing to see me again; she is desperate to talk to me. I notice that she has tears in her eyes, she has been crying, she seems to think that I had forgotten her. She stretches out her arms for me to take her, to pick her up, or for us to be in the same reality - I just don't understand. As I get closer to her, she whispers the name 'Rebekah.'

I am truly disturbed, and I sit up and try to shake off the dream - it's only a dream after all.

But what could it mean?

Figure 61 Picture of the scene with the little girl[8]

The Last Few Days of Pregnancy

My tummy was getting bigger as baby grew, and with it, my baby was getting stronger. Sometimes when I was standing, my baby would really kick or wave his or her arms about. It was just as if baby was really curious about the pumping rhythm of my heart.

Sometimes, there would be no motion, and then a kick would be aimed at my heart. Baby seemed to like to use my heart as some kind of toy or punch bag. I would often worry in case baby might give itself a black eye. Yes, my baby was definitely interested in my heart.

At times, I wondered how many mothers-to-be had suffered from heart attacks. I would try to put my hand under my left breast and push down baby's limb. I would speak quite sharply as well, until eventually, my bump would give up.

There were other days when baby seemed to be scratching the exit. It was so painful – and it made it really difficult to walk.

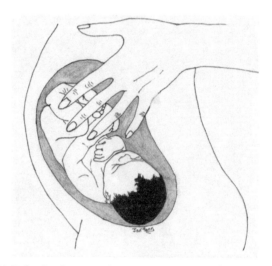

Figure 62 Baby in the womb - approximately thirty-four weeks

Every day, baby seemed to be getting bigger and stronger and ever more curious, and with it, seemingly enjoying our interaction. We would even go to the shops and watch other mums and listen to *their* babies. We were fascinated. I had never been interested in babies. I had never been one of these young women to pass a pram, look in it and say, *"Ahh."* But now, they were beautiful; they were glorious; in fact, they were God's Miracle; and not only that - but they were also so *big*!

'How was one of those going to get *out* of me?'

And this was the beginning of a real phobia that was beginning to stir within me.

Preparing for the Hospital

The doctor had said that baby was engaged - head down - and in place ready for birth. I needed to get our things ready for the hospital.

I must admit in this last period of pregnancy, that baby certainly seemed much quieter. But now, I knew baby's home was becoming too small, less freedom than before. It certainly seemed that way to me because I was getting these tightening up pressure feelings every now and again. I could feel the contractions of the womb as its muscles were limbering up for the delivery, and although they were not usually painful, they would be sharp enough to make me stop what I was doing.

I began to pack our suitcase with the things that we would need in hospital:

HOSPITAL LIST
Two nightdresses
Dressing gown
Slippers
Bed-jacket or cardigan
Two maternity brassieres
Bath and hand towels
Handkerchiefs (preferably paper)
Underwear
Toiletries
Books or other interests to pass the time
Clothes etc., put by for Bump

"The womb is practising its labour pains." I was told.

I would rub oil over my tummy to keep it supple. It's amazing how much the skin can stretch, isn't it? And hopefully 'ping' back to normal afterwards. That bit I would find out about later!

I was extremely tired during these final days. We were heavy together now, and we needed plenty of rest. Yet, even that had become difficult because baby seemed to think that when I lay on my back, it was lying on a bed of nails!

It must have been my knobbly spine that was making things uncomfortable due to lack of space and was now getting in the way.

"Lie on your side!" The nurse told me. "You will both be more comfortable that way!"

Many times, I thought baby was going to make an exit; but I couldn't keep acting on it too many times. We didn't want to cause too much fuss for this lovely couple who had so lovingly let us stay in their home.

I had been restless all day; I seemed to be feeling unwell or really strange; things were changing both physically and mentally.

Something was going to happen - that was for sure. It was like a lull and an agitation, an unknowing feeling before a storm!

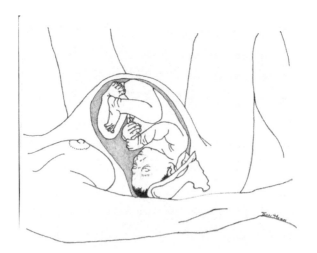

Figure 63 Baby moves down the womb

CHAPTER EIGHT

Birth in Hospital

The Hospital

I was twenty-one years of age when my baby was born. My tummy had been tightening up all day. It was doing it for longer every time, at regular intervals of around twenty to thirty minutes, and it was making me sweat. It soon got to the stage that in between the contractions, I just needed to rest. When each contraction started up again, I would start shaking and shivering, even though I didn't feel cold, and so I would have to take deep breaths.

I seemed to have lost contact with baby too at this time; he or she was more like a solid lump. Perhaps it was the shock of it all that we were suffering from; nevertheless, we were still together in spirit. I knew that baby was still there, and baby knew that I was still there, and we held each other closely in our fright. *Nothing* was going to come between us; the only difference would be that we were going to *see* each other for the very first time!

We had everything packed in our bag, ready for the journey. We really did feel that the time had come because the pains were now much stronger, and we were convinced that they were not going to go away. It came to six o'clock and then seven o'clock in the evening. We were extremely restless - overactive, actually. I decided to phone the hospital and tell them what had been happening to us all day.

A member of staff asked me a few questions, and when I told her that I had passed some clear fluid, she told me that "the waters had broken." She then explained that the bag of waters, made up of two layers of membranes, had ruptured - known as "ruptured membranes" – and the waters (the amniotic fluid) were leaking out via the cervix and vagina. She said this was a sign that I may be in labour soon and that we were to make our way to the hospital straight away.

We got help putting our bags into the car, and we were driven to the hospital. The evening was very dark and quite chilly, but it wasn't these normal things that were on our minds; it was what was going to happen to us next and how long would it take? I think that this day was the first day that I really began to worry - would my baby be alright? What I mean is: would he or she be normal? To be honest, these sorts of concerns had not entered my head before now. I suppose I had taken all this for granted, but now the exposure was going to reveal the truth!

We drove into the hospital car park, and it appeared very homely from the outside. It seemed like a relatively small hospital, more like a large house. I have recently read that the Bromhead Maternity Home is now known as the BMI Hospital in Lincoln, a private hospital that delivers high-quality private patient care. Despite the name, it will always be thought of by the majority of Lincoln residents as "The Bromhead," the name of its founder.

On 28 of May 1866, an Institution for Nurses was opened, which trained nurses at Mrs Bromhead's house on Greestone Terrace; it provided nurses for the poor of Lincoln and aided other institutions during epidemics. In 1887 this building, known at the time as The Red House, was built on the corner of Nettleham Road and Church Lane, which is not too far from the Cathedral. It was known as a memorial to the founder and first Lady Superintendent, Mrs A.F. Bromhead. The Red House was later extended and became known as the Bromhead Maternity Home, which was also a Nursing Home. It was taken over by the National Health Service in 1948, but in 2001 it was sold to the Nuffield Hospitals Group and became known as the Lincoln Nuffield Hospital until ownership passed on to the BMI Healthcare Group.[1]

The car stopped right next to the front door, and at that very moment, I started to have another tightening sensation. In fact, I'd had several all the way throughout the journey to the hospital, and they were getting to be really painful. As we got out of the car and walked to the hospital door, I remember thinking that we were going in together; however, we would be coming out as two separate entities.

Things were never going to be the same that way again.

The hospital porch-way was lit by a kind of lantern; it was a very homely, kind of cosy, calming feeling.

We rang the doorbell and waited.

It took a while before the door opened, and there in front of us, in the doorway, was a staff nurse. I was absolutely horrified. But it wasn't the staff nurse that took me by surprise; it was what she was carrying; for there in her arms was this most delightful baby. There were all the smells and aromas too, that come with freshly bathed babies. However, it was the size of the baby that petrified me. It seemed huge, and this was the reality! I had never realised before that newly born babies were that big! Perhaps I had never been so close to one as this before or taken such things on board.

"How old is the baby?" I asked gingerly.

"She was born yesterday!"

"Yesterday," I repeated in fright.

"Yes," the nurse said. "In fact, last night, so she is about twenty-four hours old now."

I was shocked. "Is she extra-large?" I asked.

"Hmmh, no, she's about average, I would think. Why?"

"Oh!" I said, looking down at my tummy, "I don't believe that I can manage a baby that size!"

"Oh, don't you worry!" she said. "When they are ready, they will come out regardless of size. You won't need to worry. Mother Nature knows what she is doing!"

I walked past this nurse and baby, but I kept my eyes fixed firmly on the baby at the same time.

I thought, 'I just can't see that it's going to be possible, I'm not big enough, and it feels so painful to even think about it!'

With every step I took along the corridor, I began to conjure up more and more fear.

'What if the womb splits as the baby is being pushed out? Would this harm the baby, or even make him or her malformed - or even dead?'

You know those circumstances where you are absolutely petrified of them, yet, there is no turning back.

I thought, 'It's too late for that!'

We walked along the hallway for a bit, and then we were ushered into a room on our left.

It was a small room, but nevertheless, it was a ward with three beds in it. There were two other mothers-to-be already in there, and I was told that my bed was the empty one by the door. It was here that baby and I began to calm down. Why? Well, because we were not alone. With two other mums-to-be in there, it meant that we were all in the same boat – well, that's what I thought at that time.

I started to unpack our suitcases: I took out various items and laid them on the bed.

After a while, we all got over our shyness and started talking to each other. I asked, "Is this the only ward for mums-to-be?"

The young woman closest to me replied, "No, we are special cases."

"Oh," I said worriedly, and then I began to wonder why 'we' had been categorised as a special case. So I plucked up courage and asked them both what they meant by 'special.'

The nearest woman to me said, "Well, my baby is facing the wrong way – it's a breech."

I looked at her curiously, and then she added, "Babies are normally born with their heads coming out first. My baby is going to be born as a breech birth, which is where the baby's buttocks emerge first - it will come out feet first!"

I then turned and looked at the other woman; she looked really pale and was lying on her side on her bed resting, with her eyes closed.

I decided to finish unpacking our cases.

A little while later, this pale woman got up and left the room. As I continued with my unpacking, the other woman came over to me and said, "Her baby has stopped moving - they think that it's, well, dead!"

I was shocked, but even more so, I was getting more and more concerned as to what 'our' problem was - and I never did find out. Nevertheless, when both these women's husbands came in to hold their hands in their final hours before their babies' births - I felt the odd one out - and then I began to reassess why we were in a special case ward.

We were on our own!

The Birth

We had arrived at the Bromhead Maternity Home on this particular evening. After our initial examination, they said they could just see what they thought was the top of baby's head, so they immediately wheeled us straight out of the ward and down the corridor to the delivery room.

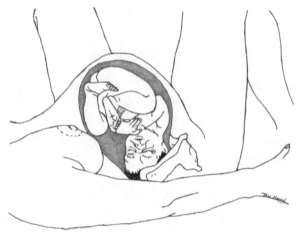

Figure 64 The start of labour

I really can't remember too much about this scene. I do know that it was a standard procedure - a normal delivery. It also seemed as if it was some kind of a relief because I was about to do something active by helping my baby come into the world.

The contractions were now coming in regular waves and were passing from the top of the womb to the bottom; they seemed to be pushing and propelling the baby down my birth canal. All the procedures that I had been taught at the ante-natal classes were now being put into use. I was told that with every contraction, I was to take a deep breath, push steadily down into my lower pelvis and keep it up for approximately ten to fifteen seconds. Under the midwife's instructions, I repeated this several times with each contraction, letting out my breath quickly and sucking in another deep breath between each push.

Needless to say, between the contractions, I was glad of a rest.

It was around here that the midwife told me that my baby was almost ready for delivery. I was so excited, and I must admit, apprehensive as well; at last, we were going to see each other for the very first time. The midwife told me that the last few contractions were coming. She told me to push with my stomach muscles and relax with my pelvic floor muscles. The staffs were extremely quiet, but they omitted to tell me that my baby's head was being delivered. I was told to stop pushing, and the staffs were very quiet. It was at this point that their silence told me they were delivering my baby's shoulders and the rest of the body.

All of a sudden, things appeared to have finished.

Had my baby begun to breathe air for him or herself? After all, until that moment of birth, he or she had received oxygen from *my* blood, as it transferred across the placenta. But this oxygen supply had obviously now stopped; the umbilical cord had now been cut - severed - to separate us from each other. There was no physical pain because the cord - made of matter - cells - contains no nerves as such. However, the mental pain caused by the division between us, at this point, was horrendous!

There was no doubt in my mind that my oxygen supply for baby had been cut off!

Gradually, around thirty seconds went by, that is, until baby's lungs had expanded for the very first time, and baby's first breath gave out its first cry.

The delivery had reached its maximum point of development; I was so relieved - and overjoyed.

There followed the final stage of labour, whereby the placenta and membranes were expelled.

But something vital was missing!

There was a lot of hustle and bustle a short distance from the bottom of the delivery table, and then I heard a trolley being wheeled out.

Things were so silent, and I felt a void - emptiness.

I looked around and began searching for my baby, but I couldn't seem to find her or him in that room.

'What has happened? Is my baby alright?'

It wasn't long before a nurse came back into the room, and I looked at her desperately. "Where is my baby?" I asked.

However, she didn't look at me. Instead, she just kept sorting things out and tidying things up.

"My baby, is my baby all right?" I asked her again, and with this, she just walked out.

I lay there and panicked. 'Has this something to do with me being a special case?' I thought.

I shouted for a nurse, and after a short while, she returned.

"What have you done with my baby? Why have you taken my baby away? I don't even know if I've had a little boy or a little girl!"

The nurse just looked at me and seemed extremely frightened, not knowing what to do or what to say, and then she disappeared again.

Shortly afterwards, a different nurse appeared, and I began to get upset again. After an intimate discussion with her, I asked, "Is my baby alright? Please tell me! There's nothing wrong with my baby, is there?" I asked desperately.

The nurse looked at me in a kind of sympathetic way and said softly and calmly, "No, everything went fine!"

I lay back on the table and felt so relieved.

The nurse asked me if I would like a cup of tea. But I refused.

I just felt extremely exhausted and wanted to go to sleep.

I was taken back to the same ward, but this time I appeared to be on my own.

'Oh!' I thought, 'This is because I am down as a special case.'

I didn't actually get to know this at the time, but the other mother-to-be had been moved somewhere else to be with the others. However, I just thought that my line of events must be the normal procedure, whereby after giving birth, the mums were taken to recover in a place on their own - somewhere quiet and peaceful, to get over the ordeal.

However, I was soon to realise that I was not a normal case - I was being isolated from the rest!

The Day After

I lay there all night, well, for the rest of that night. Of course, I felt very sore, plus all the other things that come with the delivery of a new born. I just remember that the silence seemed so wrong at this point. I had also noticed that the door to my room had been closed shut. There were these other two empty beds in there besides mine - and I felt extremely lonely. I also felt a sense of relief, but with mixed feelings. This is because there was no baby inside me - I knew I had been emptied: no more movement within me, no togetherness for the same reason. I was being made aware that the delivery had taken place - my body was telling me that. But where was he or she? I had been told that my little baby was fine, yet I hadn't seen him or her - not even a glimpse.

I seemed to be suffering from: 'No end result!'

I tried hard to go to sleep, but I felt too gloomy as I lay there in the dark. Did I want to cry? Well, no, not really, because I had given birth and I had been told that it was successful. My baby was doing okay. I seemed to have fulfilled some kind of duty, but for what?

Suddenly, the door flew open.

I screwed my eyes up through the absence of light. A shadow crossed this room. Apart from the wind caused by its movement, there was silence. I vaguely watched this dark figure as it passed rapidly across the bottom of my bed. It appeared to be making its way towards the window.

It stopped abruptly; the shape turned swiftly, and a voice came out of the gloom.

"Good morning, Janet!"

I said good morning back and began to sit up.

The figure took hold of the curtain, and as it did so, it caused a shaft of light; I could see that she was an attractive woman in her mid-thirties. She was dressed in a dark blue uniform; her blonde hair was swept up with the use of some hair-grips. Her hat, cone-shaped, was well seated on the top of her head. She was slim, neat and well-groomed.

She tugged at the curtains; they were long drapes that went down to the floor. I looked up and noted that they rose up to the ceiling - well, almost. They appeared thick and heavy as she proceeded to pull them open. As she did so, the sun began to stream into the room; it was a wonderful sight, so warm and so sunny; it was glorious!

The nurse turned slightly towards me; she was still clinging to these curtains as she spoke, "It's such a beautiful day to be born on!"

She turned a bit more, looked at me sharply and said, "And you will regret having your baby adopted for the rest of your life!"

And with that, she let go of the drapes and just walked out.

I was stunned.

I welled up inside and thought. 'Did I deserve that? I don't think that I deserved that?

And with this, I just became immersed in tears.

It was one of the worst days of my life!

Not long after, the door opened again, and a plump tea-lady appeared.

She smiled and pushed her trolley into my room; she got herself organised and then said, "Would you like a cup of tea or coffee?"

I was too choked to speak.

She looked at me and noticed my red blotchy face.

"Are you feeling all right?" she asked, with a frown and a puckered mouth.

I nodded and felt around my clothes for my handkerchief.

This kind woman went out, and a few minutes later, a nurse came in. It was not the same nurse, though, as before. She came over close to me and asked me if I was feeling all right. I poured out the episode that had happened with the nurse that had woken me up. She listened attentively, and at the same time, she made me a cup of tea. And then she left.

I later got up and had a wash and a tidy up and made myself feel a bit better - on the outside, that is. However, on the inside, I hurt – both mentally and physically.

But I never saw that nurse in the dark uniform again. Ever!

The Ten Days' Stay

When the kitchen staff came round with breakfast, I didn't feel like any of it. In fact, on this particular day, I didn't eat any of the meals that were given to me. It was strange, really, because it was a kind of a surreal day; you know, one of those days where you spend all of your time mentally trying to work things out. I had given birth to a perfectly normal baby, so it seemed, yet I had not been permitted the chance to see him or her.

It was nice, though, to feel much more comfortable, with no fidgeting or restlessness from inside me and less weight. I could actually see my feet for the first time in weeks from a straight-down view, but this wasn't the point. There had been two of us, and now, we had been separated. We had not only lost all physical contact with each other but smells and sounds as well!

It was a terrible feeling!

I lay there trying to get some sleep, but the pains in my uterus, as it was tightening up, were horrendous – worse, it seemed than they were before when it was expanding.

A member of staff, a physiotherapist, knocked on my door and then entered the room; she had come in to have a little chat with me:

She told me that in the next following weeks, my stomach would become flatter, but that did not necessarily mean that it would be firmer. She strongly advised me to do some exercises lasting around three to five minutes, four to five times every day; they were called postnatal exercises. She told me that these sessions, if done in the early days after delivery, would help to restore my original shape and re-strengthen my stomach wall and pelvic floor. I decided to ask her some questions as well - I wanted to know how the body's muscles had reacted to pregnancy and childbirth.

This member of staff told me that the pelvic floor muscles and the abdominal muscles become extremely stretched. She said that they stay like that after the baby is born and consequently do not function properly. The longer the muscles are left slack, the longer it takes to restore them back to normal, she had said. And so, it is important to begin the exercises in hospital within the first few hours of giving birth.

She made it known to me that the pelvic floor muscles surrounding the anus, vagina and urethra (the tube through which urine is passed from the bladder) support the contents of the pelvis, the womb, the bladder and the bowel. However, when they are weakened, it can give rise to incontinence and a prolapsed uterine. She said that the abdominal muscles are split into three groups: those which run straight up and down the abdomen; those which run horizontally across the abdomen; and those which run obliquely across the abdomen. Altogether, they form a 'corset' that supports the abdominal organs and the spine. However, after childbirth, these stretched and weakened muscles can often cause backache.

The physiotherapist then suggested that I do the following exercises. They were to be performed on a firm surface, preferably on the floor, but if that was not practical for reasons of space or hygiene, the next best thing was to do them on a firm bed. She also told me that once I had got into the habit of doing them, I should continue with the exercises for the rest of my child-bearing life.

"But remember," she said, "plenty of rest is just as important as exercise."

Exercises to strengthen the pelvic floor muscles

Clench and draw in the muscles in and around your anus and vagina. Continue to clench the muscles while counting slowly up to four. Relax, pause and repeat four times. At first, you may not be able to get beyond a count of one. But by the third or fourth day after childbirth, you should be able to do the full count without causing strain. The exercise is performed at hourly intervals during the day in the following three positions:

Position 1.

Lie on your side on the floor or bed, with your head on a pillow. Bend your right leg and rest it on another pillow. Then perform the exercise.

Position 2.

Turn on your back and lie with your arms outstretched at your sides and your knees raised. Keep your feet flat. Then perform the exercise.

Position 3.

Sit on a chair or lavatory seat and lean slightly forward. Then perform the exercise.

Figure 65 Me on a chair

Exercise 1.

Lie on your back with your knees bent, feet flat and arms outstretched at your sides. Clench your buttocks and simultaneously draw in your abdominal muscles. Continue until the small of your back is pressed against the floor or bed, and then relax. Perform the exercise five times running, twice a day, building up to 20 times running, twice a day.

Exercise 2.

Lie on your back with your knees bent, feet flat, and arms outstretched at your sides. Tilt your pelvis backwards. Put your heels and ankles close together. Then swing your knees as far as possible to one side.

Return to your original position, relax and repeat to the other side. Perform the exercise five times running, twice a day, building up to 20 times running, twice a day.

Exercise 3.

Lie on your back with your left leg straight, right leg bent, and arms outstretched at your sides. Tilt your pelvis backwards. Then lift your head and touch your right knee with your left hand.

Figure 66 Touching right knee with left hand

Relax and repeat to the other side. Perform the exercise five times running, twice a day, building up to 20 times running, twice a day.[2]

I did what I was told to do - several times - and I took plenty of rest in between. I never got to see anyone else much during the day, only the odd nurse and cleaner, oh, and the catering staff, but I didn't mind; I was reflecting over the whole experience trying to weigh it all up.

The next night came, and so did the following day, and although I still felt extremely sore with the pains, I continued with the exercises. I was beginning to adjust physically, but mentally I still couldn't rest.

It was now the third day and I hadn't long woken up. The usual routine was taking place: in came the nurse to pull the curtains open, followed by the tea and biscuit woman. It was then time to have a wash and change before the kitchen staff came in with my breakfast.

This particular morning, I seemed to be feeling extra sad. I was feeling more and more, a kind of loneliness. I had no idea what our future had in store for us for a start, and although I had no desire to move on anyway, as yet, I felt stuck in a groove. Suddenly the pain of not having seen my child and not knowing where he or she was and how my baby was feeling without me became unbearable. The pain of the lack of contact and yet knowing that my baby was somewhere near was awful.

How could these people do this to me?

What right had they got to separate a mother from her child?

It was then that I had this enormous pressure, this urgency from within my chest, and then an eruption, a breakthrough from my breasts. I put my hand up to the front of my blouse; it was wet through. What on earth was happening to me? I called a nurse.

I was sobbing with misery when she came in, and she just looked at me and said, "What day was the baby born on?"

"It was three days ago, and I haven't been allowed to see my baby yet. You have no right to separate a mother from her baby for so long!" I wept.

The nurse replied, "It's three days since you had the baby!"

"I know!" I cried. "And we need each other!"

The nurse continued. "I will get you some tablets."

And with this, she hastily disappeared.

She came back shortly with some pills, and she told me that it was necessary to take them to ease the pain in my breasts. She stood over and watched me as I took each pill separately with a glass of water; I sobbed as I did so.

"The milk is coming through; it does this on the third day," the nurse said. "These tablets will dry up the milk, and you will feel better!"

However, this was not what I wanted, and I told her so.

She disappeared and left me to cry on my own.

Presently, the door began to open and there in the doorway was the same nurse again, but that was not all. In her arms, all wrapped up tightly, was this parcel of joy. It was my baby. The nurse carried my baby over to me and told me to sit up and open my arms. This lovely warm bundle was placed next to my body. It was instant 'love.' We were connected once again. We belonged together, as we always had. All I could see was a kind of papoose: a beautiful North American Indian young infant with a mop of black hair - lots of it - poking up out at the top of this tightly wrapped bundle.

Figure 67 Papoose

"Is the baby really mine?" I asked.

But I heard no reply. I unwrapped the bundle just enough to see the little arms and legs. Of course, I did. I counted every single finger and toe - they were all there!

And the nurse said that my baby was a little girl.

She stared up at me with her wide-open eyes, and as I spoke to her, I just knew that she recognised my voice.

We were linked to each other once again.

There was a little hiccup, and some milk dribbled out of her mouth. I bent over my baby, and with a tissue, I started to wipe her chin and mouth. With this, the nurse came over and took her from me, saying, "I will just go and clean her up."

She walked out of the door, and unfortunately for me, they never returned again!

Visitors

My parents came all the way from Basingstoke to visit me; I was really excited. I had fulfilled my task. I had completed my mission. I hoped they would be proud of me.

On the day of their visit, which was to be in the afternoon, I was so much looking forward to seeing them. They came at what seemed to be late in the afternoon, and they appeared to be very happy to see me. We greeted each other with kisses and hugs, and I felt that they had forgiven me for everything.

Just as they were about to leave, they got up, but before leaving through the door, my mother turned to me and said, "We will come up and see you again in two to three weeks' time."

I was confused and answered, "But I thought I would be back in Basingstoke by then!"

"No," my mother replied. "We'll talk about it later, and oh, we've just been in to see the baby."

"Oh," I said; I was really excited. "And what do you think of her?"

But I can't remember how she replied - if at all - she just smiled!

It was quiet when they left.

I felt so sad.

I was back to being in there all on my own again.

However, my sister and her husband came to visit me too, and I really appreciated that!

The Bible

There was nothing for me to do in this room. There were no other mothers to share the ward with. I guess in one respect that was good because it meant that there was only one 'special' case during that period - and that was me.

My milk had dried up, and I seemed to be feeling more stable. What is more, I had been permitted to see my little baby girl, plus my family as well. Things were panning out to be not so bad after all.

On this particular day, I decided to pick up the Bible that was in my bedside cupboard. I loved Jesus, and he had always been my very best friend - ever since my first day at Sunday school at the age of five...

After Sunday school, on that very first day, I went home feeling really happy.

I remember we were all sitting at the table having dinner when halfway through, my father looked at me and said, "How did your first day at Sunday school go. Janet?"

I didn't look up at him for I was far too busy learning the art of using a knife and fork - the right-handed way. Being naturally left-handed, my grandmother had said it was wrong to put the fork in the right hand and the knife in the left; and so I found cutting food a struggle. With the knife in the right hand, the only way to manage was to use the knife as a weight to stop the food from moving about; the fork would then be plunged in and pulled towards me, hopefully ripping the morsel apart. Following on from this episode was the practice of getting the fork into my mouth, as it always seemed to want to move straight past my mouth and over to my right cheek.

"I liked Sunday School!" I replied.

"Did you sing any Hymns?" My father asked.

"The others did," I said. "I didn't know them." I carried on struggling with cutting food and eating. "But I did see Jesus," I added.

My parents had looked at each other.

"Did you say you 'saw' Jesus?" My mother asked.

"Hmmh," I replied. "Jesus came right up to me, and I touched His Hand when He took my pennies!"

They both smiled a little, but I don't remember them telling me anything different - at least, not at that point. Maybe, I was still so concerned with cutting my meat!

However, from that point on in my life, Jesus became a very real friend, especially at night, when I felt alone.

Although the rest of my family didn't go to church, except on special occasions, I continued my own Sunday morning trips. Eventually, at the age of eleven or twelve, I was asked if I would like to take the rite of Confirmation and become a member of the Christian Church. I remember that year, I asked for a Bible for my birthday. I got what I asked for: the Authorised King James

Version, complete with gilt-edged pages that were held fast in a black leather zippered binder.

I worshipped that book - as much as I do now. I adored the fact that the Book's covers could be zipped together - to keep it protected from anything outside of it. I was fascinated by the beautiful illustrations within the Book. However, I didn't understand the contents of the stories. I loved reading - as I do now - and I would start, like a storybook, at the beginning and try to read a few chapters every night, but I found it very difficult as a child.

I looked out of the hospital ward window and thought: Yes, it had always been to Jesus that I had turned to as a child; but, it had been to God that I had turned to in my days of sheer desperation later. So here I was in my maternity ward, all alone, and in some ways, I seemed to feel as if I had been put into some kind of solitary confinement – as if I had done something seriously wrong. I decided to finger through this hospital's Bible.

However, for some reason, I accidentally dropped it onto the floor. I bent down to pick it up, and as I did so, I noticed that it had fallen open at a certain page. I lifted it up carefully so as not to crumple the delicate sheets and so that I could retain the open page, and with this, I decided to settle down comfortably to read it. It was about Isaac and Rebekah…[3]

I gently closed the Bible; it was such a beautiful story to me that it touched my heart; so much so that I called my daughter Rebekah from that point onwards.

(N.B. Later on in my life, I found out that the name means: beautiful, shrewd, energetic and strong-willed.)

I would dream about my future together with Rebekah:

Figure 68 Rebekah with me
clapping hands

Figure 69 Watching
Rebekah playing

The Eighth Day

It was about the eighth day after the birth of Rebekah that I was told by the hospital staff to expect a visitor from the Adoption Society. The Adoption Officer was coming to see me that afternoon at about 2:00 pm.

I began to feel depressed again: something had been suppressed into my subconscious. Perhaps it was the reality of our situation, but now, the word *Adoption Officer* had caused a reoccurring vision of something horrific, an on-going nightmare that was now going to rear its persistent head again. Needless to say, I was chained to this room, and so I needed to tidy it up and groom myself and then wait patiently for the entrance of doom.

It was around two o'clock when I heard the hospital doorbell ring!

'This is my expected visitor,' I thought.

However, even though I heard her voice and interactions with the hospital staff, she did not enter my room. Well, not at that point. I waited a while, a good thirty to forty-five minutes went by, and then the door opened. There in front of me was a staff nurse and Miss Hardwick with a big grin on her face.

"This is Miss Hardwick to see you," said the staff nurse.

And with this, Miss Hardwick gave me a sickly grin saying, "Hello, Janet."

"Hello," I replied.

The staff nurse went out of the door closing it behind her.

Immediately, Miss Hardwick's face puckered up and turned into a sneer, with which I spontaneously felt that I had committed some kind of an offence against good taste.

She walked across this room, and as she did so, she was leaving a pungent trail, a characteristic odour of antiquated staleness. Once again, the scene of the Adoption Society's dark, dismal room flashed in front of me. My short-stay hospital room had instantly become *that* place, with which I gave out an agonising groan.

There was no chair for Miss Hardwick to sit on, nor any table for her to work from. Instead, she sat on the end of my bed and drew up the mobile bed-table, which had some flowers on it plus a jug of drinking water. Miss Hardwick moved these to one side and proceeded to place her briefcase onto this moveable flat table top. Out of her bag, which appeared to me as a doctor's bag, she pulled out some documents and then she fumbled around for a pen.

"I've got a biro," I said, "if you want something to write with?"

She scoffed a bit and soon found what she was looking for - a nib-pen with proper ink in it!

Miss Hardwick now had her back to me as she sat on the edge of my bed. The mobile table was in front of Miss Hardwick while she proceeded to spread out all her office paperwork on its top.

She did not ask me how I felt or anything else about me for that matter; instead, she said with a twisted mouth, "I don't suppose you've given the baby a name..."

"Oh yes, I have!" I said.

She looked at me with a surprised look, and then she paused for a bit.

"What is it then?" she asked.

"It's Rebekah..." I repeated it again, "Her name is Rebekah..."

Miss Hardwick seemed totally amazed.

"I'm calling her Rebekah because of a beautiful story in the Bible. The story is about how Isaac got his wife, Rebekah. It's in the Old Testament, in the Book of Genesis, in fact. I've chosen the middle name Evette, because of all the work I've done with Evette while baby and I were together..."

"Rebekah," she said hastily, overriding my words so as to cancel me out.

She resumed with a scoff with the middle name.

"Yes," I said, "And then my surname!"

She repeated the surname and continued writing it out.

Miss Hardwick kept up with her writing on the Birth Certificate.

"Occupation, What is your occupation, Janet?"

"Fashion Illustrator and Designer," I answered.

She paused a little without looking up and then carried on with her writing.

She then looked straight at me, saying, "Father's name - what is his full name?"

"David Masood."

She looked at me for a very long time, but she never wrote anything down.

"It's David Masood," I repeated.

Miss Hardwick just looked at me as if she disbelieved me, and so I nodded a Yes.

"Occupation?" she asked.

"He is a mechanic – and at the same time, he is the foreman at the company."

She stared hard at her paperwork, wrote something down, and then continued with more questions.

(N.B. I later discovered that on the Birth Certificate, the column for the Father's Name, and his Surname, has been left blank - with a stroke for a dash instead. This is also the case for the Occupation of the Father; the box has been left blank, except for the dash of acknowledgement. I suppose that means that the question was actually mentioned. Underneath the oblong box of details is written the word 'Adopted' and then the signature of the Superintendent Registrar.)

At last, she gathered up her written work and twisted the catch on her briefcase until it was shut and locked.

She glowered at me for a while, and then I plucked up the courage to ask her something, "You will find Rebekah a good home, won't you? I'm a good woman, and so is Dave; he's a good man. Please, find her a good home for us!"

She looked in my direction with her eyes staring down at me.

"What do you mean by a *good* home, Janet?"

"I am a religious person, a spiritual person," I replied quietly. "I wouldn't do anyone any harm. Can you find a good match for us? Will you make sure that my daughter goes into a religious family?"

She looked deeply at me for a while, and then she stood up. She spoke calmly but solemnly, and with an impressive manner, she replied saying, "Janet, I am working extra hard on your case, and, yes, I will find her a good home." She paused a little and then continued. "If you could pay me some extra money for that, I would be grateful."

I looked up at her and gazed in astonishment; those words didn't make sense to me.

N.B. *I later discovered on the adoption papers that Miss Hardwick had done what I had asked of her – it was a "Church" Adoption Society that she had approached for adoptive parents for Rebekah.*

Miss Hardwick waited a while for an answer, but there was none and then she began to straighten herself up.

"Here is the address of the foster mother. When you leave the hospital, you must take the baby there without any deviation."

She looked at me very haughtily, and then she turned and disappeared through the door.

My emotions were too much to bear, and I just collapsed into tears.

N.B. Taken from Forced Adoption Stories: I was 15 when I gave birth, and as soon as I went into labour, they gave me a wedding ring to wear while I was in hospital. I had long, girlish hair and quite clearly looked like a young teenager, yet I had to wear this ring to spare my shame. I was admitted to hospital in the early hours of the morning and then left completely alone in the labour room, and I was extremely frightened. There was a clock on the wall, and I could see that the midwife and nurse did not come to see how I was until 7 am - my daughter was born at 7.07 am. I was later forced to sign the adoption papers. When I said I didn't want to, I was told it was illegal for someone my age to keep their baby.[4]

CHAPTER NINE

The Foster Mother

The Hospital Departure

It was the day that we were to leave the hospital. It was a beautiful warm sunny day, and it was also the moment that I was going to be able to see Rebekah for a second time; I was really excited.

I got out her precious clothes from within her small round vanity case. We were due to leave in the afternoon at around 2:00 pm. Rebekah's clothes were already laid out on my bed when a nurse came in.

I said to her, "We are leaving today - this afternoon! Shall I come up to the babies' room to dress her, or will you be bringing her down here for me to put her clothes on?"

The nurse looked at me hesitantly and then said quietly, "If you give me her clothes, I will dress her upstairs and then bring her down to you!"

"Oh no," I said. "I want to dress her myself!"

She looked at me very sadly - almost tearfully in fact and said, "I'm sorry, Janet; it's the hospital's rules. I will bring her down when you are ready to leave!"

With this, she gathered up the clothes that I had spread out carefully on my bed and disappeared out of the room!

My driver arrived just before 2:00 pm, and he seemed eager to go. The nurse came in and asked if we were ready to leave, and we said yes.

We were told to wait by the hospital door, which we did, and shortly afterwards, the nurse came along with Rebekah in her arms. I took Rebekah off her; she felt so heavy and so warm. We went outside and walked across to the car. I just couldn't believe that she was mine. Rebekah turned her eyes away from the bright sunlight. I could only just see her face to start with because she was bound up so tightly in a shawl. I gently unfolded her plain outer attire whilst she looked all around, trying hard to focus.

I felt so proud of her!

Figure 70 Rebekah and me

It would take us around thirty minutes to drive to the foster mother's house - I just wished it could have been longer. All the while, I kept talking to Rebekah, and I felt sure that she recognised my voice. We were linked together again on this special occasion.

We were put together as a mother and baby 'should' be, for at least one more short time!

April 1968

The car that we were in was a convertible MG Midget; it was classed as a sports car with a body style of a 2-door roadster. The doors had wind-up windows, swivelling quarter lights, external handles and separate locks. The hood had a removable frame that had to be erected before the cover could be put on; plus, the rear springs had been replaced by more conventional semi-elliptic types, which provided us with a comfier ride.

Since 1962, the engines in these cars had been increased to 1098 cc, and this particular model had wire-spoked wheels.

We eventually arrived at what seemed like a fairly old type of council estate. There appeared to be lots of dogs around, and children were playing in the streets and indeed on the roads as well. My driver had to be very careful. As we moved around this estate, the children would stop playing and watch us drive past.

Figure 71 Boy on a bike

And they were everywhere along the way.

Figure 72 Toddler with toys, and one with wellies

As we turned a particular corner, we began scanning for the street name and the house number. Many a time, we had to slow down and stop for the little children to get off the road.

Figure 73 Two boys playing on the road with marbles

At last, we found the right house. I looked down at Rebekah - my warm bundle of love was fast asleep. There were two to three children outside the house, and as we pulled up, I could see that they were playing with bricks.

Figure 74 Children playing

They stopped and began to stare at us. One of them detached herself from the group and ran around the side of the house.

I opened the door of this sports car which was really quite low, and as I did so, I handed Rebekah over to the driver, who was now standing on the pavement. I got out of the car and straightened myself up, and then I gently took Rebekah out of the driver's arms - she was beginning to wake up. It felt like I was delivering some kind of Royal Baby; well, I suppose you could say that to me – that's what she was - extremely special and like a piece of gold!

I was feeling uneasy as I walked up the narrow pathway. I just felt very strange; I had never been in this situation before, and everything felt so terribly wrong.

Mrs Browning

The nearer I got to the front door I could see that it was beginning to open slowly. It wasn't long before I was confronted by a petite middle-aged lady in a navy-blue pleated skirt and a pale blue sweater. She looked very kind but extremely pale and tired.

The little girl that had run around the side of the house kept peeping out from behind this woman.

"I'm Mrs Browning," the woman said with a smile. "Shall I take her?" she asked, and at the same time, she was easing her arms slowly around Rebekah to gently separate her from me.

She looked down at Rebekah, still smiling. And as she did so, she pushed her glasses further up her nose.

"There!" she said, looking at her daughter. "This is what you've been waiting for, isn't it, Mary?"

"Mary loves babies!" she continued, looking up at me.

I looked at Rebekah, who is through the door frame by now and on the other side of it.

We had been parted!

I stood there wondering what was going to happen next. But I didn't have long to wait.

"The rule is, Janet, that you can come and see us once a week."

"Can I really?" I said excitedly.

"Yes, yes! Of course, you can! Saturday is the best day for us; can you make it in the afternoon at say - 3:00 pm?"

"Oh, I would love that!" I replied.

Mrs Browning was gently swaying from side to side and jigging her arms up and down as she held Rebekah, who by this time seemed extremely confused.

"Well, we'd better get on now, Janet," Mrs Browning said. "We have a lot of things to do. Say goodbye to Janet, Mary."

But the little girl seemed deeply involved in playing with Rebekah's fingers.

Mrs Browning moved further back inside the hallway, and as she did so, she pushed the front door a little to close off the view between us a bit more. I gave Rebekah a longing glance, but she appeared to be too fascinated with Mary.

I took a step backwards and then started to turn.

"Oh," said Mrs Browning, "Miss Hardwick said that you'll be bringing some money with you when you visit us each time! You won't forget, will you?"

I turned back round to face Mrs Browning. "No, no, of course not," I replied.

She smiled and showed her teeth. "Cheerio then, we'll see you next Saturday at 3:00 pm!"

"Yes, yes, of course!"

And with this, the door slowly shut on me with a click.

I felt so strange.

I walked down the pathway and was well aware of being watched by the neighbourhood from their windows.

*Curtains were twitching and pulled slightly bare,
whilst others had folk looking out with a stare.*

I was depressed.

I opened the door and got into the car.

'I do have a baby,' I thought. 'She is mine! But why has this woman got her and not me?

'Well, of course, she knows how to look after her properly,' I thought. 'I don't; I haven't had one before. That's all that it means.'

I peered out from this car and could see faces without reasoning;
but not so from Mrs Browning - hers had feeling!

The engine started running, and we were off!

Paying Visits

I began to settle back into life in Lincoln on this new estate.

I noticed for the first time the set routines that were taking place, like the times of the day when people would leave their houses and return, the time when the postman would arrive and the milkman and other delivery people. There were the dustmen on a set day of the week and people that would pass when they took their dogs for a walk. Across the road, there was a couple in their late middle ages. Apparently, he was the manager of a small supermarket store. They had no offspring, just the two of them, and every Sunday was the usual car-washing whilst the wife prepared the Sunday roast.

Each day I was on my own because the couple I lived with worked in offices five days a week and I would have certain chores to perform before they got back. But I really missed Rebekah., and I was always wondering how she was getting on.

Figure 75 The foster mother with Mary, two other children and
Rebekah in a pram

Every afternoon, when I had finished all my commitments,
I would go from place to place and room to room without any
settled routine or aim. Somehow, I would always end up over at
the local shops. This is because I had noticed some lovely little
babies' dresses in the wool shop. To get over my loneliness, I would
go to this shop and handle and caress these dresses around four
days a week. Eventually, I decided I would buy one, or some item
or something per week – and I did!

I also felt I needed to repay this wonderful couple for their
generosity, and I considered that a collage would be presentable as
a gift. I made a wall picture - a collage - at Southampton College,
out of fabric oddments that were either glued or sewn onto a

hessian backing. Hessian is a strong, coarse cloth of mixed hemp (rope) and jute, which is normally used for sacking and mats.

I decided to make a collage for these kind people using PVC. I had come across and worked with PVC clothing, commonly known as vinyl clothing, at Southampton College as well. PVC is a shiny plastic-coated fabric. Sometimes a kind of mixture is added to the plastic layer, which very often might be textured to make it look like leather (the leather-look), as opposed to perhaps a smooth finish (the wet-look or "patent" appearance).

These plastics were being used in all kinds of clothing in those days, but particularly in raincoats. Overall, PVC clothing had become very popular in this era - the 1960s - and later in the early 1970s due to the fashion trends. I personally had viewed PVC fabrics as the ideal material to design futuristic clothes. I had designed sheets of men's rainproof jackets in very masculine (square) styles involving straps and buckles and square pockets with flaps. I also made one or two samples and sold them. I had further designed boots and 'way-out' dresses and other PVC garments in many different colours such as black, white, red, yellow, silver and even transparent.

At this time (and later), it was also common to see PVC clothes on films and TV series such as The Avengers, for example. Since then, these shiny plastic clothes have become a fetish object.

I had lots of oddments in my 'scraps' suitcase, such as PVC in black, reds, white and transparent. I further had felts, knitting wools, braids, motifs, decorative trims, jazzy buttons, sequins, etc. It was the couple's first new home together, and there was nothing as yet on the walls of this house. They liked cars, so I decided to put my art skills to work by crafting a white vintage-type Morgan car.

The Morgan Motor Company was a family-owned British motor car manufacturer that was founded in 1910 by Henry

Frederick Stanley Morgan. The Morgan Motor Company was based in Malvern Link, an area of Malvern, Worcestershire, and today it employs approximately 163 people. The early cars were two-seat or four-seat three-wheelers and are therefore considered to be known as 'cyclecars'. Morgan's first four-wheeler was known as the 4/4; that means that it had a four-cylinder engine and four wheels. The first production of the 4-wheeled Morgan was released to the public in 1936, while the three-wheeler production continued alongside the 4/4 until 1952. Morgan cars are still going strong, with the current waiting list for a car being approximately six months - although it has been as long as ten years in the past.[1]

I made the Morgan Car out of shiny PVC fabric, complete with bumpers, head-lamps and a metallic number plate. It was finally mounted onto a dark grey hessian fabric with bamboo rings to hold it up.

The couple were extremely thrilled with it!

Figure 76 Illustration of the Morgan Collage

The time was drawing near for my first visit to see Rebekah, and I was very excited; in fact, I had been counting the hours over the last two days.

'I mustn't forget the money!' I thought.

And so, off I went to see my daughter Rebekah - we had a date!

It was Saturday and the time was nearly 3:00 pm! I eventually arrived at the estate and wended my way to the house, with which I hurriedly walked up the path.

I was very happy as I knocked on the door.

Eventually, the door opened a little way, and I could just see Mary standing there. She looked up at me sheepishly. She was a very sweet little girl with a pleasant face, and although she was probably no more than about ten to twelve years old, she appeared sensible.

"Mummy said that you will be bringing some money," she said timidly.

Figure 77 Mary

"Oh yes," I replied, "I have the money."

I opened my shoulder bag, peered inside and took out an envelope with the money in it for Mrs Browning. I handed it to Mary.

She took the envelope from me, smiled and quickly said, "See you next week, on Saturday at 3.00 pm." With this, Mary closed the door on me.

I stood there for a while feeling unexpectedly shocked, and then I realised - that was it!

As I walked down the pathway, all of a daze, I was constantly aware of curtains twitching from the neighbours' windows.

I thought, 'It's just them and me!'

But deep down inside me, what I really meant was that I was envious, because *they* all had their own children, whilst I was paying one of them to look after mine for me!

We decided to drive back home through the estate using a different route, and it wasn't long before we came across a children's playground.

Figure 78 Three children with ropes in playground

As we slowly moved past, I couldn't help but watch them; they were laughing and shouting and enjoying themselves, and I was very happy for them.

The next few days seemed to be very long and drawn-out. I had now got into a routine of set things to do during the day. I had learnt to conform to my territorial patch, but purely to mark off time leading to my next visit of seeing Rebekah.

I began to think of all sorts of things over those days, 'Was Rebekah still there, or had she been moved on to somewhere else? Why was I not invited inside? Where was Mrs Browning?'

As the days got nearer to Saturday, a kind of fear was building up; it was a fear of the unknown.

Saturday came, and we passed by those houses again with their inquisitive dwellers.

The car stopped, and I got out. As I went to open the gate, a little boy popped up from the other side and took me by surprise.

I walked up the pathway, and a rush of anxiety began to take over.

I needed to know for sure that Rebekah was being treated properly and that she was healthy and well.

I knocked on the door with my whole body shaking.

Once again, the door slowly opened, and Mary stood there.

She looked up at me and said again, "Mummy said that you would be bringing some money!"

"Oh yes," I said. "I have the money, but do you think I could see my baby?"

Mary just stared at me wide-eyed, and I knew that she didn't know what to do for the best!

"Is she well?" I asked her. "Is she asleep? I just need to see her for a while … that's all!"

Mary looked down as if she was thinking about it, and then she said, "I won't be a minute."

And with this, she closed the door on me.

I waited and waited, and then the door eventually opened again.

Mary looked up at me, saying, "You can come in."

I stepped inside. The house was really quite dark. I am now in the hallway, and Mary proceeded to walk straight through the narrow passageway towards the kitchen. I followed, and then Mary stopped. I could hear something snuffling, like somebody with a cold. I looked to my left, towards the sound, and there, underneath the stairs, was a built-in store cupboard. Inside this closed-in space was Rebekah in a pram. I couldn't believe it!

"Why is she in there?" I asked abruptly. "It's so dark and such a small place!"

Mary replied cautiously, "It's because it's the quietest place in the house for her to sleep!"

I looked closely at Rebekah, and I got upset. There was a stuffy atmosphere in there and staleness and a sickly, pungent smell.

I went to touch Rebekah, and Mary got alarmed.

"You mustn't touch the baby," she said, getting frightened. "Mummy said you mustn't touch her. She will wake up!"

I became upset and confused.

"Have you got the money?" Mary asked hurriedly.

I opened up my bag and got out the money. Mary put out her hand, and I gave it to her. She walked towards the front door, and I followed her and stepped outside. I didn't want to alarm Mary too much, and I didn't want her to see me crying either.

With my back to her, I heard her saying, "Goodbye! Mummy says to see you next Saturday at the same time."

I quickly turned round to face Mary.

"Yes, Mary," I said, "but I'm very unhappy with what I saw! You see, Rebekah needs to be out in the fresh air; it's a lovely day today. She needs to be outside, not stuck inside that stuffy old cupboard under the stairs!"

Mary looked at me, horrified.

"I'm sorry," I said as I touched her hand. "It's just that, well, it should be me looking after her - not you!"

I opened the gate in a flood of tears and nearly knocked over a father saying cheerio to his little boy.

Figure 79 Boy with his father

A few days later

I was upset all the way going home.

I just felt that this whole affair was really a business, a financial deal, a duty, which of course, that's just what it was. However, I was pining and longing to be with my baby, and she was stuck under the stairs on a lovely sunny day. I know that I sound ungrateful, but well, I had plenty of time. I could have looked after her myself!

I would dream of Rebekah and saw myself as Mrs Browning being her mother and how happy we would be together.

Figure 80 Rebekah and me

I went back to the wool shop to look at the babies' dresses again and bought another one. This time, it was a little silky one with a small cotton-lace collar and short sleeves. My plan was to take it with me for Rebekah to wear the following Saturday. It was this that also spurred me on further to start buying Rebekah gifts. The first thing would be to get her a wide silver bangle exactly like my own with engraving all around it.

'Like daughter, like mother!' I thought. 'After all, she is *mine*!'

I also continued with the shawl, which was nearly finished. Every crocheted shell was formed with love for my baby - every circle was bearing its own message!

The time came for me to make another visit to see Rebekah, and I was getting very apprehensive again. I was longing to see her, to be with her, but I didn't want to be upset. I decided to take a friend this time and a camera.

We turned into the estate, and immediately we were met with the sight of a lovely toddler sitting on the pavement, amusing herself.

Figure 81 Toddler amusing herself

Further along our now-familiar route was a young woman showing a toddler a picture book.

When we turned a corner into a side street, a little girl was busy painting by a garden gate. She was using an easel and had pots full of colourful water.

Figure 82 Toddler painting

Eventually, we arrived at our destination. I walked up Mrs Browning's pathway. It seemed weather-wise that it was quite a nice day. I remember glancing around this time; it was altogether a rather neat but small front garden. The square patch of grass was enclosed in a border of soil. Once again, I was being made aware of curtains being drawn and then opened again in neighbouring houses and figures just staring out at me.

I knocked on the front door timidly, afraid of the consequences. Whilst I waited, I also got the envelope with the money in it out of my bag.

The door slowly opened, and Mary stood there. This time, she appeared scared of me; I guess the interaction between us was a little bit the same.

I asked Mary if I could see Rebekah, and she nodded half-heartedly.

"She's out in the back garden," she said quietly, wondering how I was going to answer her back.

"Oh!" I said with my eyes wide open. "I am so glad; it's such a nice day. Can I go and see her?" I asked.

Mary nodded a yes. "If you go round to the side of the house," she said, "I will open the gate."

I turned quickly to my friend, who had a camera, "Come on!" I said, beckoning. "We can see Rebekah in the garden; bring the camera!"

I made my way around the side-path, and there was Mary waiting for me, holding open the gate.

I could see the pram in the midst of this patch of lawn, and I rushed over to it quickly; I was so excited. I peered in, and there she was, fast asleep.

My baby was out in the fresh air! That was something that I had been dreaming about all week!

I pulled down the pram hood a little so that Rebekah could be seen.

"Take a picture," I said to my friend.

I heard the camera being set up, and so I grabbed the edge of the pram. I needed to be part of this memory, somehow, to be locked in its history!

Snap went the camera.

"Got it?" I asked.

"Yes!" said my friend.

"I am so happy!" I replied. "This is something that I will never forget!"

Figure 83 Photograph of baby Rebekah in the foster mother's garden

CHAPTER TEN

What Next?

Contemplations

All in all, and up to this point, I must have held Rebekah for approximately fifty-five minutes. In addition to that, I had been permitted brief viewings - glimpses - consisting of a further total of thirty minutes by the time she was six weeks old. I would sit and make little things for Rebekah to hasten the days between the most precious parts of my life - which was another two to three minutes of quality time with my daughter at the foster mother's home.

However, unbeknown to me, there was a lot of administrative work going on behind the scenes. My caseworker, Miss Hardwick, had been busy making notes about my case.

Many years later, I was able to acquire my adoption files, being warned that I may find some puzzling things written in the documents, which I hasten to add, were correct.

As I open up these files, a description of the background of the baby states:

STORY

Introduced by a friend. He is separated from his wife (he was married six years).

He has not supported her (i.e., me) *but would like to keep the baby and let his parents bring her up. He has not seen the baby but would like to keep her.*

Within the same file and under 'parents,' it is written:

Father:… married to an English wife. His Nationality: N. Pakistan. Religion: Muslim.

His Parents: one English, one Pakistani. They live in Pakistan and would keep the baby.

I further noticed that Miss Hardwick had been sending out SOS letters. Eight days after Miss Hardwick had visited Rebekah and me in the hospital, she had written to an Adoption Organisation in London saying:

Re: Miss Janet Hann, aged 21.

"…This girl has just given birth to a female child, Rebekah…

As yet, it is early days for me to present this very sweet baby to our Adoption Committee. We do not have the baby's medical done until it is a month old, but even if my Committee accepted the child, we know that we have no adopters who would be prepared to take a child with this background. At this stage. the baby's skin is very pale and pink with a shock of jet-black hair. The mother is very pale-skinned herself with jet-black hair, which she wears parted down the middle, and I think her origins are from Somerset.

I am wondering if there would be any possibility of your Society being able to place this child? If so, would it be possible for you to interview the mother as she will be travelling home during the Easter period and then returning here? I have said she must stay up here until some sensible solution has been found for her baby.

Janet is an extremely nice girl and is extremely concerned regarding the baby and her future. When she is discharged from the Nursing Home, her baby will go as a temporary measure to one of our foster mothers. I am writing to ask if your Society would be able to help this girl, and if so, if it was helpful, we could get all the medicals and forms completed in the usual way…"

Three days later, Miss Hardwick received a reply from a Mrs Pascal at the London Adoption Society saying:

"Thank you for your letter about this girl and her baby. We can never promise to place a baby with adopters until we have seen it – which I know is very difficult for you. From what you say, there is at least a 50% chance of our finding adopters, but we will be specific when we have seen Miss Hann and the baby (separately, if necessary). Perhaps you will suggest suitable days? …"

I did go and visit Mrs Pascal at the London Adoption Organisation over the Easter Period, and the following is the letter that Mrs Pascal wrote back to Miss Hardwick.

Dear Miss Hardwick,
              <u>*Miss Janet HANN and baby Rebekah*</u>

We saw Miss Hann yesterday. She tells us that the baby's father would like to keep the baby and send her to his parents in Pakistan. This being so, before placing Rebekah, we must see this man to make sure he does not intend to apply for custody of the child. Miss Hann is to let us know his present address when she has checked on it.

We shall be glad to see Rebekah here on Monday or Tuesday… or Thursday and Friday… any time to suit your trains.

We suggest, please, that you get the baby's medicals completed first and enclose these.

Yours sincerely,
Mrs Pascal.

A few days later and Mrs Pascal had written another letter, and this one was for me:

Dear Miss Hann,
Enclosed are application forms to be completed and returned to us. As soon as we have received them and have seen Rebekah and assured ourselves that her father does not intend to claim custody of her, we will do our very best to find her a good adopting family.
With best wishes,
Yours sincerely,
Mrs Pascal.

During these final days and hours of the fostering period, I would dream of my times spent with Dave. I marvelled at how we had been put together - just one dance and then the long romance. I remembered the times spent in the countryside, those days sightseeing together, the laughter, the highs and the lows; the male power; the intimacy.

However, all the while, there appears this darkness, this hidden part to his character. Thinking back, perhaps it was some kind of a clandestine affair - as if it was a secretive encounter taking place with a complete stranger. Dave had revealed very little about himself; he seems to have played a mysterious role within a culture that was way out of my boundary - beyond my understanding. Nevertheless, his surreptitious behaviour had led to our passionate affair. The result is this beautiful baby - this remarkable life. It is as if she is a miracle, but then, surely this is what life is - one big miracle!

I began to work towards the future and wondered what the next few days would bring. Things were much calmer now and much more straightforward - like clockwork in actual fact - everything seemed settled into place. I thought about my mother. She had always treated doctors and even nurses, plus dentists etc., as if they were gods - with great respect, and she had brought me up to do the same. These 'high-ups' - as my mother would call them – these peoples' words were *the law* and very much so correct! Hence, adoption was what the doctor had said, and thus, there was no other option - no thoughts of anything different. All you have to do is to do as you are told.

But was this really what I wanted to happen? Did I truly want to hand over my baby to someone else? No, I didn't, and I tried to think of ways around it. Could I, in reality, look after Rebekah, and at the same time, could we still maintain an independent lifestyle?

I thought realistically of where we could live together on our own, not to be a nuisance or a burden to anyone else. I would need to bring in regular money to pay our bills, and at the same time, I would want to have Rebekah with me *all* the time.

However, I could not see this as being possible.

Somewhere along the line, I would need a babysitter, and for how long? I could see it as being perhaps many hours a day. Was this what I really wanted - someone else looking after Rebekah for money - and not for love? I began to think of men and perhaps getting married - and even to have other children. How would a future husband take to my child that was not his own? Would the balance be kept right - would she be left out in our home?

I began to think of other unmarried mothers and began to wonder how they were going about their circumstances…

In the 50s and 60s, single parenthood was a scandal. Women who got pregnant out of wedlock were considered little better than prostitutes. The child of an unmarried mother also faced the stigma of being "illegitimate" - whispered about and judged by the community. It was worse than murder in those days. It really was an appalling crime.[1-5]

Unmarried mothers who were under 21 were only permitted to keep their baby if their parents agreed, which, as usual - not many of them did. Moreover, they were only able to marry the father of their baby with their parent's consent, which quite often none of them would give. For most women, including those over 21 who may have had additional options at the time of their pregnancy, none of them would be given any information on resources for housing or financial support to allow them to keep their babies.[6] Therefore, for an unmarried mother to decide to keep her child and rent a flat or hold down a job, this wasn't an option because there were no such things as state allowances for women raising children alone.[1-5] It wasn't until 1973 that unmarried mothers who decided to keep their children became eligible for social welfare payments.[7]

Thus, all unmarried mothers would be encouraged to give their child up for adoption and were regularly told that it was 'best for baby and best for you.' It was not considered acceptable for a child to be raised without a mother and a father. For these pregnant women, any desire to keep their baby was perceived as immature and inconsiderate to the child's needs. There was further, never any discussion as to the birth mother's needs as far as her mental or emotional state was concerned regarding the pregnancy and relinquishment of her child.

Most women in these kinds of circumstances would speak of 'getting on a track they could not step off' once they had confessed their pregnancy to their parents. From that moment onwards, they were told what to do, where to go and how to feel about it. They unanimously believed there were 'no other options,' and for many, they were just pushed along by the flow of the social worker's process.

If a woman fought desperately to keep her child, applying for every kind of employment and aid she could think of, no one would help her, and she would be consistently told she had to give up her baby and move on with her life. The common belief at the time was that a child would be better off in a two-parent family. A woman who could become pregnant outside of marriage was not considered mature enough to raise a child on her own, and that it was best to give up the child for adoption and never speak of it again, thus 'moving on' with their life. As a result, women had entered a process they could not extract themselves from and were never given any kind of counselling or therapy to help them deal with the difficult emotions that arose from such a process.[8]

Magdalene Laundries

For more than two centuries, unmarried mothers were sent to a series of refuges. They were forced to sleep in large, communal dormitories, attend daily prayers, and help domestic staff with their duties, whilst they would find themselves being pressed relentlessly to give up their child.[9] The women in Ireland were sent to institutions as a punishment for having sex outside of marriage. Unwed mothers, flirtatious women and others deemed unfit for society were forced to labour under the strict supervision of nuns for months or years - sometimes even for life.

Over the years, the Magdalene laundries - named for the Biblical figure Mary Magdalene - had become primarily Catholic institutions. Although most residents had not been convicted of any crime, conditions inside were prison-like, including shaven heads, institutional uniforms, bread and water diets, restricted visiting, supervised correspondence, solitary confinement and even perhaps flogging. There were inmates imported from psychiatric institutions and jails, women with special needs, rape and sexual assault victims, pregnant teenagers sent there by their parents, and girls deemed too flirtatious or tempting to men. Others were there for no obvious reason. Though the institutions were run by Catholic orders, they were supported by the Irish government, which funnelled money toward the system in exchange for laundry services. As women came forward to share their experiences of being held against their will in these restrictive workhouses, the Irish public reacted with outrage.

The following is an example:

It was 1960 when Susan arrived with a single suitcase, and she immediately felt uneasy. This was because everything was hidden from the outside world due to the shrubbery and trees. Once through the door, her clothes, savings book, small stud earrings and bracelet were taken away from her. She was given a uniform - clogs and a starched denim dress. Susan - like the other arrivals - was told not to speak about her past life. All of them were given a different name. Hers was Ann - but she couldn't get used to it.

None of the girls had committed any crime. But they had two things in common. They were all unmarried, and they were all pregnant.

At this institution, the long rooms of the girls' quarters were on the top floor, looking out towards the cemetery. The nuns called them all "girls", but in truth, the residents were anything from 13 to 30 years of age. Susan was 17 when she arrived. She was there because she had sinned, or so the nuns told her, by falling pregnant. This was a mother and baby home, not a prison. Legally, Susan and the other girls could have left at any time. However, in practice, it wasn't as simple as that; any girl who ran away might find themselves rounded up by the police, and in any case, for the vast majority, there was just nowhere else for them to go.

Each girl admitted to the home knew they would give birth there and stay until their baby was adopted – which could be as long as three years. They weren't allowed outside except for short walks around the grounds, and they had to be accompanied. They were all given jobs. Some worked in the kitchens or in the red-bricked laundry building. Susan worked nights in a small room off the labour ward. Occasionally she fed babies in a nursery lined with rows of cots, but she was only allowed to spend about 30 minutes with each child. Another nursery held toddlers up until the age of three, but she doesn't remember ever seeing any toys.

Nuns ruled the laundries with impunity. Some girls were incarcerated after being raped, and the nuns told them it was "in case they got pregnant." Once there, they were forced to cut their hair, they were not allowed to talk and were assigned backbreaking work in the laundry, where nuns regularly beat them for minor infractions and forced them to sleep in the cold. Often, women were referred to by numbers or as "child" or "penitent."

Babies were usually taken from their mothers and handed over to other families.

In one of the most notorious homes, scores of babies died. In 2014, the remains of at least 796 babies were found in a septic tank in the home's yard; the facility is still being investigated to reconstruct the story of what happened.

Why did such an abusive system endure for 231 years in Ireland? Well, to start with, any talk of harsh treatment at the Magdalene laundries and mothers' homes tended to be dismissed by the public since the institutions were run by religious orders. Survivors who told others what they had been through were often shamed or ignored. Other women were too embarrassed to talk about their past and never told anyone about their experiences.

How these circumstances got to be known was when the Sisters of Our Lady of Charity decided to sell some land they owned in Dublin, Ireland, to pay their debts in 1992. The nuns petitioned officials for permission to move the bodies of women buried in the cemetery at their Donnybrook laundry, which between 1837 and 1992 served as a workhouse and home for "fallen women."

Estimates of the number of women who went through Irish Magdalene laundries vary, and most religious orders have refused to provide archival information for investigators and historians. Up to 300,000 women are thought to have passed through the laundries in total, at least 10,000 of them since 1922. But despite a large number of survivors, the laundries went unchallenged until the 1990s.

The accusations against these homes include:

- Burying babies in unmarked and unrecorded graves
- Coercing women and girls to remain

- Poor medical care
- High mortality rates for babies
- Overwhelming pressure on mothers to allow babies to be adopted
- Emotional and physical abuse
- Illicit adoption: babies were effectively "sold" to families in the US and elsewhere without proper procedures or consent
- Allowing medical trials without informed consent
- Use of dead babies in anatomical research
- Falsification of records

The Irish Government has now apologised to thousands of women locked up in Catholic-run workhouses known as Magdalene laundries between 1922 and 1996.[1-5]

Action

I had been toying with an idea for a few days now! I had been thinking more and more that I needed to contact Dave. After all, he had not got to know whether his offspring was a boy or a girl. As the days had moved on, the feeling had got stronger and stronger - I needed to tell Dave that we had a beautiful little girl — and that her name is Rebekah.

This particular morning, I went upstairs and searched my suitcase for my address book.

"There it is!" I said aloud.

I fingered through the pages until eventually, I found what I was looking for: the telephone number to contact Dave!

I looked up out of the window.

It felt good.

Yes! It seemed as if there were three of us in this together again!

'When would be the right time?' I thought excitedly. 'Well now!'

'No, not now; I'm too excited. I would mess things up!

I knew that I had to be alone in the house to make the telephone call, so this would have to take place during the day between 8:30 am and 5:30 pm, Monday to Friday. However, I also realised that Dave too worked the same kind of hours, and so that meant if I rang during those periods, he wouldn't be available. I considered an evening call as an occasion when Dave might be in. However, I wanted to be alone when I phoned him, and I knew that the evenings were not a good time - because I was never alone.

I started to take into account the weekends, maybe during the day. Sometimes the people I lodged with would go shopping on a Saturday afternoon; maybe I could telephone Dave then.

Saturday soon arrived, and there was talk of these people going to town; I began to realise that this was my opportunity to make my call.

I was all of a jitter as I dialled the number; I had so much important news to tell Dave.

The phone was ringing; I could hear it.

I hung on for a while, and it was still ringing.

My excitement level began to lower.

No one seemed to want to answer my call.

I got sadder and sadder until I eventually put the phone down.

I decided to dial again - but a bit later, in a few minutes - or even half an hour.

And that's what I did.

Once again, the telephone was ringing - around three minutes in fact; but to no avail. There was seemingly no one there.

As you do, I started to think of all sorts of things for the worst: they knew that it was me somehow, and they didn't want to speak to me.

I felt depressed.

I looked around this family home, and I felt lonely.

This was when it dawned on me – "Well, of course, they are not there because they have gone shopping as well!"

So this is where I changed my perspective to a positive view, "They have all gone shopping in London!"

This made me cheer up!

My plan B now came into action:

I would telephone during the week at a time when I was alone. Dave might not be there, but at least his friend possibly would be. He could pass on the message to Dave that I had been in contact and ask him to phone me back where I have been living for the past four and a half months.

I chose Monday - it would be sooner than all the other weekdays, and with this, I really enjoyed my weekend!

It was Monday, and I had asked my friends if I could telephone Dave that day. They said that they would be eager to know what he had to say when they got back in the evening. So, with permission granted and without any fuss, I decided to make the phone call - the earlier, the better.

It was approximately 8:50 am when I telephoned, and this time, much to my surprise, Dave's friend answered the phone.

I said, "Hello Taz, this is Janet!"

"Well, hello," he replied. "And how are you?"

"I am well," I said. "It's really good to speak to you again!"

"And you!" he replied.

"Is Dave there?" I asked.

"No, he's not Janet."

"Oh," I said. "Do you know what time he will be back?"

There was a little pause.

"I'm afraid I don't, Janet."

There was a pause again.

"You see," he continued, "Dave has been gone some four weeks now!"

I was shattered, and I didn't know how to answer.

At last, I plucked up courage. "What do you mean he's been gone four weeks?"

There was silence for a while, and then he spoke again.

"You see, Janet, Dave's wife arrived at the house, something she had never done before. I could hear them having this massive argument in his room. She was with him for some time, and then she left."

There was silence for a bit, and then he continued, "Dave said that the argument was to do with money."

I listened very carefully.

There was a break, and then Taz said, "It must have been a few days later, perhaps a week, when his wife returned again; she stayed quite a while this time, and then they both left together."

I carried on talking to Taz for a few minutes, and then we said our farewells and I put the receiver down.

I slumped back in the red swivel chair.

It so happened, in fact, that Dave had gone back to live with his wife and family.

One part of me felt sad and dejected; the other side of me was perhaps pleased for his wife and children.

I decided to reply to the secretary at the adoption society:
Dear Mrs Pascal,

With reference to our meeting on Thursday, I am now able to complete Dave's full address. However, on contacting this address, I find Dave no longer lives there and has left no forwarding address or any other information as to where he is. I am sure that now he agrees to Rebekah's adoption.

I will be contacting you also on Tuesday to tell you when and what time the foster mother, Mrs Browning, will be bringing Rebekah down to you.

Yours sincerely,
Janet Hann.

I oscillated the red fabric chair on its chrome swivel-base, and as I did so, I began to think of Dave.

He had obviously been planning to change his lifestyle; I guess he had been searching for freshness and freedom; perhaps he had been longing for innocence and purity.

The red chair went leftwards and rightwards, leftwards and rightwards.

Maybe his goal had been self-transformation; what I mean is, perhaps he had wanted a chance for a radical change through his relationships with women.

Rebekah used to like me doing this when we were together; she really enjoyed me swinging leftwards and rightwards on this red swivel chair.

Did I say three of us?

Well, no, there's now just one!

CHAPTER ELEVEN

Journey to London

The Day of the Handing Over: The Four of Us

It was the beginning of May and the day before the Handing-Over. I already felt numb. My mother's arrival was due pretty soon now, and I knew what that meant!

We met my mother at the train station.
"It works better that I come by train this time," she had said.
But I didn't really understand why.
The one thing that I did notice was that my mother had travelled light! What I mean is that her toothbrush and essentials were all kept in a plastic toiletry bag, which was tucked just inside her shopping bag.

I was pleased to see my mother in one sense; she had been very faithful to me. All the way through my stay in Lincoln, my mother had kept in contact with us. She had worried about the pair of us, but at the same time, I knew she was really glad that we were out of the way.
We all chatted in the evening around a wholesome meal, and I must admit that I did enjoy my mother's company on that particular evening. She was a chatty, bubbly, friendly woman –

amongst other things. We all spoke of the events of the last few weeks, and my mother and I were very grateful to these people for putting us up for so long – or should I write, putting up with us for so long – but things were about to change.

As usual, I was to sleep in my bedroom by the front door. My mother was going to sleep on a camp-bed in the main room. I had got used to going to bed at a relatively early time, but my mother was used to staying up later; and so as normal, I said my goodnights and went off to bed. I could hear the three of them talking in the other room; they seemed to have plenty to say. Sometimes they spoke loudly; sometimes, I knew they were whispering, and at other times, they were laughing wholeheartedly, as if they were telling really good jokes.

Eventually, the meeting seemed to break up; the toilet was being flushed and taps being turned on; the shower as well; cupboard doors opening and shutting – all the normal procedures – except there was an extra one!

I heard all their goodnights, and everything went quiet.

I had a secret.

It was a very precious piece of knowledge, and I was not prepared to tell it or share it with anyone!

And with this, I thanked God in my prayers that night.

We had planned the secret together!

As always, I was woken up by the sound of the alarm in the upstairs bedroom. There were the usual sounds, including someone running downstairs and a kettle being boiled in the kitchen next door. It was like clockwork on an early weekday. So much so that

I could tell the time by the different sounds. In fact, I could tell what particular minute it was. Eventually, the front door would be unlocked and then there would be a quick peep in at me to say cheerio. A door would click shut, and the sound of the car engine would start up. They would roll back out of the drive, and then 'Brrrmh' they would be off! That is until tea time!

However, *this* morning, things were different! They did not peep in my bedroom to say cheerio. This *particular* morning, I got out of bed to receive emotional hugs and squeezes – and a choked cheerio. I watched them get into their car, roll backwards out of the drive and with a tearful wave between the three of us - the couple were gone.

I didn't bother to get back into bed, and my mother was also busy in the kitchen preparing our breakfast.

"Make sure that you leave your room tidy, Janet."

I always did!

Well, if my mother was there!

My mother just wanted to make sure that she succeeded in her duties; she needed to make certain that her plan would come together. She also wanted to leave her special mark, that the place was to be left neat and clean.

That was 'our' mark.

My mother and I were in a bit of a rush. We were expecting a visitor, well two, and we needed to be washed and dressed before they arrived.

It wasn't long before the doorbell rang.

My mother went to answer it, and there on the doorstep was not the postman; but this beautiful baby all wrapped up and being delivered in the arms of the foster mother – Mrs Browning.

Preparation Time

That fearful day had arrived! It was now in the present!

Nevertheless, I needed to balance things out to be able to cope with it.

It was going to be a good day in one respect; after all, I would see my daughter for such a long time. However, what the event actually meant, in reality, was beyond thinking about - something I couldn't even bear to comprehend.

I just wanted to savour every minute of Rebekah's presence. Beyond that, nothing else existed; that's how I would deal with it!

The foster mother looked very pale and weary when she arrived; she had on a nice navy-blue-and-white checked coat and a hairgrip in her short dark soft hair, which looked as if it had been recently cut, restyled and set. My mother beckoned them in, and then she shut the front door.

"Would you like a cup of tea?" my mother asked Mrs Browning.

Mrs Browning just stood there, and I knew she was feeling very uncomfortable. I asked her if she would like to come in and sit down, but I was very careful that she did not choose the 'sacred' red chair. That chair belonged to Rebekah and me – especially now we were back in this room together!

I went to take Rebekah out of Mrs Browning's arms, but her words were, "No, that's all right, we are quite comfortable, thank you!"

I wanted so much to be as one with Rebekah as we had prepared for before. Here we were in the same setting, yet *seeing* each other physically like never before. It was amazing - extraordinary! I needed so much to hold her, cuddle her, kiss and stroke her, but Mrs Browning had taken Rebekah way over to the other side of the room as far away as possible from me - and the front door!

I got up in a kind of surreal state; it seemed a weird day - a mixed event.

I attempted to try and sort things out.

Anyhow, I was going to be able to make a big fuss of Rebekah!

Out came the bootees that Pat had knitted and the beautiful matinee jacket that my mother had made. The crotched shawl was laid out on the back of the settee. I had also bought a special dress from the wool shop, plus a frilly panty to cover Rebekah's nappy. My mother had further knitted Rebekah a bonnet in case it was cold.

This was to be the special day that we adorned my offspring with gifts.

We were like three wise women, not men, around a treasured baby.

However, first, I wanted to bathe Rebekah; I needed to inspect my entire infant for the very first time. But that was not going to happen, I was told - it was unnecessary!

Nevertheless, we needed to put on the presents of clothing, and so, very carefully, we took off all her outer garments. This left just her nappy and vest, and on went the luxurious dress from the wool shop.

"There!" my mother said. "Keep her on your lap Janet; I am just going to get my camera!" And she did.

"Wait a minute!" I said. "I just need to brush Rebekah's hair." And I did!

I must tell you that I felt like I was in heaven as I groomed my baby. I brushed her hair gently forward and then kissed her forehead; she felt so warm, and her smell was becoming more like mine – we were becoming one again!

"Look at me, Janet!" my mother had said.

But there was no way I was going to take my eyes off Rebekah – nor ever again, if I could have had my way.

Click went the camera; it was Rebekah and Mum!

Figure 84 Rebekah and me

My mother put the camera down and then asked that we change places, which we did.

All the while, Mrs Browning was watching us like a hawk. Her nose was in her cup, which was full of tea, while her eyes scanned the scene just up over the top. In *her* mind, that baby was not mine at all! The ruling had it that she was already signed up for someone else's!

Mrs Browning sat there and observed what
I couldn't do at all;
Because between me and my daughter was an
invisible brick wall.
For Mrs Browning worked for the other side;
She was the one that had supplied the divide.
Janet, she was told, was a surrogate mother;
She was having her babe for someone other.
Mrs Browning was here to maintain the gap,
Between birth mother and child - without any mishap!

My mother put the matinee jacket on Rebekah, and then she asked me to take a picture of herself with Rebekah.

I got the camera poised when my mother said, "Wait a minute, Janet, I will get the shawl from behind me and sit Rebekah on it," which she did!

Click went the camera, and another picture was taken.

Figure 85 Rebekah on my mother's lap

It was shortly time for us all to leave.

We all did the essentials and then gathered our belongings. My mother carefully put on Rebekah's bonnet. It fitted so nicely; she really did look cute and cosy.

"Let's have just one more picture!" My mother announced.

This time it was the foster mother and Rebekah outside by the gate.

Figure 86 Rebekah with the foster mother

Taxi

The taxi arrived on time - well, a little before time, which was good.

The taxi driver helped us put all our things into the cab, and then we clambered inside ourselves.

Mrs Browning went and sat with Rebekah on the left-hand side of the back seat. My mother got into the middle. That left me on the right-hand side of the back seat - to look out of the right-side window.

The cab's engine started up, and we were off. I glanced back at the house that I had been in for some four and a half months. I felt all mixed up.

"How long does it take to get to the railway station?" my mother asked the driver.

"Oh, not long," he replied. "About fifteen to twenty minutes. But we're in good time!" he said.

That's because my mother had told him what time our train was due to depart.

"Going on holiday, are we?" he said, turning his head to one side to listen for the reply.

But he needn't have bothered.

We all just stared solemnly, looking straight ahead.

And *none* of us replied!

We headed towards Leyburn Road, and then we turned left onto Newark Road (A1434). From here, we turned left onto what seemed like a long straight route - Tritton Road (B1003).

After this part, it wasn't long before we came to a roundabout, where we took the third exit onto Rope Walk; and from here, we turned left onto Brayford Wharfe East.

"Not long now!" the taxi driver announced. He was obviously trying to break the silence.

But *none* of us uttered a word.

Soon, we turned right onto Wigford Way (A57) and then right again; keeping left, we met our destination on the right, with which the taxi came to a halt.

The taxi driver was right - it did take us around fifteen to twenty minutes to get to Lincoln Central Railway Station, which was in Saint Mary's Street.

The Journey to London

I got out first, and then my mother; I went round to the other side to open the door for Mrs Browning - and so did my mother. Mrs Browning passed Rebekah to my mother whilst she climbed out of the taxi. She straightened her clothes and then took Rebekah off my mother.

"Can I hold her for a while?" I asked earnestly.

"No!" said Mrs Browning quite abruptly, but at the same time, I could tell that she was very nervous. "I can manage!" she said.

We stood waiting for the train on the railway station's platform; we were like three separate entities, living worlds apart. Rebekah was in Mrs Browning's arms, but it wasn't long before the train arrived.

My mother and I let Mrs Browning get on first. We both asked her if we could hold Rebekah whilst she got up into the carriage, but she flatly refused and struggled her way through the carriage doorway, moving slowly inwards until she found herself a seat by a window.

My mother sat next to Rebekah and Mrs Browning.

I had chosen the seat opposite Rebekah - the opposite window seat.

Mrs Browning and Rebekah were facing the way we were travelling whilst I was going backwards - with my back in the direction of our destination. However, I could sit there and watch Rebekah - my child - for the whole of the journey.

And I did!

We were told that we had two changes to make; this meant that we had to change from one train to another train twice; and all in all, it would take us around three hours twenty minutes. We sat on the train, but we knew that we shouldn't really relax because this first part of the journey was only 27 miles (43.45 kilometres). We appeared to be sitting there, all clutching our bags, expecting something to happen.

We all seemed to be tense; nevertheless, it wasn't long before we arrived at Newark Castle Station where we made our first change. We were lucky; our second train was already waiting alongside the other platform, and we just had to move across. We settled into our new seats (same positions, though), took a few things out of our luggage and put our bags up on the rack above our heads.

My mother fell asleep. I think that Mrs Browning would have liked to have done the same too. Rebekah did - she fell asleep!

Did I fall asleep - of course not!

I was savouring every little strand of hair on Rebekah's head, every eyelash; every cell; every atom of her being; plus all of her movements and behaviour that these things produce.

I think I could tell you all of the thoughts that had gone into the shawl that she wore.

Each crocheted shell contained specific memories locked in time.

Then there were the bootees that Pat had made, the words that we spoke as she knitted them, and the discussion of working as a student for Walt Disney in America and not knowing whether to follow it through. All of these things came flooding back and were being mixed together and crocheted to the scenes passing by the window, all stitched together to the rhythm of the train.

There was:

The bonneted clouds,
The ribboned fields,
The patchwork scenes,
The embroidered edges,

The buttoned bushes,
The lacy trees,
Clickety Clack; Clickety Clack; how about that! This
and that!
I began to relax and felt rested,
But this cannot be - I am being tested.
Oh, Janet, please don't cry,
You have no reason as to why,
Wipe your eyes afore they haze,
There's no time to be in a daze.
Just think, it's not a normal day,
Because you're both on holiday.

I got out my handkerchief.

"Oh! Rebekah's yawning! Has she got any teeth?" I bent over sharply to cash in on the opportunity.

But Mrs Browning was on the alert!

She must have had one eye open because, as quick as a flash, her arm had tightened around Rebekah so as to draw her closer to her being.

But it didn't matter because I still had plenty of time to make observations and dream.

My mother's head moved a little, then one eye opened; it gazed a little without blinking, and then the other eye popped open; both seemed to be focussing and remembering.

"Would anyone like a sweet?" my mother said as she rustled a bag of boiled sweets. "They help to keep your mouth moist!" she said. "I'm dry, is anyone else?"

But apart from that, I think I can safely say we really didn't talk much. None of us had anything much to say!

We were all in our own little worlds - except for Rebekah and me - we were linked - there was no doubt about that!

It took us around an hour to get to Newark Northgate Station, and this was to be our second change. This transfer was not as easy as the first one since we had to pack things back up in our bags. Besides, we had relaxed more here in the warmth of the train, and it was a struggle to get out and hurry over to the other platform. We also had to wait a while for our connection to arrive this time, and it was proving chilly standing on the station platform.

At last, our transfer was complete. I fell back into my seat and stared longingly at Rebekah. We were just centimetres away from each other, yet seemingly, I had been banned from touching her.

'What have I done wrong?' I thought to myself. 'Just tell me, what have I done wrong? I have given birth to a baby! What's wrong with that? I suppose there is another way of looking at it, and that is that I have become a surrogate mother: I have conceived and given birth on behalf of a stranger, another woman who is unable to have her own baby. But is this what I really wanted to be? Did I truly want to give my baby away?'

I looked out of the carriage window again and watched as everything passed me by.

'No! My daughter is being taken away from me,' I thought. 'This is not *my* choice! The circumstances themselves are making it this way.'

I looked at Rebekah passionately, 'If I were able to turn the clock back, say two years, would I want to change my life?' I thought to myself.

'What? And deny this little girl a life? No! Never!'

Already she has given me so much happiness, and with this, I began to think of Mary.

I looked across at Mrs Browning, who was half-asleep. She looked pale and tired, but a sensible woman, I could see. I wondered if she had been awake in the night with Rebekah. I wondered if it had been Mary that had been feeding Rebekah and changing her nappy in the night.

I thought of Mary; she will certainly regret Rebekah's absence. I guess she cried this morning when she bade Rebekah goodbye.

A tear splashed down my cheek. 'Already, Rebekah had brought happiness into other people's lives. I wonder what the future will hold for her. Will I ever get to know? One thing God knows is that *I will always Love Rebekah, Forever.*'

I got out my handkerchief and wiped my tears. 'If the others don't see them, they won't need to worry about me. That's what I feel.'

CHAPTER TWELVE

Destination:
Bloomsbury - London

The Journey across London

Eventually, the train pulled into London's Kings Cross Railway Station; this latter part of our journey had taken us approximately two hours.

We all scrambled out of the carriage, and from there, we made our way to the Waiting Room. The first thing that we needed to do was to have a bite to eat and drink, which included Rebekah, too, of course. My mother had made us some ham sandwiches and a flask of coffee. She had also brought us some apples and bananas, plus some moist tissues to wipe our hands, bless her - she was very thoughtful like that!

Figure 87 Mrs Browning feeding Rebekah

We tidied ourselves up. Rebekah also had her nappy changed, albeit whilst I was out of sight in the Ladies Toilet. I did manage to catch sight of her with her legs kicking whilst she handled and played with the shopping bag. I further noticed that all her soiled items were being put into an empty carrier bag.

We now had to find our way across London, and we decided that the best way to do it was to take the underground Tube.

Once down in the underground, we were soon forced with gusty pressure into the network of tunnels; but we knew which way to head because I was given the directions in the letter I had received.

You need to get off at Tottenham Court Road Underground Station, it said.

And so, at Kings Cross, St. Pancras, we took the blue Piccadilly line.

As always, the underground railway was full of gushes of wind, clangs and crashes as doors were automatically being opened and shut. There were these crowded carriages whereby some people were standing up whilst holding on to swinging safety straps, fastened to the carriage roof, whereas others would be clinging onto seat bars or poles. Other folks were sat down for the ride, yet no-one really wanted to be friendly. It was the usual thing where people just like to 'stare into space.'

I thought, 'Nothing's changed.'

We had just two stops: the first was at Russell Square, and the second was at Holborn; this is where we had to make a change to another line - the red line.

Whilst we were being jostled on the underground train, I thought, 'These underground tube trains have always been depressing to me, and this day was definitely no different.'

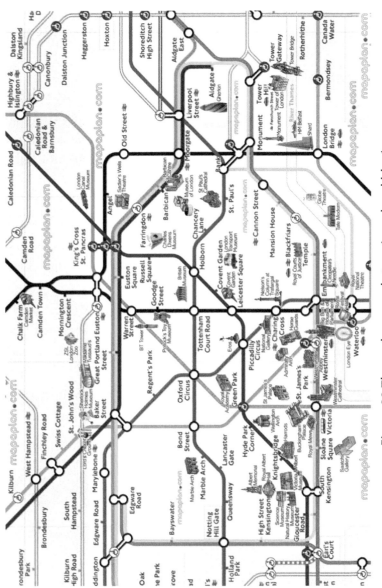

Figure 88 The underground stops in red and blue[1]

I was used to this environment; however, today, things were much worse. Nevertheless, I did feel truly sorry for Mrs Browning: Rebekah must have been very heavy, and Mrs Browning's arms must have really ached.

It wasn't long before we arrived at the next stop, which was our exit stop - Tottenham Court Road. All in all, our underground journey had taken us around 18 minutes, though they do tell me that the distance we had travelled was no more than 1¼ miles (2.01 kilometres).

We battled our way through the rush of people, trying hard not to lose one another as we rose up out of the underground, only to be met with yet another rising staircase. We had risen up into Tottenham Court Road's tube station, and it became one of the strangest of sensations, for as we turned right, it had now become my all-familiar route.

The four of us country folk were now fully absorbed into the melee of the Big City's life. But we did know where we were heading, and Rebekah seemed to be taking it all in.

Shortly, we all passed *The Sound of Music* at the cinema one more time, and then we took a sharp turn to the right onto Great Russell Street.

Rebekah was placed upwards in Mrs Browning's arms, and from behind, you could see her head just above Mrs Browning's right shoulder. She was peeping out from her bonnet and peering round from left to right.

Soon, we would be passing the British Museum on our left and Helen Graham House on our right. I watched Rebekah all the time with a surge of pain as she bobbed up and down in front of me.

'This is where your father and I would meet up on these steps,' I said to her under my breath. 'This is where we parted as well on these steps,' I continued.

I swallowed hard!

"It's not far now, Janet! It's just around the corner; it says so on this paper!" my mother said.

I glanced up at the entrance doors of the YWCA, and mixed emotions flooded into my mind.

We clip-clopped onwards, and Rebekah was bob-bob-bobbing.

'What a story I could tell her,' I thought, 'about her origins! Perhaps one day that might be possible - if only it would!

I choked back my emotions as we passed this place. 'This was once *our* home,' I said quietly, looking at her face.

We all turned the corner to arrive in Bloomsbury Square.

We started scanning the buildings' numbers – that's how close we were!

With the square on our left, we walked straight ahead. There were car meters in those days, dotted around the square, and there always seemed to be plenty of cars taking advantage of them. Yet on this day, there seemed to be only a few - not that I could see or hear anything much.

"There it is!" my mother shouted as she pointed in front of her. "There!" she said. "It's straight in front of us!"

For some reason, Rebekah started to cry. I think she wanted to be still for a while.

Well, that's what I wanted to think!

Figure 89 Rebekah crying

We made our way straight ahead - not more than about 50 yards (approximately 46 metres). My mother was first in the queue and then Mrs Browning carrying my daughter. Of course, I was last in the line - I could see Rebekah better from behind.

Her eyes were still wet, whilst within her bonnet,
They were looking around, as she bobbed up and down,
To the military sound, of our solemn footsteps.

If you were to ask me what time the appointment was, well, to be truthful, I haven't a clue. I just know that it was sometime in the afternoon.

Bloomsbury Square

Some of the buildings in Bloomsbury Square were of the 18th and early 19th century period, and although they were mostly all of the same style, they each seemed to be making their own statement with pride. Bloomsbury Square is a location that also has gardens in its centre. To the north of the square is Great Russell Street and Bedford Place, leading to Russell Square. To the south is Bloomsbury Way and to the west is the British Museum.[2]

As I looked at the ascribed building, I could feel that it was drawing us nearer.

It knew we were advancing along and jutted out to beckon us on.

It was a tall, bold, strong-looking angular structure - definitely suggestive of business. But, at the same time, it gave out a *secretive* sense; there were no signs, no labels to indicate what it was all about. However, you knew that once inside, you would be closed off from the outside world, and indeed, from time and space.

Rebekah began to cry once again.

I quickly moved towards her to wipe the tears from her face.

It was time to cross this road; we were now outside this place.

The Adoption Society

There were three high steps to travel on, to get us up to the front door;
I will be honest with you, for I wished there were more.

I felt really numb, I looked around,
All was a haze, within my daze.

There was some kind of a shuffle taking place that brought me round.

My mother seemed to have changed her position; she was no longer in the front of the queue; she was standing on the pavement and looking down. Mrs Browning also seemed to be all of a dither. She had been standing on the second step up to this door, but now, she seemed to be changing her mind.

She was turning around and looking at me; her eyes were red, her face very wrenched, "Here!" she announced, with her arms outstretched. "You have Rebekah now!"

I was bewildered; I wasn't sure whether I had heard properly; but yes, this misty shape appeared to be holding her arms out towards me.

I held out my arms.

Rebekah was going to be *my* baby once more!

Rebekah moved closer towards me. She looked up, confused yet lovingly.

Suddenly, a third shape stepped in - not between us, but beside us. "Our Secret." it said.

"Don't forget Our Secret," God said.

The haze cleared for a while.

"Oh, yes," I whispered. "Our Secret."

I sat down on this step as I held Rebekah, and I moved my arms closer together until they overlapped. I slid my left hand up my right sleeve and pulled out a piece of paper. I looked at Rebekah, then took hold of her tiny hand and kissed it. And as I did so, 'The Secret Handing-Over' took place.

I did what God had said!

The written message on paper was carefully slipped up her sleeve - just as God said.

I kissed Rebekah and nuzzled her nose;
For, what's behind this door?
Well, only heaven knows.

"I will love you always, Rebekah. Forever," I whispered as I bonded our arms. "God Bless."

I felt myself being gently eased up off the step.

"Knock the Door!" God said. "Now, Knock the Door!"

And I did what God said.

I stood there with baby as light as a feather,
But, nevertheless, we were still together - Forever; because
that's what God had said.

I looked up at this high door - this Gateway to the Unknown and it suddenly swung open.

A woman stood there, from within this dark space, and at last, she took her chance to smile and then beckoned us through this mysterious place.

I hugged Rebekah tight and with eyes red, and wide,
We both carefully moved to step inside.
We turned to see if the others were following.
Mrs Browning and my mother had picked up their belongings,
And with a shrug of fear,
They moved in - relatively near.

We looked around; it was so dark and gloomy, but nevertheless roomy.

We all made our way up some stairs; there were no carpets, only bare floorboards, which creaked with every step that we made.

We turned the corner to see a room, or rather we were met by an enormous vacuum.

The Room

This middle-aged woman turned to look at us. "Come in!" she said.

We were all huddled together like timid field mice.

She gave us a welcoming smile and then pointed to her left.

"If you would care to take a seat over there," she said.

We walked in with caution and in silence. As we turned and looked to our right, there was a neat little round table with chairs set out by a window. The woman pulled out the chairs smiling, and with open arms, beckoned us all to take a seat. She was tall and office-like, wearing a black straight skirt, cardigan and a white blouse - plus I noticed that she was wearing court shoes. As we sat down, she turned around and strode across the room and then disappeared through a different exit door.

We all looked at each other, but we said not a word. In fact, you would've heard a pin drop, for nothing else was to be heard.

Our eyes were drawn to this window, and so that was where we kept looking and watching. We were on the first floor, it seemed, and as I looked out of the window, I could see where we had come from. Straight in front of this window, down below, was a road that had brought us up to this building. On the right was Bloomsbury Square's garden, and in it was a bronze statue.

I watched the cars moving away from their parking meters and driving towards our window. They would then bear to our right to follow the road round. One car had just pulled out, and as it did, so another one moved into its place.

All of a sudden, I remembered the silver bangle. That was something that I must not forget. I stretched over Rebekah to get to my bag. I opened it up, unzipped a little pocket inside and lifted out the silver bangle that I had purchased for Rebekah.

'Which arm shall I put it on?' I thought to myself. 'Put it on her left arm, like mine! Yes, that was it.'

I carefully undid it and pulled it up around her wrist. Rebekah moved her arm a little as I gently snapped it shut. I looked at her bracelet and then looked at mine. I put our arms together so that each bracelet touched the other.

"Like mother, like daughter," I said. "We will always be linked together!"

Rebekah looked up at me.

She was *mine!*"

Figure 90 Mother and baby with bangles on wrists

The Door

It was around here that there was something different going on. It was like a tidying up; or moving about. A kind of kerfuffle, and it was coming from another room. I thought I could hear a small child, and I felt that there were other members of staff around. They seemed to be working in a room nearby.

Mrs Browning bent over and started fumbling in her bag. I thought that perhaps she was looking for some sweets or something. Instead, she pulled out an item that appeared knitted. She went to shut her bag, and as she did so, she dropped the knitted shape. I bent over to pick it up for her, and it was then that I realised that it was a knitted teddy bear.

"Oh!" I said.

"It's Mary," she said, looking up at me in fear. "Mary made it."

Her face was really ashen. I just stared at her in a daze.

Figure 91 Teddy

Suddenly, from the far side of this huge room, a large door began to open, and there, in the doorway, was a different member of staff. She strode over to us, looking down at Rebekah all the while. She took Rebekah out of my arms and then walked back into the other room and closed the door.

I heard a young woman's voice exclaim, "Oh! She is so beautiful!"

I remember vaguely thinking that this member of staff must have taken Rebekah to show her to her colleagues in the other room. I could hear some kind of commotion again, and I began to wonder what the procedure would be and what sort of forms I would be given to fill in for the handing-over. The disturbance seemed to die down, and the office staff seemed to be quiet again.

I looked up at the ceiling, and I remember thinking how high it was and how these doors all seemed to nearly reach this upper limit.

'This place must have been meant for giants!' I thought.

I decided to get out my pen, ready to fill in the paperwork; it would be easier to find now rather than to struggle when they handed Rebekah back over to me.

That huge door opened again, and this same member of staff was now standing in the doorway. She looked across at me and said, "You can go now!"

I looked back at her, puzzled. "Pardon?" I said.

"You can go now!"

I was confused. "My baby! Where's my baby?"

The woman spoke in a very formal voice, and said, "Oh, she's gone!"

There was this sudden burst of sobbing.

I looked across to where it came from. It was my mother. She looked up at me helplessly, "Come on, Janet. It's time to go home!"

The foster mother was weeping.

But for me - it just wouldn't sink in.

It was as if *Time* itself had stood still!

Farewell: The Outside Steps

I am numb with shock as I walk out of this building. The sun was shining brightly as I squinted outwards from this place; its door, between five and fifty feet high - all I could think of, was - WHY?

I stood on the doorway's three steps and started scanning the area.

'Somewhere out there, somebody has *my* baby!' I thought, 'And they can't be too far away!'

Suddenly, a car pulled out of a parking space alongside the square. It had obviously been parked on one of those meters, and with this, it started coming towards me whilst I stood on the steps. I put my hand up to my forehead to shade my eyes because all of a sudden, the bright sun peeped out again from behind a cloud.

Between these rays of light, I could see some people in this car. In the back was a woman carrying my baby - Rebekah. The first thing I noticed was that she had a happy smile. Next to this woman sat an older woman, and I do believe that I could see a little toddler in there. These people were coming towards me now, and then the driver turned right to follow the road round. I squinted to see more through these streams of sunlight.

The driver of this vehicle was a man in a suit, and he too was smiling and appeared very happy.

Then…
They were gone!

I will *always* remember this scene because it is tinged with so much pain and suffering - so much sadness. Yet, those happy faces will stay with me forever. They provide me with comfort in knowing that my baby was with a family that would give her lots of love - just as I would have done.

As I stood there, I wondered where they were going. It seemed ironic to have been living in Lincoln for the last part of my pregnancy - some four and a half months - and it was in Lincoln that the handing-over had been organised. But yet, the very place where Rebekah and I were to part was in an adoption society building - just three minutes away from where I had been living in London and where I used to meet up with her father. 'Beautiful Memories.'

I looked around me in a daze; everyone seemed to be going about their business as if it was just some kind of a normal day - but, to me, it was as if time itself had stood still!

There was a gentle tug on my arm which brought me back to reality.

"Come on, Janet! If we don't hurry up, we will miss the next train home to Basingstoke!"

Good Night and May God Bless You, Rebekah
- Forever -
Just as He did at that Door
With Love and in Peace
Your Birth Mother
Janet

The next day, back in Basingstoke, I wrote the following letter:

Dear Mrs Pascal,

I felt so distressed and upset that I have got to write to you to settle my mind. When Rebekah was handed over to the parents yesterday, I noticed that the foster mother had brought next to nothing of Rebekah's clothes that I had bought for her. I feel so hurt that I had to make this list out for you of all the things Rebekah should have had. If I ring you up on Monday between 1:30 pm and 2:30 pm, perhaps you could tell me what was missing? Then I shall go and fetch them from Rebekah's foster mother in Lincoln and give them to you to pass on for Rebekah. I really don't see why Rebekah has been deprived of all her clothes to be kept for the next baby.

Please apologise deeply to the parents about the colour and conditions of Rebekah's clothes. I do believe the foster mother has been ill whilst looking after Rebekah. Also, some of the clothes Rebekah took with her were the foster mothers. Why, when she had her own, I don't know.

I do hope you can help me.
Yours sincerely,
Janet Hann.

Rebekah's Clothes

24 shaped nappies
Hairbrush and comb
Baby powder and baby sponge
Bibs:- 1 large, 2 small fancy ones
7 pairs of bootees
7 pairs of mittens
3 vests
3 nighties
2 winceyette petticoats
1 feeding bottle
1 pram set and bonnet
5 matinee coats
4 dresses
1 shawl
Tights (lacy)
Rubber pants

N.B. Mothers were encouraged to buy a pack of baby clothes to hand over to the adoptive parents of their child. This custom may be fondly seen as 'the last thing they could do for their babies.' However, it can also be viewed as 'the final humiliation.'[3]

A few days later, there was a letter in the post:

Dear Miss Hann,

You will be pleased to hear how well baby Rebekah has settled in with her new family. She slept most of the way home with them and has gained a few ounces in the first day or so when they took her to the clinic. She is such a happy baby – always smiling when awake, and they are so delighted with her that they are already applying to the Court for their papers.

We have sent baby's clothes on to the adopters, so please do not feel upset about this anymore. We shall write when we have more news.

Yours sincerely,
Secretary

Postscript

Unwed Motherhood

Impoverished single mothers have always been a favourite soft target for critics of the welfare state. However, having a child out of wedlock had not always been looked upon so poorly. It was only as social, moral, and economic attitudes changed that women, who found themselves unmarried and pregnant, became stigmatised. To understand how the mid-1960s came to become the peak period for adoption in the UK (as well as other countries) and the stigma that drove this apex of adoption, we must first understand the history affecting attitudes towards illegitimacy.

To begin with, we must look to a time when illegitimacy was not necessarily stigmatised. Medieval Britain did not view illegitimacy as a problem. This is because the children were absorbed into the mother's own community and contributed to the labour necessary to support the community. The only disadvantage to the illegitimate child was their inability to inherit. However, with the growing practice of primogeniture, where only the eldest child inherits, this disadvantage was shared with any child who was not the first born.

Industrialism, the growth of capitalism and the ethics of the sixteenth-century Puritanism changed all this. Illegitimate children who may once have been an asset in a labour-based economy would grow to become a liability if they could not find paid employment in the factories of later years. Rearing children became an expense rather than a benefit to the family's upkeep. This reduced the desire to care for children not of one's own family, which caused an overall reduction in family size. Unmarried women who could not provide for their children fell upon the parish and the Poor Law for aid and thus became a serious offence against the community.

The Poor Law Act of 1576 aptly captures attitudes towards illegitimacy of the day:

'Concerning bastards begotten and born out of lawful matrimony (an offence against God's and Man's laws) the said bastards being now left to be kept at the charge of the parish where they were born, to be the great burden of the same parish and in defrauding of the relief of the impotent and aged true poor of the same Parish, and to the evil example and the encouragement of the lewd life, it is ordered and enacted.'

It was believed that the Poor Law had to be harsh and humiliating; otherwise, the poor would abandon their children. In conjunction with the economic burden, illegitimate children were seen to cause the parish a moral stigma. Sexual intercourse outside marriage was perceived as morally wrong; therefore, any child conceived by an unmarried woman was viewed as the wages of sin.

Over the next two hundred years, the plight of the unmarried mother grew even more strained. As laws became harsher, she was condemned morally and spiritually and punished socially and materially. Due to the harshness of the Bastardy Clauses of the 1834 Poor Law Amendment Act, there grew a great increase in infanticide. This was punishable by death according to the Act of 1832, to Prevent the Destroying and Murdering of Bastard Children. Women without access to any real effective birth control methods who found themselves pregnant were then damned by any choice they made.

At this time, however, there was one organisation in London that sought to help unmarried women in their plight. In the early eighteenth century, Captain Thomas Coram was shocked to discover the number of infant children left to die as a result of attitudes around unmarried motherhood. Unable to turn his back on this problem, Mr Coram began a petition to open an institution, the Foundling Hospital. This would allow women to give up their children without retribution, to be fostered and then later trained for employment.

With much effort, the Foundling Hospital was opened in 1737. The demand was so great it was immediately filled, and children became part of a lottery to see who would be allowed in. In need of funding to expand their services, the hospital eventually secured the necessary funds under the direction that they must then accept any child in need. It became so, and the hospital operated a facility serving up to 400 children at any given time straight through to the early twentieth century when it restructured its services to become the Coram Foundation today.

The history of the Foundling Hospital demonstrates that women with illegitimate children were suffering. They had few resources, no access to birth control, and suffered harsh penalties and stigmatisation if they fell pregnant out of wedlock. Coram's institution may have partially eased their suffering; however, adoption was still looked down upon as it was thought tantamount to giving poor 'lewd' women a license to indulge their sexual passions with impunity.

It was the Victorians who began to consider other reasons for illegitimacy beyond the mothers' perceived corrupt morals. Most notably, they looked to the harsh conditions under which many of the poor lived and that brought the sexes in close proximity. Victorian society contemplated factors other than the spiritual condition of the unmarried mother for her situation; however, the middle classes of Victorian Britain still looked down on the lower classes, whom they saw as unable or unwilling to control their errant sexual desires.

It was the First World War that shifted attitudes in favour of adoption, though attitudes towards unmarried mothers were still arguably heavily stigmatised. It was estimated that in the early twentieth century, at any one time, there were 80,000 children in residential care under the provisions of the Poor Law. It was the First World War and the need to provide orphaned children with a decent home that tipped the balance in favour of legalising adoption. This led to the Adoption Act of 1926, which severed a birth mother's legal right to her child and allowed the child to be brought up by another set of parents. This addressed only the circumstances for the illegitimate, now adopted child, and did nothing to change the way pregnancy outside of marriage was viewed. Furthermore, adoptions were conducted under a strong cloak of secrecy, thus contributing to the notion of shame for the woman who bore and lost her child to adoption.

The twentieth century continued to regard illegitimacy as a social problem; however, moral reasoning began to be replaced with scientific explanations. So, while these women were perhaps no longer seen as guilty of a moral lapse, they were still regarded as deviant and as psychiatric cases in need of treatment.

By the 1940s and 1950s, elaborate psychological models existed to explain why some unmarried women had babies, frequently attributed to emotional issues with their parents.

In 1961, it was stated, 'when an adolescent girl in our society becomes pregnant outside of wedlock, this is indicative that something has gone wrong in the relationship between the girl and her parents.' No wonder young women were terrified of telling their parents and of the inherent shame when their community discovered their pregnancy when 'science' suggested they were psychologically defective and that their parents failed in their parental duties.

In extreme cases, women who became pregnant outside of marriage were even confined to psychological institutions as parts of the scientific community perceived them as feeble-minded, emotionally disturbed, or mentally disordered.

This brings us to the 1960s, the period of this memoir. New forms of popular culture and sexual freedom were balanced against continued intolerance and stigmatisation of illegitimacy, thus producing record numbers of children outside of marriage with no further assistance to unmarried mothers to provide for their offspring. It was a time of increased sexual activity amongst the young, without increased sexual education or contraception, while the shame of unmarried motherhood remained strong. This led to Britain's peak year for adoption in 1968, with a total of 16,164 adoptions in England and Wales in that year alone.

Attitudes towards illegitimacy and support structures for how to address it are deeply rooted in social conditioning. It is the cultural context in which the unmarried mother finds herself and the attitudes towards having children outside marriage that most contribute to whether or not she keeps her child. There are many non-Western societies that have completely different cultural contexts for illegitimacy.

In African, Caribbean, Indian, Polynesian and Eskimo communities, they appear to practice kinship fostering and outright adoption to a much greater extent than in white Western societies, encouraging a communal responsibility for the next generation. For adoption to exist in a society where possession, ownership and materialism reign supreme, such as most Western cultures, then it will (and has) become something exclusive of any communal support.

Unmarried motherhood in any form, whether a woman raises her child or forfeits for adoption, comes with many challenges. The attitudes that govern her experience have changed drastically over the last few centuries. After 1968, with the availability of birth control to unmarried women in Britain, there was a sharp decline in illegitimate pregnancies and associated adoptions. Organisations formed, such as Gingerbread in the 1970s, to support single mothers by raising awareness and addressing policy concerns to shift attitudes around childbirth outside of marriage. However, while the moral panic of the 1960s that focused on the perceived sins of the unmarried mother had faded, in many ways, it shifted to new conversations around the creation of a welfare state and current struggles with children being taken from their mothers over conditions of care.[1]

Now that we have charted illegitimacy from medieval times through to the twenty-first century, we can see that the lesson in all of this appears to be as follows. Being an unmarried mother is a problem only to the extent that society has defined

it as a problem, and it is only through shifting our attitudes
that we can change the way women and children are perceived
and cared for in our communities.[1]

Records of the National Council for One Parent Families

The National Council for One Parent Families (NCOPF) (1918-fl.2006) was originally established in February 1918, under the name the National Council for the Unmarried Mother and her Child (NCUMC).

Its primary concern at that time was infant mortality and the welfare of unmarried mothers and their illegitimate children. The organisation was formed following a National Conference organised by the Child Welfare Council of the Social Welfare Association for London, which was held at Mansion House on the 14 of February 1918. The conference was the result of a Child Welfare Inquiry, which had been established by the Social Welfare Association in London in 1914.

The first Council meeting in April 1918 appointed a Chair, Hon. Secretaries and an Executive Committee. The original functions were: 1) To obtain reform of the existing Bastardy Acts and Affiliation Acts; 2) To secure the provision of adequate accommodation to meet the varying needs of mothers and babies throughout the country, with the special aim of keeping mother and child together; 3) To deal with individual enquiries from, or on behalf of, unmarried mothers.

Funds were acquired via public funding and voluntary donations. On the 4th of January 1946, the Society was incorporated.

World War II saw a huge increase in the number of women turning to the Council for assistance.

The election of a Labour government after the war saw the expansion of the Welfare State following the findings of the Beveridge Report. This changed the focus of the Council away from providing direct aid towards explaining the complexities of the benefits system.

The 1960s and 1970s saw the Council return to its original function as a pressure group. The change of name to the National Council for One Parent Families occurred in 1973. It had been proposed in February 1972, and the new name reflected the Council catering for all lone parents.

With the election of a Conservative government in 1979, the Council's priorities changed, and a Back to Work strategy was launched that promoted employment opportunities for lone parents.

In 2004, the Council aimed to promote the welfare of lone parents and their children by helping to overcome the poverty, isolation and social exclusion faced by many.

In 2007, National Council for One Parent Families and Gingerbread merged to become one organisation.[2]

N.B. An exhibition at the Women's Library in London considers the history of single parenthood, exploring the many reasons why women have become lone mothers, including relationship breakdown, widowhood and family separation as a result of exile. Although its findings challenge the stereotypes, it also looks at how heavily lone mothers have been stigmatised over the years - and such attitudes still persist. For instance, Former Prime Minister, David Cameron of the UK (2010 to 2016), described unmarried mothers as a key sign of a "broken society."[3]

Endnotes

Places & Facts of Interest concerning the Memoir

CHAPTER ONE

1. The early uses of this term referred to a narrow platform or a gangway, whilst the first reference to the use of this name in fashion dates from only 1970. The height and narrowness of the *catwalk* at a fashion show are designed to highlight and dramatize the appearance and movements of the models who walk with a distinctive strut. *'Catwalk'* is sometimes used as a verb meaning, 'to walk like a model on a *catwalk.'*

2. From a historical point of view, Southampton (Hampshire, England) had remained the foremost passenger port in Britain in the 1950s and 1960s as with 4% of the cargoes imported into Britain. In the 1970s, the port went through a change brought about by containerisation. The number of passengers travelling through the port also declined as air travel became common in the 1960s. During more recent years, tourism has become an increasingly important industry, and in the 21st century, Southampton has continued to flourish with a population of around 236,000.

3. The Castle itself in Southampton was constructed after the Norman conquest of England and was located in the northwest segment of the town overlooking the River Test. The initial castle was a timber motte-and-bailey design, with a motte approximately forty-five feet (fourteen metres) across. The bailey contained a royal apartment said to be in the southwest corner of the castle. It also had a chapel and a hall, although exact locations have been difficult to discover. Only fragments of the medieval castle remain visible in Southampton today - the castle hall and the castle vaults, along with surviving parts of the south bailey wall. The castle water-gate can also still be seen, and fragments of the north wall.

4. Historic Winchester, which is further known as the 'City of Kings,' is a County Town of Hampshire in the UK. Once upon a time, it used to be known as the ancient capital of Wessex. Winchester's School of Art was founded over one hundred and twenty years ago and is now one of the twenty-five schools that make up the University of Southampton. The college already had an international reputation for fabric design, while now it further houses the Textile Conservation Centre, with its global reputation for the conservation of historic and contemporary textiles. The school was originally based at Hampton Court Palace and was later relocated to Winchester in 1999, where new buildings were added. One of the buildings houses the administration for the college and new facilities for fashion design and photo and digital media. There are many courses offered there now, including new facilities for fashion design and photo and digital media; foundation in Art & Design, Textile Art, Textile Design and many more.

6. It was only on the 30th of September 1958 that Independent Television (ITV) had reached the South of England in the appearance of Southern Television. It started its service using an old Southampton cinema (The Plaza) in the district of Northam as its main studio, whilst a custom-built studio complex was being built on land reclaimed from the River Itchen nearby. The service extended into South-East England, Kent, in Sussex in 1960 when the Dover transmitter opened.

9. A painter named Benjamin Waddy Maughan, who lived in London (England) in 1868, invented the first instantaneous domestic water heater that did not use solid fuel. It was called a *geyser* after an Icelandic gushing hot spring. Maughan's invention made cold water at the top flow through pipes heated by hot gases from a burner at the bottom. The hot water then flowed into a sink or a bathtub. The invention was somewhat dangerous because there was no flu to remove heated gases from the bathroom.

A water heater is still sometimes called a *geyser* today in the UK.

10. This quaint little place called Eastleigh is known as a railway town in Hampshire, but once upon a time, as long ago as the year 932 AD, it was a little village called East Leah (The Saxon word Leah means a clearing in a forest). Two little hamlets known as Eastley and Barton continued to exist until 1838, and in that year, the London and South-Western Railway Company built a railway from Southampton to Winchester. In 1839, the railway was extended to Basingstoke and London, and it passed through the small village of Barton, which became known as Bishopstoke Junction.

By 1851, Barton had a population of 194, and Eastley had a population of 213. In 1852, a cheese market opened by the railway station, and it wasn't long before it became Hampshire's leading cheese market. In 1868, the two villages of Barton and Eastley were combined into one parish, and its name became Eastleigh to make it more modern. It then grew rapidly, and there were three streets: High Street, Market Street and Southampton Road. However, the roads were in very poor condition, and so in 1893, a Local Board set about creating drains and streetlights. They also built pavements and kerbs, but roads were not made up until the 20th century. By 1901, Eastleigh had grown into a small town with a population of over 9,000. Today, the population of Eastleigh is nearer 55,000.

CHAPTER TWO

1. In 1892, Arthur Turnure founded *Vogue* as a weekly newspaper in the United States. From its beginning, the magazine targeted the new New York aristocracy, being primarily concerned with fashion, plus sports and social affairs included for its male readership.

Condé Montrose Nast bought *Vogue* in 1905 and gradually expanded the publication. He changed it to a bi-weekly magazine and also started *Vogue* overseas in the 1910s. He started first in Britain, followed by Spain, Italy and France in 1920, collecting a reputation that it continues to maintain.

In the period that I am writing about - the 1960s - the magazine began to appeal to the youth of the sexual revolution. At the same time, it continued making household names out of models such as Twiggy, Jean Shrimpton, and several others. With more than 120 years in print, the publication boasts of having reached 11 million readers in the U.S. and 12.5 million internationally.

2. David Bailey was born in 1938 in London's East End. As a youth, he had very limited choices in the job market; it was only after being posted to Singapore whilst in the British Royal Air Force in 1956 that he started to get involved in the field of photography. In 1959 he became an assistant to fashion photographer John French in London[3] and was a leading figure in the Swinging Sixties.

In 1960, at 22, he began photographing for British *Vogue*, and his work transformed British fashion and celebrity photography. His work reflects the 1960s British cultural trend of breaking down antiquated and rigid class barriers by injecting a 'punk' look into both clothing and artistic products.

3. Soon, Bailey became almost as famous as the people he was photographing, for example, the Beatles and the Rolling Stones, The Who, singers such as Marianne Faithfull and Sandie Shaw, actress Mia Farrow, and actors Peter Sellers and Michael Caine. There were also the well-known models Jean Shrimpton, Twiggy and Penelope Tree. Bailey also photographed the period's current fashions on the streets of London and New York for magazines like American *Vogue* and *Glamour*. Today, he is still active and shows no signs of slowing down.

4. Jean Shrimpton was born in Buckinghamshire in 1942, raised on a farm with dogs and horses and educated at a convent school in Slough. She went on to attend the Lucie Clayton Charm Academy, which is a modelling school in London. Jean was one of the first models to be associated with the term Supermodel, with *TIME* magazine labelling her as one in 1971.

5. Bailey, as Jean always called David Bailey, insisted on using her as his model. She had a very clean, pure look which was different to all the other models working for *Vogue*. Bailey broke all the classic guidelines for poses and expressions, which changed fashion forever and made David Bailey and Jean Shrimpton fashion icons.

6. The term Haute Couture is French. *Haute* means 'high' or 'elegant' while *Couture* literally means 'sewing,' although it has come to indicate the business of designing, creating, and selling custom-made high fashion women's clothes. To be called an haute couture house, an organisation must belong to the Syndical Chamber for Haute Couture in Paris, which is regulated by the French Department of Industry.

Members must employ 15 or more people and present their collections twice a year. Each presentation must include at least 35 separate outfits for day and eveningwear. Each customer's outfit is made exclusively for them with haute couture clothing typically requiring three fittings. It usually takes from 100 to 400 hours to make each garment. The syndicate has about 18 members, including such fashion houses as Coco Chanel, Christian Dior and Pierre Cardin.

During fashion's 'golden age,' after World War II, some 15,000 women wore couture. Today only 2,000 women in the world buy couture clothes, of which approximately 60% are American.

7. By the time of the Domesday Book (1086), Basingstoke had a population of about 200. There were three watermills that ground grain to flour; it also had a weekly market. In the Middle Ages, Basingstoke grew into a small town, and by the 13th century, it probably had a population of around 600 or 700 people. There were really only four streets: in the middle was the Market Square; on the west was Church Road that led to St Michael of the Mount church; and on the east side was Mote Street and the Mote Hall, which was where the townsmen met together (N.B. Mote is the old English word for meeting). In the north, there was the main Winchester to London road, and in the south, there was a lane which was called Frog Lane or Lower Brook Lane.

The people of Medieval Basingstoke grew most of their own food because all around it were three large fields, the west, south and north fields. However, the prosperity of Basingstoke depended on wool which was woven locally. There were tanners and tailors at Basingstoke, as well as other craftsmen, such as blacksmiths, bakers, brewers and coopers.

In 1392, Basingstoke was devastated by fire, yet the king granted Basingstoke a charter that made the 'good men' into a corporation and gave them the right to use a common seal (which was pressed into the wax seal on documents). Basingstoke was now entirely independent.

However, during the 17th century, the wool trade declined as Basingstoke faced increasing competition from the north of England. At the time of the first census in 1801, Basingstoke had a population of 2,589. The railway reached Basingstoke from London in 1839, which was extended to Southampton in 1840 and in 1848, a line to Reading opened. In 1865, the Haymarket was built as a corn exchange, where grain was bought and sold. By the early 1930s, the population had risen to around 14,000, and in the 1940s and 1950s, new council housing estates were built. Eventually, in 1961, it was decided to make Basingstoke an overspill town for London.

8. Buckingham Palace is one of the several palaces owned by the British Royal family; it is also one of the major tourist attractions in London. It has been the official London residence of Britain's monarchy since 1837. The Palace is not only the home of the Queen but also the London residence of the Duke of York (Prince Andrew), the Earl and Countess of Wessex (Prince Edward and his wife) and their daughter. There is also a number of staff members living there too.

9. Buckingham Palace is often used for other functions as well. For example, there is the administrative work for the monarchy, and it is here also in the state apartments that Her Majesty receives and entertains guests invited to the Palace. Every year more than

50,000 people go to the Palace as guests to attend banquets, lunches, dinners, receptions and Royal Garden Parties. The Palace has about 600 rooms, including 19 State Rooms, 52 royal and guest bedrooms, 78 bathrooms, 92 offices, a throne room, a ballroom, a picture gallery and even a cinema, swimming pool, post office and police station. Some of these rooms can be visited when the Royal Family is not in the Palace. The Palace's Stables and the Royal Mews can also be visited, and the front of the Palace is further celebrated for the Changing of the Guard, which always attracts plenty of spectators.

10. The Tower of London's sinister reputation with its rich and varied history ensures it remains a much-visited tourist spot today. The Tower is also celebrated for being known as the home of the Crown Jewels. They include the crown of Queen Elizabeth, the Queen Mother's, which contains the famous Indian diamond and St Edward's Crown, which is used for the actual crowning of the Sovereign.

The Tower is also well known for its Yeoman Warders, or Beefeaters, and their striking Tudor uniform, which has hardly changed since 1485. Their distinctive white neck ruff was introduced by Queen Elizabeth I. Nevertheless, no visit to the Tower is complete without seeing the huge black ravens. Legend states that if the ravens were to leave the Tower, the Crown would fall and Britain with it - but there is no danger of them flying away because their wings have been clipped.

11. The term "parasol" comes from the Latin *para* for shelter or shield and *sol*, which means sun. Basically, a parasol can be referred to as an "umbrella", but the implication is that it can shield someone from the sunlight, whereas an umbrella offers protection from the wet rain. However, parasols today are further designed to be mounted to tables or planted in the sand, providing hands-free shade for a gathering of people along with food and drink. This tool has a long history, having been used thousands of years ago in countries that are extremely hot. For instance, parasols pop up in bas-reliefs, paintings and writings in places like Ancient Greece and Rome, China, Mesoamerica, the Middle East, and North Africa. They seem to have originated in the East Indies about 5,000 years ago.

In 3000 BC, the Egyptians used parasols as a royal privilege, and bearers did the carrying. In the United States, a parasol appeared on a street corner in Windsor, Connecticut, in 1740 carried by a fashionable lady; it had been brought all the way from the West Indies. A century later, no one would have taken much notice, for wealthy women throughout America and Europe considered parasols an essential part of any well-dressed lady's wardrobe.

The parasol is most often thought of in connection with Victorian society in England and the U.S. Perhaps the chief reason for its popularity at the time was the Victorians' obsession for a fair complexion. This proved to the world that a woman was a lady who didn't have to work outdoors like "common" females did.

12. The parasol also bears religious connotations: in Oriental thought, the mountain is identified with the 'axis mundi,' or the central axis holding up the world. Above the mountain is the dome of the sky, symbolised by the umbrella. Its important function is to cast a shadow of protection from the heat of suffering, desire and other spiritually harmful forces. Umbrellas seem to be especially important in processional rites, appearing as mobile temples providing honour and respect. Octagonal and square parasols commonly represent the Noble Eightfold Path and the four directional quarters, respectively.

13. Michelangelo was an Italian Renaissance sculptor, painter, architect, and poet who exerted an unparalleled influence on the development of Western art. He was considered the greatest living artist in his lifetime, and ever since then, he has been held to be one of the greatest artists of all time. A number of his works in painting, sculpture, and architecture rank among the most famous in existence.

Although the frescoes on the ceiling of the Sistine Chapel are probably the best known of his works today, the artist thought of himself primarily as a sculptor. His practice of several arts, however, was not unusual in his time, when all of them were thought of as based on design or drawing. Michelangelo worked in marble sculpture all his life, but he only did the other arts during certain periods. The high regard for the Sistine ceiling is partly a reflection of the greater attention paid to his painting in the 20th century and partly too because many of Michelangelo's works in other media were left unfinished.

14. Apparently, a local company called Thornycroft manufactured military and civilian vehicles and required a skilled workforce to do so. Thornycroft had run their own 'Works School' very successfully for many years before the Second World War, but in 1942, Hampshire Education Authority took over the running of classes, forming a new Basingstoke Technical Institute. In 1947, the Technical Institute moved to the Worting Road site, and in 1954, it was re-named Basingstoke Technical College. The Ministry of Education soon authorised a new college building programme with which the college was officially opened on the 30th of May 1961. Nowadays, Basingstoke College of Technology (BCOT) offers students a wide range of further and higher education courses and relevant training skills for most occupations.

15. Upholstery is the craft of providing furniture, especially seats, with padding, springs, webbing, and fabric or leather covers. A person who works with upholstery is called an upholsterer, while an apprentice upholsterer is sometimes called an outsider or trimmer. The word *upholstery* comes from the Middle English word *upholder*, which appears to have a connotation of *repairing* furniture rather than creating 'new' upholstered pieces from scratch.

In 18th-century London, upholders frequently served as interior decorators, being responsible for all aspects of a room's decor. These individuals were members of the Worshipful Company of Upholders, whose traditional role, prior to the 18th century, was to provide upholstery and textiles and the fittings for funerals. In the London furniture-making partnerships of the 18th century, a cabinet-maker usually worked together with an upholder.

Traditional upholstery, involving padding and covering chairs, seats and sofas, evolved for many centuries before the development of sewing machines, synthetic fabrics and plastic foam. Using a solid wood or webbed platform, it might include the use of springs, lashings and any type of stuffing from animal hair to grasses and coir, wool, hessian, scrims, bridle ties, stuffing-ties, blind-stitching, top-stitching, flocks and wadding - all built up by hand. In contrast, modern upholsterers employ synthetic materials like Dacron and vinyl, serpentine springs, and so on. Furniture reupholstery continues to thrive in the UK today, with several businesses, both small and large, providing this service.

16. The movement that resulted in the World YWCA began in England in 1855 amid the Industrial Revolution and the Crimean War. It was founded through the convergence of social activist Lady Mary Jane Kinnaird's *General Female Training Institute* and committed Christian Emma Robarts' *Prayer Union*. It sought to be a social and spiritual support system for young English women.

Originally founded as the Young Women's Christian Association, the abbreviation no longer has that meaning, as their staff and the people they serve are not all young, women, or Christian. The name has been kept to maintain brand equity. The original Christian focus is still strong in many of the national associations, but some have changed their focus to social programmes, services and mission-based topics.

The YWCA is independent of the YMCA (Young Men's Christian Association), though many local YMCA and YWCA associations have amalgamated into YM/YWCAs or YMCA-YWCAs, and belong to both organisations while providing the programs of each.

17. Located in the East End's Spitalfields area, Petticoat Lane is one of the oldest and most famous markets in London. Over the years, the market has been best known for selling fashion and clothes, but it actually sells just about everything now, from designer goods to fruit and vegetables and bargain goods. Petticoat Lane is really two markets in two locations: the market on Wentworth Street runs six days a week, and the Middlesex Street market is only open on Sundays. This is a popular day to visit for both locals and tourists alike, and you can see up to 1,000 stalls if you visit on a Sunday.

By the way, don't expect to find this market in Petticoat Lane, as the street name no longer exists. It was changed in the 1800s to Middlesex Street to spare the blushes of the Victorians, who didn't like to have a street name that referred to underwear. It was originally known as Hogs Lane as early as the Tudor period. Street names tended to be descriptive in the days before street signs, or literacy and their names would tell people what went on in the area. It is thought that Hogs Lane got its name from the pigs that bakers kept in the street, although it may also have been a reference to an old droving road used to bring livestock into the city, dating back many centuries earlier.

CHAPTER THREE

1. The Windmill Theatre, Great Windmill Street, London, was named as such due to being built on the same site as an earlier windmill that existed until the later part of the eighteenth century. It began as nothing more than a reconstruction of a small playhouse replacing the once-famous Britain's first art-house cinema, The Palais de Luxe, bought by a Mrs Laura Henderson in 1930. The new auditorium was built on two levels - stalls and one circle - with views to a spectacular stage.

The Windmill Theatre first opened on the 15th of June 1931. Mrs Henderson and her manager Vivian Van Damm decided to use the theatre as a variety house with non-stop performances. It was also the only theatre in London to stay open throughout WWII. The Windmill Girls were the actual cause of the Revudeville's immense success. The dancers appeared in nude tableaux throughout the performances, having to remain absolutely still due to the licensing restrictions. Should they move a muscle, the theatre would have been closed down.

On the 31st of October 1964, the Windmill Theatre shut its doors on Revudeville for the last time. The next day it opened as a cinema; the Windmill had been taken over by the Compton Group, the film production and distribution organisation.

2. Ladybird made clothing and footwear for children aged 0 to 13 years old and was of late, owned by Shop Direct, the UK's largest online retailer and parent company to household names like Littlewoods, K&Co, Woolworths, Very and Isme. Ladybird first appeared on the UK clothing rails in 1938. The brand was owned by Adolf Pasold & Son, and according to legend, company founder Johannes George Pasold had seen a ladybird in a dream when first starting the family firm in the 18th century.

In 1965, as British manufacturing started to decline, Ladybird merged with the world's largest sewing thread manufacturer Coats Patons. The deal gave Ladybird access to a huge range of wool and thread, opening up possibilities for new ranges. Over the next few years, it became the most favourite children's clothing in the UK for under-5s and was sold globally through stores in countries as diverse as China, Saudi Arabia, India and Malaysia.

However, there were problems with the credit crunch of 2008, and the organisation went into administration in 2009. This is when both Woolworths and Ladybird were rescued by Shop Direct, with the age-old brand values remaining.

3. In 1959, the Street Offences Act became law. In 1960, London's first sex cinema, the Compton Cinema Club (a members-only club to get around the law), opened at 56 Old Compton Street. As post-war austerity relaxed in the swinging 60s, Clip Joints also surfaced. Typically, Clip Joints suggest the possibility of sex, charge inflated prices for watered-down alcoholic drinks, and then throw out customers when they become unwilling or unable to spend more money.

4. The British Museum was involved in much excavation abroad. For example, its Assyrian collections formed the basis for understanding cuneiform (an ancient Middle Eastern script) in the same way that the Rosetta Stone unlocked the Egyptian hieroglyphic script (a symbol-based script). Visitor numbers increased greatly during the nineteenth century.

The British Museum attracted crowds of all ages and social classes, particularly on public holidays. Alongside their academic work, curators took an interest in broadening the museum's appeal through lectures, improving the displays and writing popular guides to the collections. During the beginning of the twenty-first century, the museum has continued to expand its public facilities. Visitor numbers have grown from around 5,000 a year in the eighteenth century to almost six million today.

8. The finished mummy and a portrait of the dead person were placed inside a coffin. This protected it from the attentions of robbers and maybe even wild animals. The first coffins were plain wooden boxes, but later ones were made in the shape of a mummified body. For extra protection, the mummies of wealthy people were placed in two coffins or sometimes in a whole nest of coffins like a series of Russian dolls. The outer coffin was often painted with an idealised picture of the owner, which, as I have already said, in most cases, bore no resemblance to its owner. A mummy was often laid to face east. That was so that it could see the sunrise, a symbol of rebirth. I was further surprised to discover that mummification had not been confined to humans alone. The collections included mummified bodies of cats and ibises, crocodiles, fish, falcons, dogs and even a calf.

9. The ancient Egyptians believed that it was necessary for the body to be preserved for the next life so that the spirit of a man or woman, who had safely passed the judgement of the gods, would be transfigured into a divine being. These *akhu* or blessed dwelt in a realm that included features like those of their earthly surroundings. They also sampled pleasures like those they had known on earth. I further became familiar with the 'Book of the Dead.' The museum holds over two hundred of these - most of which are fragmentary.

The Book of the Dead is a name Egyptologists gave to sheets of papyrus covered with magical funerary texts and accompanying illustrations called 'vignettes.' The ancient Egyptians placed these with their dead in order to help them pass through the dangers of the Underworld and attain an afterlife of bliss in the Fields of Reeds - the Egyptian heaven.

11. The word sepia, in photography, refers to a brown tint that could occur in the production of photographs. The reddish-brown colour originated at the turn of the 20th century when photographs were being treated with sepia ink. The ink, derived from the secretion of the cuttlefish, was used as a primitive pigment, although nowadays, it has been replaced by modern dyes. By using moderate dilutions, sepia ink is quite opaque, but applying very dilute (weak) washes makes the photograph much more transparent, with red undertones.

CHAPTER FIVE

2. By the early 13th century, Medieval Portsmouth was described as 'one of our most important ports.' Its main exports were wool and grain, whereas its main imports were wine, woad for dyeing, wax for candles and iron. However, the town was burned down four times during the 14th century during a period of almost continuous warfare between England and France. It was not fortified until after the last attack in 1380.

In about 1418, a tower was erected at the entrance of the Harbour called the Round Tower; the cannons on it could fire at any enemy ship attempting to enter. In the 16th century, a giant chain was stretched across the mouth of the ships sheltering place. The winch was by the Round Tower, and the chain could be lowered to let in friendly ships but raised to prevent enemy ones from entering.

In 1494, Henry VII strengthened the town's fortification by building the square tower. Henry also changed the destiny of Portsmouth when he built a dockyard in 1495 whereby royal warships could be built or repaired. From then on, Portsmouth became a naval port. A naval academy for training naval officers was opened in the dockyard in 1733. Meanwhile, the town had reached bursting point.

In 1764, a body of men called the Improvement Commissioners was set up in Portsea. They had the power to pave and clean the streets. They also appointed a man called a scavenger who collected rubbish with a cart once a week. In 1768, a similar body was set up in Old Portsmouth. In 1776, they were given the power to light the streets with oil lamps, and from 1783, they appointed night watchmen to patrol the streets.

There were many improvements in amenities during the 19th century. For instance, in 1811, it gained its first piped water supply; but you had to pay to be connected, and only the rich and middle-class could afford it. In 1820, the Portsea Improvement Commissioners installed gas street lighting. Old Portsmouth followed in 1823. In 1818-22, a canal was built across Portsea Island. It ran along the site of the railway between Portsmouth and Fratton. The barges were then towed by steam tugs across the sea into Chichester Harbour, where the canal began again. Nevertheless, the canal closed in 1838.

Meanwhile, the old horse-drawn trams were replaced by electric ones in 1901-03, and the first motor buses began running in 1919. Other facilities also continued to improve; for instance, in 1939, there were more than 30 cinemas.

During the Second World War, Portsmouth was an obvious target for German bombing because it was a major naval base. After the war, the most pressing need was for new housing. Some were erected on bomb sites, while others were constructed on Portsdown Hill above Cosham. More than 700 prefab houses were built between 1945 and 1947.

Apart from wartime bombing, another reason for building new houses was slum clearance. In 1955 a survey showed that 7,000 houses were unfit for human habitation, and so, in the 1960s and early 1970s, a whole section of central Portsmouth was rebuilt. As well as demolishing slums, the council gave people grants to improve their homes.

In the early 20th century, the main employer was the dockyard. During the First World War, the number rose to 23,000, but it fell to 9,000 when the war ended. Traditional industries like brewing and corset making vanished, but electrical and electronic engineering became a major employer. There was also a large increase in the number of jobs in service industries.

Tourism also became a major industry. The Mary Rose, the Tudor warship, was raised from the seabed in 1982 and became a museum. The D-Day museum opened in 1984, and in 1987, HMS Warrior, Britain's first iron warship, was moved to Portsmouth. In the early 21st century, Portsmouth is still a thriving city with a population of 205,000.

CHAPTER EIGHT

3. The Marriage of Isaac and Rebekah (Genesis 24:1-67)

24 Now Abraham was old, well advanced in years; and the Lord had blessed Abraham in all things. 2 And Abraham said to his servant, the oldest of his house, who had charge of all that he had, 3 "Put your hand under my thigh, and I will make you swear by the Lord, the God of heaven and of the earth, that you will not take a wife for my son from the daughters of the Canaanites, among whom I dwell, 4 but will go to my country and to my kindred, and take a wife for my son Isaac." 5 The servant said to him, "Perhaps the woman may not be willing to follow me to this land; must I then take your son back to the land from which you came?" 6 Abraham said to him, "See to it that you do not take my son back there. 7 The Lord, the God of heaven, who took me from my father's house and from the land of my birth, and who spoke to me and swore to me, 'To your descendants I will give the land,' he will send his angel before you, and you shall take a wife for my son from there. 8 But if the woman is not willing to follow you, then you will be free from this oath of mine; only you must not take my son back there." 9 So the servant put his hand under the thigh of Abraham his master, and swore to him concerning this matter.

10 Then the servant took ten of his master's camels and departed, taking all sorts of choice gifts from his master; and he arose, and went to Mesopotamia, to the City of Nahor. 11 And he made the camels kneel down outside the city by the well of water at the time of evening, the time when women go out to draw water. 12 And he said, "Oh Lord, God of my master Abraham, grant me success today, I pray thee, and show steadfast love to my master Abraham. 13 Behold, I am standing by the spring of

water, and the daughters of the men of the city are coming out to draw water. 14 Let the maiden to whom I shall say, 'Pray let down your jar that I may drink,' and who shall say, 'Drink, and I will water your camels' – let her be the one thou hast appointed for thy servant Isaac. By this I shall know that thou hast shown steadfast love to my master."

15 Before he had done speaking, behold, Rebekah, who was born to Bethu'el the son of Milcah, the wife of Nahor, Abraham's brother, came out with her water jar upon her shoulder. 16 The maiden was very fair to look upon, a virgin, whom no man had known. She went down to the spring, and filled her jar, and came up. 17 Then the servant ran to meet her, and said, "Pray give me a little water to drink from your jar." 18 She said, "Drink my lord"; and she quickly let down her jar upon her hand, and gave him a drink. 19 When she had finished giving him a drink, she said, "I will draw for your camels also, until they have done drinking." 20 So she quickly emptied her jar into the trough and ran again to the well to draw, and she drew for all his camels. 21 The man gazed at her in silence to learn whether the Lord had prospered his journey or not.

22 When the camels had done drinking, the man took a gold ring weighing a half shekel, and two bracelets for her [the maiden's] arms weighing ten gold shekels, and said, 23 "Tell me whose daughter you are. Is there room in your father's house for us to lodge in?" 24 She said to him, "I am the daughter of Bethu'el the son of Milcah, whom she bore to Nahor." 25 She added, "We have both straw and provider enough, and room to lodge in." The man bowed his head and worshipped the Lord, and said. 27 "Blessed be the Lord, the God of my master Abraham, who has not forsaken his steadfast love and his faithfulness towards my

master. As for me, the Lord has led me in the way to the house of my master's kinsmen."

28 Then the maiden ran and told her mother's household about these things. 29 Rebekah had a brother whose name was Laban; and Laban ran out to the man, to the spring. 30 When he saw the ring, and the bracelets on his sister's arms and when he heard the words of Rebekah his sister, "Thus the man spoke to me," he went to the man; and behold, he was standing by the camels at the spring. 31 He said, "Come in, O blessed of the Lord; why do you stand outside? For I have prepared the house and a place for the camels," 32 So the man came into the house; and Laban un-girded the camels and gave him straw and provender for the camels, and water to wash his feet and the feet of the men who were with him. 33 Then food was set before him to eat; but he said, "I will not eat until I have told my errand." He said, "Speak on."

34 So he said, "I am Abraham's servant. 35 The Lord has greatly blessed my master, and he has become great; he [the Lord] has given him flocks and herds, silver and gold, men-servants and maid-servants, camels and asses. 36 And Sarah my master's wife bore a son to my master when she was old; and to him he has given all that he has. 37 My master made me swear, saying, "You will not take a wife for my son from the daughters of the Canaanites, in whose land I dwell; 38 but you shall go to my father's house and my kindred, and take a wife for my son.' 39 I said to my master, 40 'Perhaps the woman will not follow me.' But he said to me, "The Lord, before whom I walk, will send his angel with you and prosper your way; and you shall take a wife for my son from my kindred and from my father's house; then you will be free from my oath, when you come to my kindred; and if they will not give her to you, you will be free from my oath.'

42 "I came today to the spring, and said, 'O Lord, the God of my master Abraham, if now thou wilt prosper the way which I go, 43 behold, I am standing by the spring of water; let the young woman who comes out to draw, to whom I shall say, "Pray give me a little water from your jar to drink," 44 and who will say to me, "Drink, and I will draw for your camels also," let her be the woman whom the Lord has appointed for my master's son.'

45 "Before I had done speaking in my heart, behold, Rebekah came out with her water jar on her shoulder, and she went down to the spring and drew. I said to her, 'Pray, let me drink.' 46 She quickly let down her jar from her shoulder, and said, 'Drink, and I will give your camels drink also.' So I drank, and she gave the camels drink also. 47 Then I asked her, 'Whose daughter are you?' She said, "The daughter of Bethu'el, Nahor's son, whom Milcah bore to him.' So I put the ring on her nose and the bracelets on her arms. 48 Then I bowed my head and worshipped the Lord, and blessed the Lord, the God of my master Abraham,

who had led me by the right way to take the daughter of my master's kinsman for his son. 49 Now then, if you will deal loyally and truly with my master, tell me; and if not, tell me; that I may turn to the right hand or to the left."

50 Then Laban and Bethu'el answered, "The thing comes from the Lord; we cannot speak to you bad or well. 51 Behold, Rebekah is before you, take her and go, and let her be the wife of your master's son, as the Lord has spoken."

52 When Abraham's servant heard their words, he bowed himself to the earth before the Lord. 53 And the servant brought forth jewellery of silver and of gold, and raiment, and gave them to Rebekah; he also gave to her brother and to her mother costly ornaments. 54 And he and the men who were with him ate and

drank, and they spent the night there. When they arose in the morning, he said, "Send me back to my master." 55 Her brother and her mother said, "Let the maiden remain with us a while, at least ten days; after that she may go." 56 But he said to them, "Do not delay me, since the Lord has prospered my way; let me go that I may go to my master." 57 They said, "We will call the maiden, and ask her." 58 And they called Rebekah, and said to her, "Will you go with this man?" 59 She said, "I will go," So they sent away Rebekah their sister and her nurse, and Abraham's servant and his men. 60 And they blessed Rebekah, and said to her, "Our sister, be the mother of thousands of ten thousands; and may your descendants possess the gate of those who hate them!" 61 Then Rebekah and her maids arose, and rode upon the camels and followed the man; thus the servant took Rebekah, and went his way.

62 Now Isaac had come from Beer-la'hai-roi, and was dwelling in Negeb. 63 And Isaac went out to meditate in the field in the evening; and he lifted up his eyes and looked, and behold there were camels coming. 64 And Rebekah lifted up her eyes, and when she saw Isaac, she alighted from the camel, 65 and said to the servant, "Who is the man yonder, walking in the field to meet us?" The servant said, "It is my master." So she took her veil and covered herself. 66 And the servant told Isaac all the things that he had done. 67 Then Isaac brought her into the tent, and took Rebekah, and she became his wife; and he loved her. So Isaac was comforted after his mother's death.

CHAPTER TWELVE

1. Bloomsbury Square was developed by the 4th Earl of Southampton in the late 17th century and was initially known as

Southampton Square. It was one of the earliest London squares, with the Earl's own house occupying the whole of the north side of the square, where Bedford Place is now located. The other sides were lined with typical terraced houses of the time, which were initially occupied by members of the aristocracy and gentry.

By the early 19th century, Bloomsbury was no longer fashionable with the upper classes. Consequently, the Duke of Bedford of the day moved out of Bedford House, which was demolished and replaced with further terraced houses. During the 19th century, the square was occupied mainly by middle-class professionals, while in the 20th century, most of the buildings came to be used as offices. None of the original 17th-century buildings now survive, but there are many handsome 18th and early 19th-century houses, and the garden is open to the public.

References

Chapter One

2. Tim Lambert: http://www.localhistories.org/southampton.html (retrieved 08-02-2016)
3. Tim Lambert: https://www.wessexscene.co.uk/your-city-the-castle-lost-to-history/ (retrieved: 09-02-2016)
4. http://www.cityofwinchester.co.uk/Education/Art_College/art_college.html# (retrieved 13-02-16)
5. A History of the Paper Pattern Industry: The Home Dressmaking Fashion Revolution | Reviews in History.
6. Extracts from: http://www.78rpm.co.uk/southern.htm#top (retrieved: 12-02-16)
7. The Corset Controversy is from: https://en.wikipedia.org/wiki/Corset_controversy
8. https://en.wikipedia.org/wiki/Ernie_The_Fastest_Milkman_in_the_West (retrieved: 21-02-16)
9. *https://en.wikipedia.org/wiki/Water_heating* (retrieved: 21-02-16)
10. Tim Lambert: http://www.localhistories.org/eastleigh.html (retrieved: 21-02-16)
11. https://en.wikipedia.org/wiki/Gibson Girl (retrieved: 21-02-16)

Chapter Two

1. Extract from: https://en.wikipedia.org/wiki/Vogue_(magazine) (retrieved: 20-02-16)
2. http://www.biography.com/people/david-bailey-38755 (retrieved: 21-02-16)
3. http://pdngallery.com/legends/bailey/bio.shtml (retrieved: 21-02-16)

4. http://www.vogue.co.uk/person/jean-shrimpton (By Brian Duffy) (retrieved: 21-02-16)
5. http://agnautacouture.com/2012/12/09/jean-shrimpton-made-a-major-contribution-to-fashion/ (retrieved: 21-02-16)
6. http://www.infoplease.com/spot/fashionside1.html (By David Johnson) (retrieved: 21-02-16)
7. Tim Lambert: http://www.localhistories.org/basingstoke.html (retrieved: 22-02-16)
8. http://www.aviewoncities.com/london/buckinghampalace.htm Buckingham Palace (retrieved: 22-02-16)
9. http://resources.woodlands-junior.kent.sch.uk/customs/questions/london/buckinghampalace.htm (retrieved: 22-02-16)
10. http://www.langust.ru/review/100qa_ti.shtml (retrieved: 22-02-16)
11. http://www.sarasparasols.com/parasol_history.html (retrieved: 24-02-16)
12. http://www.religionfacts.com/parasol (Nitin Kumar of Exotic India) (retrieved: 24-02-16)
13. http://www.britannica.com/biography/Michelangelo (retrieved: 24-02-16)
14. http://www.bcot.ac.uk/bcot-history/ (retrieved: 29-02-16)
15. https://en.wikipedia.org/wiki/Upholstery (retrieved: 29-02-16)
16. https://en.wikipedia.org/wiki/YWCA (retrieved 29-02-16)
17. http://www.eastlondonhistory.co.uk/history-petticoat-lane-market/ Posted on 1st February 2014 by Malcolm Oakley (retrieved: 31-12-16)

Chapter Three

1. https://www.windmillinternational.com/about/history-of-the-windmill-theatre/ (retrieved: 03-03-16)
2. http://www.woolworthsmuseum.co.uk/fashion-ladybirdhistory.htm (retrieved: 31-12-2016)
3. https://en.wikipedia.org/wiki/Soho (retrieved: 05-03-2016)
4. http://www.britishmuseum.org/about_us/the_museums_story/general_history.aspx (retrieved: 01- 03-16)
5. *The British Museum A-Z Companion* (1999)

6. *Who's Who in Mythology* (1985)
7. *The How and Why of Ancient Egypt* (1978)
8. *The Complete Book of Mummies* (2001)
9. *The British Museum A-Z Companion* (1999)
10. *The British Museum A-Z Companion* (1999)
11. http://index.about.com/index?gclid=CMWw7ujwxMsCFQmNGwodp qMPIw&qo=semQuery&am=broad&q=what+is+sepia+photography& an=google_s&askid=d7941a17-3952-4b8a-8c3e-59bcefdf7f08-0-ab_ gsb&dqi=&qsrc=999&ad=semD&o=35381&l=sem (retrieved: 16-03-16)

Chapter Four

1. https://en.wikipedia.org/wiki/Leicester_Square (retrieved: 15-03-16)
2. https://en.wikipedia.org/wiki/Leicester_Square (retrieved: 15-03-16)
3. https://en.wikipedia.org/wiki/Empire,_Leicester_Square (retrieved: 15-03-16)
4. https://en.wikipedia.org/wiki/Mecca_Leisure_Group (retrieved: 15-03-16)
5. https://en.wikipedia.org/wiki/Wilson%2C_Keppel_and_Betty (retrieved: 12-03-16)
6. http://www.sbs.com.au/food/cuisine/pakistani
7. http://www.sbs.com.au/food/article/2008/07/01/about-pakistani-food
8. http://www.foodbycountry.com/Kazakhstan-to-South-Africa/Pakistan. html
9. https://en.wikipedia.org/wiki/Pakistani_cuisine
10. https://en.wikipedia.org/wiki/Trafalgar_Square (retrieved: 12-03-16)
11. https://en.wikipedia.org/wiki/Strand,_London (retrieved: 12-03-16)
12. http://www.slideshare.net/stupidsalman/the-role-of-music-in-pakistani-culture (Retrieved: 20-01-17)
13. http://www.sbs.com.au/food/cuisine/pakistani
14. http://www.slideshare.net/stupidsalman/the-role-of-music-in-pakistani-culture (Retrieved: 20-01-17)
15. https://www.cs.mcgill.ca/~rwest/link-suggestion/wpcd_200809_ augmented/wp/m/Music_of_Pakistan.htm (Retrieved: 20-01-17)

16. Dr Anna Machin Published: The 'biological bribery' that explains why humans fall in love – BBC Science Focus Magazine, (Retrieved: 22nd August, 2021 at 04:00)

17. Tim Lambert: http://www.localhistories.org/brighton.html (retrieved: 12-03-16)

18. http://www.thisbrighton.co.uk/culturepiers.htm

19. http://www.arthurlloyd.co.uk/Brighton/WestPier.htm

20. http://brightonpier.co.uk/history-of-the-pier (retrieved: 16-03-16)

Chapter Five

1. Rose Bell, 2013. Sex and Contraception @ motherandbabyhomes.com

2. Tim Lambert: http://www.localhistories.org/portsmouth.html (retrieved: 23-03-16)

3. http://portsmouthtempleofspiritualism.co.uk/index.php (retrieved: 26-03-16)

4. http://portsmouthtempleofspiritualism.co.uk/spiritualism.php (retrieved: 26-03-16)

5. http://portsmouthtempleofspiritualism.co.uk/spiritualism.php (retrieved: 26-03-16)

6. http://portsmouthtempleofspiritualism.co.uk/history.php (retrieved: 26-03-16)

7. Horsley, E.M. (1986). *Hutchinson Factfinder: Concise Encyclopedia*, London: Guild Publishing, p.266. (retrieved: 26-03-16)

8. http://portsmouthtempleofspiritualism.co.uk/spiritualism.php (retrieved: 26-03-16)

9. http://www.islamcan.com/common-questions-about-islam/why-does-quran-allow-muslim-men-to-have-four-wives.shtml#.VvFXBLnJ-M8 (retrieved: 22-03-16)

Chapter Six

1. What Getting An Abortion Was Like In The '60s, '70s, And '80s Compared To Now (bustle.com)

2. Abortion Rights » History of Abortion Law in the UK

3. https://en.wikipedia.org/wiki/Liberty_(department_store) (retrieved: 26-03-16)

4. http://www.reallyusefultheatres.co.uk/our-theatres/london-palladium (retrieved: 26-03-16)

5. https://downstairslounge.wordpress.com/2011/12/18/ken-dodd-diddles-with-the-diddymen/

6. https://en.wikipedia.org/wiki/Diddy Men (retrieved: 26-03-16)

Chapter Seven

1. http://www.webmd.com/digestive-disorders/hiatal-hernia (retrieved: 05-04-16)

2. https://en.wikipedia.org/wiki/North_Hykeham (retrieved: 08-04-16)

3. *Family Medical Adviser* (1991), Reader's Digest, pp.416-433

4. http://www.allfreecrochet.com/Tutorials/How-to-Crochet-the-Magic-Circle (retrieved: 01-02-16)

5. https://en.wikipedia.org/wiki/Lincoln,_England (Retrieved: 01-04-16)

6. http://www.virtualmuseum.ca/sgc-cms/expositions-exhibitions/mains-hands/storyofwool/crafts/teasingcarding.html (retrieved: 10-04-16)

7. pictures of victorian london street gas light - Bing images (retrieved: 08-04-16)

8. pictures of victorian london slums - Bing images (retrieved: 08-04-16)

Chapter Eight

1. https://www.flickr.com/photos/lincolnian/2782978633/ (retrieved: 08-04-16)

2. *Family Medical Adviser* (1991), Reader's Digest, pp.248-249

3. *The Bible: Revised Standard Version*, Genesis 24: vv 1-67

4. Forced adoption stories by mothers made to give up their babies revealed | Daily Mail Online. By DAILY MAIL REPORTER PUBLISHED: 01:18, 17 April 2015 | UPDATED: 09:50, 17 April 2015

Chapter Nine

1. *https://www.morgan-motor.com/history*

Chapter Ten

1. Magdalene Laundries in Ireland. Wikipedia, the free encyclopedia
2. How Ireland Turned 'Fallen Women' Into Slaves - HISTORY Retrieved: April 2021DATED:
3. Paulo Nunes dos Santos/The New York Times/Redux
4. The girls of Bessborough - BBC News
5. Nuns and children at Bessborough
6. No Other Options (motherandbabyhomes.com) Rose Bell (2013), Mother & Baby Homes
7. *www.independent.co.uk/news/uk/this-britain/sin-and-single-women/*
8. No Other Options (motherandbabyhomes.com) Rose Bell (2013), Mother & Baby Homes
9. Houses of shame | Family | The Guardian Wed 31 Oct 2007 10.36 GMT

Chapter Twelve

1. https://www.bing.com/images/londontubemap
2. https://en.wikipedia.org/wiki/Bloomsbury_Square (retrieved: 10-01-17)
3. Houses of shame | Family | The Guardian Wed 31 Oct 2007 10.36 GMT

Postscript

1. Rose Bell, 2013. Unwed Motherhood (motherandbabyhomes.com)
2. Records of the National Council for One Parent Families | The National Archives
3. Houses of shame | Family | The Guardian Wed 31 Oct 2007 10.36 GMT

Printed in Great Britain
by Amazon

32571534R00205